Praise for *52 Loaves*

"Alexander writes aromatic crumbs of baking wisdom, trailing them on his dogged quest for the perfect loaf. He tucks in his experiences with a meditation and a final revelation in a French monastery. The end is what they call an oven rise, where the dough magically doubles in size and pleasure." —*The Cleveland Plain Dealer*

"I love a man who has real passion and William Alexander has it in spades . . . Whether you think he's genius or just plain insane you will be awed by his relentless pursuit . . . What's even better is that in this book he shares every single lesson that he's learned, so you too can make that perfect loaf." —*Project Foodie*

"Serious, irreverent, funny, and informative at the same time, *52 Loaves* reflects precisely the frustrating and infuriating—if not impossible—process of creating the perfect bread." —Jacques Pépin

"Laugh out loud funny . . . Alexander definitely doesn't hold back, whether it's confessing to tending a loaf of bread over an afternoon tryst with his wife or describing the looks of pity he received after unwittingly asking a 'stupid' question at a lecture . . . A great book, simultaneously funny and thoughtful."

—TheKitchn.com

"Nitpicking obsessiveness was never so appetizing . . . A–."

—*Entertainment Weekly*

"As Alexander takes readers along on his quest for the perfect loaf, he also invites us into his life—and, thanks to his honesty and his sense of humor, he's somebody you'll want to know." —*American Way*

"An engaging and instructive read with great rhythm, and if you've been on your own quest for good home-baked bread, I think you'll find it as engrossing as I did. It is the book I was reading in Japan and well, I blame William Alexander for making me miss Mount Fuji while riding the bullet train."

—Clotilde Dusoulier, *Chocolate & Zucchini*

"Alexander's breathless, witty memoir is a joy to read. It's equal parts fact and fun . . . Alexander is wildly entertaining on the page, dropping clever one-liners in the form of footnotes and parenthetical afterthoughts throughout."

—*The Boston Globe*

"Anyone who has baked bread—or yearns to—will recognize William Alexander's *52 Loaves* as a quest book. The quest? To re-create the perfect loaf of peasant bread he tasted at a restaurant. Once. Many years ago . . . The funny, often self-deprecating style he used in *The $64 Tomato* transfers well to *52 Loaves*."

—*Richmond Times-Dispatch*

"A warm, laugh-out-loud [memoir] . . . Alexander writes about the ups (few), the downs (numerous) and a lively history of bread itself, all recounted in a self-effacing but often irreverent voice . . . There is much to savor here, and Alexander entertainingly unravels many of the staff of life's deep mysteries for the uninitiated." —*The Oregonian*

"Engaging and enjoyable." —*Gastronomica*

"The world would be a less interesting place without the William Alexanders who walk among us—the people who pursue all sorts of Holy Grails and latch like ticks onto particular passions, yet who have the good grace to tell us all about their exploits with humor, rather than with pomposity . . . Alexander's pursuit may be bread, but anyone in pursuit of an ideal will probably recognize his musings on whether it's possible to re-create a memory, much less seek perfection. When those around him question his obsession, you find yourself agreeing with them—while also wondering how exhilarating it might feel to be so passionate about something." —*Minneapolis Star Tribune*

"[A] funny, informative book." —*Birmingham* magazine

"A clever weekend baker learns some life lessons, loaf by loaf . . . His bright writing highlights a pleasing variety of comical misadventures . . . Entertaining and educative." —*Kirkus Reviews*

"Alexander gives a funny, week-by-week account of his year-long quest to bake a perfect loaf." —*New Haven Advocate*

"Whether one sees this as an obsession or an odyssey, the result is a book that is more memoir than cookbook and is rife with reflection, peppered with science and punctuated with humor." —*Poughkeepsie Journal*

"In his outrageously witty book *52 Loaves*, William Alexander . . . covers a myriad of fascinating and informative historical and culinary material." —*The Rocky Mount Telegram*

"*52 Loaves* describes [William Alexander's] entertaining and more-than-slightly obsessive quest to bake the perfect loaf." —*New Haven Register*

"This humorous memoir is recommended for anyone who has ever tried to bake a loaf." —*Library Journal*

"What *Zen and the Art of Motorcycle Maintenance* did for, well, motorcycles, William Alexander's *52 Loaves* will do for bread and bakers of bread. That is, his story takes you so deeply into the literal reality of the staff of life that you effortlessly pop out into the mystic. I can think of no higher praise than that!" —Peter Reinhart, author of *Peter Reinhart's Artisan Breads Every Day*

52
Loaves

A HALF-BAKED ADVENTURE

William Alexander

ALGONQUIN BOOKS OF CHAPEL HILL | 2011

ALSO BY WILLIAM ALEXANDER

The $64 Tomato:
How One Man Nearly Lost His Sanity,
Spent a Fortune, and Endured an Existential
Crisis in the Quest for the Perfect Garden

Published by
ALGONQUIN BOOKS OF CHAPEL HILL
Post Office Box 2225
Chapel Hill, North Carolina 27515-2225

a division of
Workman Publishing
225 Varick Street
New York, New York 10014

First paperback edition, Algonquin Books of Chapel Hill, October 2011.
Originally published by Algonquin Books of Chapel Hill in 2010.
Printed in the United States of America.
Published simultaneously in Canada by
Thomas Allen & Son Limited.

Descriptions of the seven Divine Offices used with
permission from the Abbey of the Genesee.

Leeuwenhoek's sketches of yeast cells © The Royal Society.

The Library of Congress has cataloged the hardcover edition
of this books as follows:
Alexander, William, [date]
52 loaves : one man's relentless pursuit of truth, meaning,
and a perfect crust / William Alexander.
p. cm.
Includes bibliographical references.
ISBN 978-1-56512-583-4 (alk. paper) (HC)
1. Bread. 2. Bread—Anecdotes.
3. Alexander, William, [date]. I. Title.
TX769.A4858 2010
641.8'15—dc22   2009049656

ISBN 978-1-61620-050-3 (PB)

10 9 8 7 6 5 4 3 2 1
First Paperback Edition

I am going to learn to make bread tomorrow.
So if you may imagine me with my sleeves rolled
up, mixing flour, milk, saleratus, etc., with a deal of
grace. I advise you if you don't know how to make
the staff of life to learn with dispatch.
— Emily Dickinson

They say bread is life. And I bake bread, bread,
bread. And I sweat and shovel this stinkin' dough
in and out of this hot hole in the wall, and I
should be so happy! Huh, sweetie?
— Nicolas Cage in *Moonstruck*

Contents

IV. Sext

V. None

Recipes

A Baker's Bookshelf

Acknowledgments

Prologue

"Next!"

My heart was pounding so hard at the airport security checkpoint, I was certain the TSA agent would see it thrusting through my jacket.

"Laptop," I blurted out for no apparent reason, my voice cracking like a teenager's on a first date as I placed my computer into the plastic tray.

"Liquids." The TSA inspector held up my regulation Baggie stuffed with three-ounce bottles and nodded approvingly.

I reached into my backpack and casually pulled out a half-gallon plastic container filled with a bubbling, foul-smelling substance. "Sourdough." I might just as well have said, "Gun!"

"Uh-uh, you can't bring that on a plane!" a TSA official stationed at *the next line* called out. I wanted to say, "Who asked you?" but sensibly kept my mouth shut as I looked around nervously. Thanks to that blabbermouth, every passenger and TSA employee at the security checkpoint was looking my way.

"Can he bring dough?" another inspector yelled.

A buzz had now started, with murmurs of "dough" audible from the passengers behind me, all of whom, I'm sure, hoped they weren't on my flight.

A tense and chaotic ten minutes later, I found myself talking with a stone-faced supervisor.

"Sourdough?" He sighed with the heavy air of someone who didn't want to deal with a situation — any situation.

"Twelve years old!" I beamed. So that I could say it wasn't a liquid and thus subject to the three-ounce rule, I'd added half a pound of flour to the wet sourdough before leaving the house. Unfortunately, this had the effect of stiffening it into something with an uncanny resemblance to plastique explosive. As the supervisor started to run a wand around it, I held my breath, half expecting it to beep myself.

"A thirteen-hundred-year-old monastery in France is expecting this," I offered.

His trained poker face remained blank, forcing me to pretend he'd asked why.

"They managed to keep science, religion, and the arts alive during the Dark Ages, even risking their lives to protect their library from the barbarians who burned everything else in sight. After thirteen centuries, though, they've forgotten how to make bread."

Still no reaction. None. Trying to lighten the mood, I added, "The future of Western civilization is in your hands."

That bit of hyperbole got his attention. "You're a professional baker?"

My wife coughed.

"Um, no."

He arched an eyebrow. But no matter. Whatever transpired in the next few minutes, I was boarding that plane with my starter. I had to. During nearly a year of weekly bread making, I'd disappointed my wife, subjected my poor kids to countless variations on the same leaden loaf, and, most of all, let myself down, time and time again, loaf after loaf, week after week. Well, I was not going to let down the monks at l'Abbaye Saint-Wandrille de Fontenelle.

Granted, I was as unlikely a savior of a monastery as you could imagine — a novice baker who'd lost his faith and hadn't set foot in a church in years, carrying a possibly illegal cargo of wild yeast and bacteria practically forced on me by an avowed atheist — but nevertheless I was determined to succeed, for I was on a mission.

A mission from God.

I.
Vigils

Vigils, or watching in the night, is prayer to
be celebrated in the middle of the night. In
monastic communities the concentration on
vigilance begins with this office, enveloped in
and supported by darkness and silence.

Rarin' to Go

How can a nation be great if its bread tastes like Kleenex?
—Julia Child

I was up before dawn, watching and waiting for daylight, and was rewarded with a promising sunrise that delivered a glorious, sparkling October day, a Flemish landscape painting come to life. With the low mountains of New York's Hudson Highlands as my backdrop, I set out across the fields, endless rows of rich red soil stretching to the horizon, a sack of wheat slung over my breast, swinging my arm to and fro in an easy rhythm, sowing while startled birds furiously flapped their wings into flight, fleeing the advancing rain of seed. The silence of late October was interrupted only by the laughter of barefoot children playing hide-and-seek among the crisp, golden cornstalks and by the church bells in the distance, which marked the passing of every quarter hour. What a great day to be alive and to be sowing life.

"Are you going to weed or stand there daydreaming?" Anne asked, snapping me out of my reverie.

My wife was on her knees, pulling weeds, her face streaked with sweat and dirt, her nose runny.

I dismissed her comment with a grunt but reluctantly joined her. "How did we ever let these beds get so out of hand?" I wondered aloud as I yanked another foot-tall clump of thistle from the earth and flung it into the wheelbarrow. We pulled and tossed, tugged and heaved, the weeds having progressed far beyond the stage where they could be removed with a hoe.

Two hours later, the neglected beds, more used to being a home to beans and tomatoes than to grain, were cleaned, raked, and ready for winter wheat. I drew shallow furrows through the earth with a triangle hoe as Anne, on all fours, her drippy nose almost touching the earth, poked seeds into the soil, four inches apart, as if planting peas, not sowing wheat. The scene was more phlegmish than Flemish, but as much as I loved the romantic notion of turning my yard into a wheat field, of *sowing* wheat instead of *planting* it, I wasn't about to till up my lawn and construct a deer-proof fence when I already had good soil, good fencing, and available beds in the vegetable garden. And planting in neat rows, rather than broadcasting seed, would allow for efficient weeding with a hoe later.

"We need Jethro Tull's seed drill," I remarked as Anne continued to press seeds into the earth.

She didn't take the bait.

"Sitting on a park bench, da, da-daaaa, eyeing little girls with bad intent," I sang, getting her attention, not to mention thoroughly irritating her. Anne had once unbuckled her seat belt and threatened to get out of the car — at sixty miles an hour — if I didn't remove *Aqualung* from the CD player.

"Jethro Tull invented the seed drill, you know."

"First of all, Jethro Tull is the group, not the lead singer. He's Ian somebody."

I knew that, of course, because during my freshman year in college I'd thoroughly embarrassed myself while trying to impress my dorm mates by exclaiming, "Man, I love the way that guy Tull handles the flute." Thirty-odd years later, I was apparently still trying to redeem myself vis-à-vis Mr. Tull.

"No, no, the original Jethro Tull. His seed drill drilled the hole, dropped in the seed, and covered it up, all in one shot. Amazing invention for seventeen hundred, wasn't it?"

"I'm out of seed."

I retrieved the second packet. I'd spent about five dollars on two packets of wheat seeds, not the most efficient way to buy wheat, but little did I know at the time what a bargain I'd gotten. No sooner would I have the seed watered in than wheat prices would start to climb.

A neighbor walked by. "What're you up to?" he called from the street, surprised to see us planting so late in the year.

"Baking a loaf of bread," I answered enthusiastically.

I could see this wasn't a satisfactory answer. "From scratch!" I added.

Still baffled, but deciding not to ask any more questions, he moved on. Just as well. Explaining what I was really up to was a good deal more complicated. I'm not sure I fully understood it myself. I was growing wheat because I was about to embark on a year of bread making, fifty-two loaves, fifty-two chances to re-create in my own kitchen a perfect loaf of bread I'd tasted only once, years ago, and I'd realized, with both surprise and embarrassment, that I really had no idea what flour was. I'd look at the white fluffy powder in the sack, at photographs of wheat fields in Nebraska, and couldn't connect the two. They weren't even the same color!

If I was going to master bread, I thought I should first understand wheat, and what better way than to plant it, to see it grow from a seed to a blade of grass, to keep vigil over its long winter sleep until the miraculous spring awakening, when it would spurt, with adolescent abruptness, into a tall golden stalk of grain to be harvested and ground into flour.

Besides, I just liked saying I was baking a loaf of bread "from scratch."

"*Really* from scratch," Anne muttered, poking another wheat kernel into the earth. "When will it be ready for bread?"

"If all goes well, I guess this summer."

If all goes well. The Hudson River valley is apple country, not wheat country, and I worried there was good reason for that. My little plot was very possibly the only wheat growing within fifty miles. Not to mention the fact that I didn't know if I was even planting the right kind of wheat for the artisan bread I planned to make, or if the wheat I'd chosen would grow in this region, or if I'd planted it too early or too late. I had no idea how I'd know when it was ripe or what to do with it when it was.

I explained all this to Anne, the better to start building the cushion for the likely disappointment later.

"So I don't actually know how to grow wheat," I confessed.

This was apparently her cue to invite a most unwelcome eight-hundred-pound gorilla into the garden.

"That's all right. You don't exactly know how to bake, either."

She meant this optimistically, but I took it as a slightly harsh if accurate indictment. Of course, Anne was right. I didn't really know how to bake, and I certainly didn't know how to bake so-called artisan bread.

My wife often says that I was born too late, that because I dislike cars and other machines (which is why we were preparing the soil by hand rather than using a small rototiller), I would've been happier in an earlier century. She says this only because she's never seen me on a horse. In the time she refers to, all bread was "artisan," except no one knew it. It was made in small quantities from stone-ground flour, leavened with wild yeast, given a long, slow rise, and baked on a stone in a wood-fired brick or clay oven — the very definition, give or take, of artisan bread.

Not that it was all good bread. Far from it. Until the last century or two, wheat was a luxury in much of the world, and bread for the commoners was more often than not made of rye, barley, or other inferior grains — if it was even all grain. The preserved teeth of many of our ancestors show premature wear from the grit that was in every loaf, and unscrupulous millers were often accused of supplementing the grain with the sweepings from the sawmill downstream (the resulting bread thus being merely a precursor to the 1970s brand Fresh Horizons, which got its whopping fiber boost from added wood pulp).

Good, bad, or flammable, it was nevertheless what we would today broadly consider artisan bread, made by independent bakers or baked by women in communal ovens. Then the industrial age dawned, and the next thing we knew, we were all eating Wonder bread. I grew up in the fifties on cellophane-wrapped, rectangular loaves like Wonder and Silvercup (which promised to be "even whiter and softer!"), although I insisted my mom switch to Sunbeam after Hopalong Cassidy and Gene Autry lassoed me into believing that a slice of their energy-packed favorite brand would have me "rarin' to go!" That it did, but where it had me rarin' to go was to hot lunches. I came to despise sandwiches as a kid, and no doubt the tasteless, gummy bread that stuck to the back of your teeth and the roof of your mouth was a factor.

My view of bread as something to be avoided at all costs persisted well into adulthood, and then into fatherhood, even as Hoppy and Gene rode off into the sunset, until a chance breakfast at a swanky New York restaurant changed everything. It was one of those places we could never have afforded for dinner, and even at breakfast, there were way too many forks and glasses for me to be comfortable. I surveyed the baffling landscape of silver and crystal before me.

"Is someone else going to be sitting at our table?" I asked Anne as I reached for a glass of water. "Is this yours or mine?"

"Mine is whichever one you don't choose."

"We should leave. I didn't dress properly." I tugged at the lapel of my ratty wide-wale corduroy jacket, a sandy tan island in a sea of dark blue suits. "I mean, who wears a suit to breakfast on a Sunday morning?"

"People who go to church."

"Who goes to church in Manhattan? This is the most godless city on earth."

As I finished that sentence, a basket of bread was delivered by a server padding on silent feet.

"Bread's here. Can't leave now," Anne said.

Ugh. The dreary breadbasket. I would've greatly preferred a sticky bun, but needing something to do with my fidgety hands, I quickly tore off a corner from a thick, crusty, wheat-colored piece and took a bite. The dark brown, caramelized crust gave a satisfying crackle when you bit into it — not a crunch, but an actual crackle — and managed to defy physics by remaining both crispy and chewy at the same time. It was a crust to be eaten slowly, first with the teeth, then with the tongue, and it possessed a natural sweetness and yeastiness unlike any I'd ever tasted.

The bread clinging to the crust was every bit as good. It wasn't white, wasn't whole wheat; it was something in between, and it had a rustic quality — a coarse texture that managed to be light and airy, with plenty of holes, yet also had real substance and a satisfying resistance to the bite. This bread didn't ball up in your mouth like white bread, and like the crust, it was yeasty and just slightly sweet, and it exhaled (yes, the bread exhaled) an incredible perfume that, cartoonlike, wafted up from the table, did a curl, and, it seemed, levitated me from the table. I was seduced, body and soul, my senses overloaded. This bread demanded the attention of more than the taste buds: it was a delight to the eyes, the nose, and the tongue as well. But years later, what I remember most about this moment is the utter surprise, the almost mystical revelation that bread could be *this good*. True, I had grown up with plastic-wrapped white bread, but I'd also had the occasional baguette or decent restaurant bread and had never tasted anything like this.

"Excuse me?" I finally realized that Anne was talking to me.

"I said, how's the bread?"

"I think you'd better try it."

When the waiter brought my eggs Benedict (at a price that should have included the rest of the chicken), I asked him what kind of bread this was.

"I think we call it peasant bread."

Peasant bread! This was the stuff of kings. "I've got to learn to make this," I said to Anne as we left the restaurant.

That was five or six or more years ago. I hadn't learned to make it, though I'd tried halfheartedly, and I hadn't tasted bread anywhere near as good since. It seemed likely that if I was ever going to have the kind of bread I wanted to eat, I was going to have to apply myself. And I'd better do it soon; I feared that if I waited much longer, I'd forget what the perfect loaf tasted like. As it was, it was going to be difficult enough to reconstruct those complex tastes, textures, and aromas, and I figured it was now or never.

That makes it all sound like a very pragmatic undertaking, like growing tomatoes simply because they taste better than store-bought. Bread, however, is such a *loaded* food, full of symbolism and rich in history, whose very preparation produces what surely must be the most recognizable food aroma in the world, that it arguably occupies its own shelf in the food hierarchy.

This was made shockingly clear from a newspaper story I'd recently come across while munching on a slice of toast. The *New York Times* reported that Sunni militants in Baghdad had come up with a horrifying new strategy, every bit as effective as car bombs and sniper fire, to force Shiites out of targeted neighborhoods.

Kill all the bakers.

The toll so far was a dozen and counting, as militants systematically hunted down the bakers, closing one bakery after another by killing, kidnapping, or threatening those who made the bread. The attacks often took place in broad daylight, the customers left unharmed. The militants didn't have to kill them; without bread, they left the neighborhood on their own. "To shut down a well-known bakery in a neighborhood, that means you paralyze life there," one baker said.

I was shocked that bread, in the twenty-first century, still occupied such a major social — and now political — role. How little I understood about this alchemy of wheat, water, yeast, and salt. I suppose this story might have turned me off to bread, discouraging me from what I fully expected to be a lighthearted kitchen fling, but it apparently had the opposite effect, providing me with the final nudge I needed. I wanted to understand bread, to bake exceptional bread more than ever, to *become a baker.*

"I'm going to make bread every week for a year," I announced to my family not long afterward, "until I bake the perfect loaf of peasant bread."

"Every week — great! What other kinds of bread are you going to make?" Katie, sixteen, wondered.

"Nothing. Just peasant bread."

Her face fell.

"I wouldn't mind some croissants."

"Or pizza," Zach, home from college for the week, added. "Cinnamon buns . . . stuffed bread . . . baguettes . . ."

"Peasant bread," I said flatly. "It may take me a year to perfect it."

"I think your bread's pretty good now," Katie offered.

"It's too dense and moist, and it has no air holes. And you need a hacksaw to cut through the crust," I said, trying not to show my irritation at the compliment.

"Well, that's true about the crust . . ."

So true that the kids refused to slice my loaves themselves, it was so difficult — not to mention hazardous.

"Fifty-two weeks of peasant bread, huh?" Zach said with more than a touch of sarcasm. "Sorry I'll be missing that, Dad."

"I'll make sure you come home a year from now to the perfect loaf."

I said this with confidence even though I'm not very good at resolutions and had already failed miserably at a dozen or so prior attempts to make this bread. Regardless, this seemed an eminently achievable goal. I wasn't planning on mastering the violin or learning particle physics. I was merely baking a loaf of bread, and this time, I told myself, would be different. I would be disciplined and methodical; I would take a scientific approach; I would talk to bakers and read books; and mainly I would stay focused, keep my eye on the prize and my ass in the kitchen and not get diverted by interesting but irrelevant distractions, my usual undoing.

"I've got a year to learn," I said with a mix of cockiness and trepidation, aware that I was staring down the eight-hundred-pound gorilla's flared nostrils. "Fifty-two weeks. Fifty-two loaves. I'm going to bake the perfect loaf of bread in a year. End of story."

Actually, beginning of story.

II.

Lauds

This prayer breathes the atmosphere
of bright youth, of beginning, of innocence,
of blossoming spring. It is a joyful, optimistic
hour reflected by the hymn, psalms
and canticles.

Bake Like an Egyptian

Acorns were good until bread was found.
— Sir Francis Bacon

Weight: 196 pounds
Bread bookshelf weight:* 2 pounds

I needed a recipe.

Right now. I had somehow arrived at the advent of fifty-two weeks of baking, poised at the very threshold of my project, without having yet decided on a recipe for the first loaf. This oversight was no trifling matter. The inaugural loaf was important: It would be the benchmark against which all the other loaves would be measured, the starting point upon which fifty-one subsequent loaves would be built. This was my foundation, my touchstone, the zeroing of my scale, the calibration of my gas meter, the —

You get the point.

"I need a recipe," I said. Aloud. To myself. The nice thing about baking alone in the kitchen before dawn is that you can talk to yourself like a crazy person and no one suspects you're a crazy person. I considered my options. There really aren't that many differences in bread formulas; the variations are mainly in technique. The basic recipe for bread has been around now for

---

*That is, the weight of the bread books on my shelf, not the weight of the shelf itself.

about — well, let's see, this is the seventeenth . . . minus . . . hmm . . . borrow a one . . . that leaves — *six thousand years,* which means the copyright has expired and I can repeat it here:

> Mix flour, water, salt, and yeast. Let rise, then form a loaf and bake.

This recipe (or something close to it) was found scratched on the inside of a pyramid. It turns out that Egypt, in addition to its more widely known contributions to civilization — the Sphinx, hieroglyphics, Omar Sharif — also gave us bread. Plus something to wash it down with (more about that in a moment). Yet the ancient Egyptians weren't the first to eat wheat. Early forms of wheat, including emmer and einkorn, had been domesticated in the Fertile Crescent since Neolithic times. Most commonly, these grains were cooked with water and eaten as gruel. Eventually it occurred to someone to press the gruel into a disk shape and grill it on a hot stone, and flatbread was born (if the inventor had realized that said innovation would culminate in the McDonald's Snack Wrap, he might have buried it with Tutankhamen).

That might have been the end of it, were it not for another culinary invention of the Egyptians. They liked to tip a cold one back now and then (or, more likely, a warm one) and had numerous small breweries where they cultivated brewer's yeast. Now, maybe it happened this way and maybe it didn't, but it seems quite likely that one day a tipsy cook spilled a little beer into the dough, and the inevitable happened: yeast and dough were accidentally mixed, and leavened bread was born.*

It didn't take long for bread — an obvious improvement over

---

*An alternative theory is that some dough was left out too long in the sun, and wild yeast naturally present in the flour made the dough rise. I prefer my version.

gruel — to become a staple of the Middle Eastern diet. Bread makes a pretty complete food. The wheat kernel, or seed, provides protein, starch, fat, and fiber and is rich in a number of important vitamins. Bread became such a major part of life in Egypt, with laborers paid in loaves, that this food would come to be known, in Egyptian Arabic, as *aish,* literally "life."

I rather fancied the notion that I was trying to perfect life and that my method for doing so wasn't appreciably different from that of Pharaoh's baker. My life would have no more than four simple ingredients: flour, water, yeast, and salt. I would make my life free-form, without a pan, directly on a stone in the oven.

Of course, to make a loaf, I needed a little more to go on than a hieroglyphic scrawl. The day after my bread epiphany in that upper-crust restaurant, I'd called my younger brother, Rob, and told him I wanted to learn to bake bread. He was a pretty fair baker himself, and my request might have triggered some sibling rivalry — if it were me, I'd have been tempted to borrow a page from our grandmother's book and leave out one crucial ingredient (like salt) — but Rob welcomed me into the fraternity of home bakers, giving me his complete recipe (as far as I know), his encouragement, and, shortly after, my first artisan bread cookbook.

I had been tinkering on and off with Rob's recipe, keeping track of the variations and results in a log, but it looked to be an evolutionary dead end: the bread had changed, but it was never as good as Rob's, let alone the sublime object of my desire. I've mentioned the rock-hard crust, but the crumb — the term bakers use to describe the texture of the bread's interior, not the little bits that fall to the table — was just as bad. No matter how much or how little yeast I added, how long or how short the rising time, or how long I left the bread in the oven, the loaves invariably had a dense, undercooked crumb most notable for its complete lack of gas pockets. Frustrated, I'd stopped baking bread altogether over a year earlier.

"All right," I finally announced on this morning of renaissance. "The last shall be first." Meaning I'd begin this touchstone loaf by using the same recipe I'd used for the last loaf I'd baked. Following this latest variation of Rob's recipe, I began by mixing the flours, mostly all-purpose white flour, with a little whole wheat and rye for flavor. I took about a third of this flour mixture and added it to all the water, along with a mere teaspoon of active dry yeast, making a batter called a sponge or *poolish* (the word most likely refers to the Polish bakers who introduced this method to France in the nineteenth century). I then let the *poolish* — with the consistency of thin pancake batter — sit. After four or five hours, it would be aromatic and bubbly, full of complex compounds that would contribute flavor and aroma to the finished bread. Only then would I mix in the rest of the flour and salt and knead the dough.

Use of a preferment, as the *poolish* and other methods (such as a *biga* or a *pâte fermentée*) are called, is a technique you won't find in your mother's copy of Fannie Farmer or likely even at your local bakery, where a "straight dough" — in which everything is mixed at once, kneaded, and set aside to rise — is generally the rule. A straight dough is a much faster way to make bread and lends itself well to automation.

The Egyptians didn't have to worry about preferments, as their bread was leavened by saving a little of today's dough to use in tomorrow's bread — the original preferment. Most modern bakers start from scratch with fresh commercial yeast for each new batch, but this just doesn't provide the kind of flavor that old yeast brings to the table. The *poolish,* even though it is started with fresh yeast, is one way to recapture some of that lost flavor, to bake more like an Egyptian.

Thanks to the custom of decorating their tombs with paintings of everyday life and their penchant for record keeping, we actually know more about how Egyptians baked four thousand years ago than we do about baking in, say, medieval England. We know, for example, that during the thirty-year reign of Ramses III, his royal bakery distributed 7 million loaves of bread to the temples. We know how the bread was made; a detailed tomb painting of the bakery illustrates every phase of the process, including a detail of a large trough of dough being kneaded by foot. We know that Egyptian bakers had a repertoire of over fifteen varieties of bread. They had round breads, braided breads, even breads shaped like pyramids; breads with poppy seeds and sesame seeds; and bread with camphor.

And yet here I was, thousands of years later, restricting myself for the next year to a single type of loaf, with just four ingredients. I was baking like an Egyptian, but less so. There's nothing like progress.

WEEK

2

Naturally Pure and Wholesome

Wildlife experts in Scotland have urged the public to help save swans by feeding them brown loaves instead of white. A lack of nutrients in white bread is leaving the birds crippled with a condition similar to rickets in humans.
— *The Scotsman,* February 15, 2008

It's a sad state of affairs when the only thing you have to read over breakfast is a bag of flour.

Thanks to Anne, I've become so accustomed to having the *New York Times* delivered early every morning — home delivery was a de facto condition of our marriage — that when I beat the person we used to call "the paper boy" to the kitchen and have nothing to read over breakfast, I go a little stir crazy and will read anything: I'll peruse the back of the cereal box for the tenth time (just in case it's changed or they have a new mail-in offer); I'll study the junk mail to see what the local Chinese food buffet place is offering for their special, romantic Valentine's Day buffet (all-you-can-eat king crab legs, in case you're wondering what turns a girl on — just try to keep those specks of crab off your cheek); I will in fact even read a flour bag to stave off *Times* withdrawal.

Thanks, as I say, to Anne. I'll admit that I was attracted to Anne some twenty-five years ago by her looks, but I became intrigued when I saw her reading the *Times* over lunch one day at the office where we both worked. Suffice it to say, I hadn't dated a lot of women who read anything more challenging than *TV Guide,* much less the *Times.* Thus Anne's reading this paper in front of me so blatantly was the erotic equivalent of an ovulating baboon displaying her swollen red rump, and I eventually worked up the courage to ask her to lunch, figuring that at the least we'd have something to talk about. Which we did.

Not long after, Anne left the research institute where I still work today to begin medical school, and we subsequently married, had two kids, yada yada, and as Anne was finishing up her residency in internal medicine in the Bronx, we were eager (well, I was eager) to move to a more rural area. Anne was willing to indulge me, to follow me anywhere — almost. She had merely one nonnegotiable demand. One evening after the kids were in bed, she came over to the regional map I was studying at the kitchen table and drew a rough circle, indicating the approximate home-delivery limit of the *Times.*

"Anywhere inside the circle is fine," she said, smiling.

Fair enough. I found a small town in the Mid-Hudson Valley, just inside the northern edge of the circle, and indeed, before closing on the house, Anne called the paper to make sure the address was in their delivery area. Seventeen years later, Bobbie Davis still tosses the paper onto (or close to) our patio, 365 days a year.

So what does this have to do with the price of bread, as they say? Well, I was downstairs at five thirty to start the *poolish* and I was going a little nuts because the paper hadn't come yet, giving me nothing to read over breakfast. Nothing but a bag of King Arthur flour. It turns out there's a lot to read on a bag of King Arthur, a northeastern brand highly regarded by both commercial and serious home bakers. I learned from the bag that the company is 100 percent employee-owned. There was a glowing testimonial from "I. M." (hmm . . . sounds like an inside gag: "I. M. really the CEO") plus a greeting from the president, and a recipe. I read the slogan "Naturally Pure and Wholesome" and saw that King Arthur flour was "Never Bleached. Never Bromated." That was reassuring. Much of the flour sold in America is still treated with peroxides and/or bromides at the mill — practices outlawed in the European Union owing to overwhelming evidence of the carcinogenic properties of these chemicals, used to both whiten the flour (pure, fresh flour has a creamy color) and "age" it (artificial aging is cheaper than storing the flour for several weeks while it undergoes natural oxidation), which improves the baking properties.

Finally I turned the bag to its side and read the small print near the bottom.

Ingredients: Unbleached hard wheat flour, malted barley flour (a natural yeast food), niacin (a B vitamin), reduced iron, thiamin mononitrate (vitamin B₁), riboflavin (vitamin B₂), folic acid (a B vitamin).

Odd. If it was so "naturally pure and wholesome," why was it loaded up with all those B vitamins?

I thought about other enriched foods we eat. Some breakfast cereals contain the equivalent of a multivitamin for marketing purposes, but among the staple foods, milk (with added vitamin D) and salt (with iodine) were the only others that came to mind. And they have only a single additive. Was this just King Arthur's thing? I pulled another bag of flour, a generic brand, from our cupboard. Same ingredients.

I wasn't sure I was crazy about this. Why did I have to take a supplement with my bread?

A good question, and one that deserved an answer. But first I had to start some bread. Last week's touchstone loaf was well named: hard as rock and nearly as heavy, even though the dough had risen quite nicely. To an outsider — say, my wife — it may have looked as if I was making the exact same loaf this week, but not so! Today I was omitting the second quarter teaspoon of yeast from the dough, relying only on the yeast in the *poolish,* on the theory that the heaviness might be the result of too much, not too little, yeast, causing the bread to overrise, then collapse in the oven.

A mere quarter teaspoon seems like an awfully small amount of yeast. Most recipes call for between one and two teaspoons of yeast, but those recipes make bread in a few hours. Mine would take eight or nine hours, giving a smaller amount of yeast more time to do the job, especially while in the *poolish,* which is a breeding ground for yeast.

Four hours later, the surface of the *poolish,* dotted with small bubbles, was already smelling vaguely of bread. After adding the remaining flour and two teaspoons of salt, I attached the dough hook to the mixer and set the timer for twelve minutes. This should've been twelve minutes I had available to do something else, but as the mixer flung the dough around the bowel with the dough hook, it started dancing across the countertop with an unerring instinct for the edge, keeping me standing at the counter with one hand on the mixer the entire time. The kneaded dough was slightly elastic and just a bit sticky, which I'd read is exactly what you're after. It should provide some "tack" to a hard surface but pull away nearly cleanly when you apply a little force. I misted some plastic wrap with vegetable-oil spray and covered the dough, leaving it to rise for two hours.

While the dough was rising, I went up to my office to call the King Arthur Flour Baker's Hotline to find out why their "naturally wholesome" flour had an ingredient list that read like a medicine chest inventory. A pleasant woman with just a snowflake of New England in her voice answered on the second ring. "For flours that are used to make staple products like bread, it's federally mandated that we add vitamins and minerals to flour," she explained. This had been true since the 1940s, "when refined flour was becoming popular and Americans were becoming vitamin-deficient."

Wait a second — the "Greatest Generation" was vitamin-deficient? Tom Brokaw had left that part out. Interesting.

"You're probably not the person to ask," I said apologetically, "but do you know why these particular vitamins were chosen?"

"Well, actually, I am," she said, a little put off.

"Sorry." I found myself apologizing again.

"These are vitamins that are known to prevent certain nutritional diseases — diseases of nutritional deficiency — like rickets." That would be the riboflavin. Thiamin was to prevent beriberi, which had disabled almost as many Japanese soldiers as the Russians had in the Russo-Japanese War, and iron, of course, prevents anemia. Folic acid was to prevent birth defects like spina bifida. I asked her about the fourth B vitamin in the flour, niacin.

"Niacin prevents something called, I think, pellagra."

"Pellagra? What's that?"

"You're right. I'm really not the person to ask."

I apologized yet again, thanked her for her help, and hung up, almost satisfied. Something bothered me. Rickets, beriberi, anemia — I had heard of these diseases, but not pellagra. Why was there a vitamin in my flour and in every slice of commercial bread sold in America in the past sixty years to prevent a disease I'd never heard of? Maybe there was some other, more familiar name for it (like "polio" or something). I scribbled "pellagra" on a piece of paper and shoved it into my desk drawer along with receipts, rubber bands, pens new and old, and the other detritus of the home office.

Then I went downstairs to read the *Times*.

WEEK

3

The Winter Wheat of Our Discontent

> "A loaf of bread," the Walrus said,
> "Is what we chiefly need."
> — Lewis Carroll, *Through the Looking-Glass,* 1871

"It sure looks dead," I said to Anne, examining the stubble of wheat that poked through the snow.

"But so does the lawn this time of year."

Good point. And to be expected. After all, both were grasses; one just had an edible seed head. I had a greater reason to be concerned, however. I'd just come across the following quotation from a baker: "I use wheat flour from spring wheat in all my traditional country breads."

Spring wheat? I was growing *winter* wheat, which I thought was the preferred variety! Hard spring wheat, which is planted in the spring and harvested in the fall, has more protein (13 to 16 percent before milling), and therefore gluten, than hard winter wheat (10 to 13 percent), planted in the fall. Gluten is what makes the dough elastic, allowing it to trap gases released from the yeast, which in turn allows the dough to rise. Although you can have too much of a good thing. An excess of gluten can make the dough too tight. I suppose gluten is like rubber bands: A single thin one will break easily if stretched too far, but a handful together, while stronger, may provide too much resistance to stretching. The trick is in finding the right number of bands to do the job.

I'd thought the right number was to be found in the King Arthur all-purpose flour I'd been baking with. All-purpose flour has a moderate protein (or gluten) level, between cake flour and bread flour. King Arthur's all-purpose is high in protein for an all-purpose flour, but not nearly as high as its bread flour, which is recommended for use in bread machines. Yet reading that this artisan baker used harder wheat, I wondered if I needed more gluten. The next morning, I made a loaf of peasant bread using King Arthur bread flour, made from the hardest of hard spring wheat. After a *poolish,* followed by kneading in the stand mixer and a two-hour rise, the dough had nearly "doubled in bulk," as just about every bread cookbook in the world describes it. I gave it a vigorous whomp down the center, as I'd seen Julia Child do on TV decades ago, watched the dough sadly deflate onto the counter, flattened it out, and pulled the sides together to form a ball, or *boule,* the characteristic shape of rustic breads.

The round *boule* is the original peasant loaf, so original that it lent itself to the French word for baker, *boulanger.** You wouldn't know it, walking past a Parisian bakery window today, but it wasn't until 1750 that elongated loaves surpassed round loaves in popularity. Because the fantastic bread I'd eaten that fateful morning in New York City years ago was a *boule,* it was the only loaf I was interested in making. To me, it wasn't peasant bread if it wasn't a *boule.* Plus, I loved the look of a *boule,* with the bold, decorative slashes on top that sometimes open up like a flower, revealing the crumb within. In bakeries, you can see *boules* that have lovely concentric ridges rimmed in flour, the result of the bread's having risen in the basket the French call a *banneton,* whose circular rings leave their imprint on the dough. Lacking such a classy (and expensive) container, I simply lined a colander with an old, well-floured linen napkin and placed the *boule* inside, seam side up. After covering with plastic wrap again, I put the loaf aside for the second rise, also called the proofing. This would take another ninety minutes.

It was all quite easy and calming. Until it came time to load the oven, when too often the easy rhythm of bread making yields to chaos, and all sorts of objects start flying around the kitchen as I try to flip the loaf from the colander onto the wooden baker's peel, dust the top (with flour) for that country *boule* look, quickly make a few slashes (with a razor), slide the loaf into the oven (with a peel), and give the oven walls a shot of mist (with

---

*By contrast, the Turkmen word for bread is more recent, having been changed in 2006 to the name of the ruler's mother, Gurbansoltanedzhe.

a plant sprayer), all with a minimum of time and jostling, so as not to lose any of the precious gas I've spent hours building up in the dough.

More often than not, I end up forgetting one of the steps, or realize I don't have my razor or mister handy, or do something out of sequence, or something else goes wrong, and I panic. Today was no different. The bread would not release from the peel, which I thought I'd dusted well with cornmeal, the loaf clinging from one end as if hanging on for dear life — "No, not the hot stone, I won't go!" A few more vigorous shakes and it plopped off, but by then my loaf, which had risen so beautifully, was totally deflated, and it baked into a brick.

There was no way I could serve this to my family. What to do? I remembered a recipe I'd seen recently that called for a piece of cod to be supported by a thick, dense slice of country bread in a bowl of light broth. Perfect! No one would notice how terrible the bread was in the bottom of a bowl of soup. This also gave me an opportunity to show off at dinner.

"Did you know that the Gallic word *soupe* originally referred to the slice of bread placed in the bottom of the bowl of broth?"

"Mmm. Good fish." Katie is wonderful to cook for, always appreciative of my efforts.

"And eventually the bread moved outside the bowl — "

"Um, Dad?"

" — but the name stayed with the thickened broth — now 'soup.' "

"Where'd my broth go?"

The dense bread on the bottom was a preternatural sponge, soaking up a hundred times its own weight in broth. I swear, you could almost hear a whooshing sound as the bowls dried up before our eyes.

We all put down our spoons and watched, mesmerized. The show over, everyone looked to me for an explanation. "It's fast food," I said. No one seemed amused.

"Can we go out for dessert?"

WEEK

4

The Purloined Letter

Water is a particular thing. You cannot pick it up with a pitchfork.
— George Eliot, *The Mill on the Floss,* 1860

Water?

Stunned, I stared at the letters on the page. W-a-t-e-r. In a baker's version of "The Purloined Letter," the source of my despair had apparently been in plain sight all along, flowing out of the faucet. The reason my bread wasn't rising properly, wasn't developing gas holes, was simply that I'd been using tap water!

It's true; I'd just read that bread must be made with spring water, for chlorine and other impurities found in municipal water inhibit yeast activity. Furthermore, the author stated it in such a matter-of-fact way that she made me feel I must be the only creature on the planet not to have realized this.

Naturally, chlorine isn't good for microorganisms! That's precisely why I dump it into my swimming pool every day. This suddenly seemed so obvious that I wondered how I could have overlooked it. But could it really be that simple? Was my quest for perfect bread about to end almost before it had begun?

While I waited for the weekend and my next opportunity to bake, the mailman delivered my ninety-nine-dollar, two-volume, fourteen-hundred-page set of E. J. Pyler's *Baking Science and Technology,* a book more suited for a graduate student than a home baker, but I devoured it like a good novel. Chlorine, it turned out, wasn't even the half of it. I learned from Pyler that hard water will produce a firmer dough, and acidic water — say, the kind of water found in our northeastern reservoirs, which are filled with acid rain — weakens the gluten structure, diminishing the ability of the dough to rise.

I grabbed some swimming pool testing strips to analyze my tap water. The pH was so low (that is, acidic) as to be off the scale! But then I realized that the scale on these strips ended at 6.8, just a little under the neutral 7.0. But how much lower was it? I expressed my concern to Anne. Being married to a doctor is a mixed bag. Once again, she arrived home late — very late — for dinner, but at least armed tonight with a handful of urinalysis dip strips.

"Try these," she said. The bad news was that the water's pH was about 6.2 or 6.3, quite acidic. The good news was, it wasn't pregnant.

Chlorine, low pH — the evidence pointing to water as the culprit was mounting. And there was more: Not long before, someone had told me she'd heard that the secret to authentic French bread is authentic French spring water. At the time I was dubious, but considering that bread is (by weight) about 40 percent water, it didn't seem at all unreasonable that water might affect not only the texture of the bread but the taste. Thus I figured if I was going to use spring water for my French *boule,* it might as well be French.

I picked up a bottle of Evian, delivered straight from the French Alps, fully expecting that my bread, once liberated from its chlorinated, acidic manacles, would rise in the oven like a soufflé, tasting of the Alps, evoking the character of Jean-Paul Belmondo and the eroticism of Brigitte Bardot.

Yet as I measured out the Evian, the very act of watching this stream of water flow from France into my bread bowl depressed me. I always feel guilty about drinking bottled water, particularly water that has made a transatlantic journey. Or worse, a trans-pacific journey. (Why this is worse, I don't exactly know, but it feels worse.) How much energy was expended to transport it here, how much carbon emitted into the atmosphere? In my writing, I've urged people to buy locally grown farm products, and here I was, using water shipped four thousand miles.

When did drinking water become such a burden? My father didn't spend one moment of his life worrying about the ethics (or the purity) of the water he drank, I guarantee it. He was just happy to have indoor plumbing. Every trip to the faucet was a small miracle, and he thankfully drank whatever came out.

In fact, my parents' generation didn't have to deal with half the decisions, ethical or otherwise, we have to make today. Forget paper or plastic. They didn't have to select from a dozen cable TV packages or choose between a PC and a Macintosh; they didn't have to decide between free-range and mass-produced chicken, between well-traveled organic and local conventional carrots; and they certainly never had to pick their own flights (and seats) from a zillion listings on the Internet. Sometimes I feel as if my head is going to explode. Fortunately I have a usually reliable antidote to this neuron overload: I retreat to the kitchen to do what men and women have been doing for six thousand years — bake bread on a stone.

As I watched the loaf rise in the oven (and truthfully, it did seem to be rising a bit more than usual), I had mixed feelings. As badly as I wanted this loaf to be *the one,* what was I to do if it indeed was the perfect loaf, if when I sliced into it, Belmondo and Bardot phantasmata came streaming out, swirling around my kitchen, anointing me the god — or devil — of bread? Make bread for the rest of my life from imported water? Environmental issues aside, I wanted my bread to have that *terroir,* the taste of the land, and when the Hudson Valley wheat growing in my garden matured, I wanted to bake it with Hudson Valley water.

Calm down, I said to myself. It's only bread.

It's only bread.

WEEK 5

To Die For

"Nothing in Christianity is original."
— Dan Brown, *The Da Vinci Code,* 2003

I always know when it's Passover because a box of matzo invariably materializes in the office kitchen. I don't know who brings it; I never see anyone eating from it; and a week later the box is empty. Very strange. This season of celebrating miracle and mysticism, of Passover and Easter, is also a season of bread, unleavened and rich, so I couldn't help noticing how in one work of art, the mystery and the bread coincided.

Contrary to popular opinion, the biggest mystery to be found among Leonardo da Vinci's paintings isn't Mona Lisa's smile. Nor is it a thin yarn about secret codes that reveal the existence of Jesus's descendants or some such nonsense. This true-life puzzle is in plain sight, in arguably Leonardo's greatest painting, *The Last Supper.* Look at a reproduction, the larger the better. Notice the dinner rolls. The world's most famous representation of the final meal Jesus shared with his disciples shows a table strewn with plump, unmistakably leavened dinner rolls to die for. So what's wrong with this picture? It was *Passover.* Jesus was a Jew. What's he doing eating leavened bread? There's nary a matzo in sight!

Matzo, of course, is a variety of unleavened bread. You might say *strenuously* unleavened bread. Not only is it made without yeast, but it must go from mixing to oven in no more than eighteen minutes, Jewish tradition specifying eighteen minutes as the time it takes for the leavening process to begin, even without the addition of yeast.

Christianity in effect co-opted bread as an important religious symbol when Jesus uttered the famous words at the Last Supper, speaking of bread as his body, an event Christians continue to commemorate in the form of Holy Communion. In the Catholic Church and some Protestant denominations, the bread that is eaten at Communion is unleavened; more accurately, it's an ultrathin wafer with the consistency of blotting paper that has the annoying knack of sticking to the roof of your mouth. Yet it wasn't always this way. The bread used to be leavened bread, as it still is today in the Eastern Orthodox Church. Around the year 1000, the pope, reasoning that the bread at the Last Supper must have been unleavened, given that it was Passover (and certainly

Jesus was already in enough trouble with the temple priests that he would not have been eating leavened bread at Passover), transformed the Eucharist bread into the unleavened wafer.*

The pope's argument for unleavened Communion bread seems pretty convincing, even as it makes for a poor gastronomic experience. Why, then, does the Orthodox Church use leavened bread to mark this holiest of holy Christian ceremonies? Partly it's because *risen* bread is symbolic of the Resurrection and the ascension to heaven of all believers. But how do they get around Passover? Well, they cite scripture that suggests the Last Supper actually took place the day *before* Passover. It has also been suggested that the Orthodox Church had another motivation: unleavened bread is the symbolic bread of the Jews, representing a tradition from which the church was quite happy to make a clean break.

Of course, the leavening of the bread at the Last Supper is the least of the bread debates between churches. In 1215, the Fourth Lateran Council decreed that when blessed bread is eaten during the Eucharist, it literally becomes, through transubstantiation, the flesh of Christ, a doctrine the Catholic Church holds firmly to today, and a belief that contributed to the Protestant separation from the Church of Rome.

Ecumenical debates aside, it is traditional in many parts of the world to celebrate the end of Lent with a special, rich Easter bread, often made with eggs, butter, and sugar, and I had a sudden urge to do the same, to participate in this worldwide celebration of bread. (This was as close as I came to celebrating Easter

---

*Coincidentally creating a nice little cottage industry for the monasteries that make Communion wafers to this day. One French abbey produces 22 million of them a year.

these days, not having been to church for two years.) Maybe I was also looking for an excuse not to make peasant bread, after the previous week's disappointment with the spring water, which had produced a loaf indistinguishable from the first three.

The Easter bread I was making, from Carol Field's *The Italian Baker,* was said to be adapted from "an old Roman recipe." (Hmm. Pre- or post-Crucifixion Rome? I wondered.) Surprisingly, the ancient recipe started with a *poolish* (my guess is that the *poolish* was part of said adaptation) and was loaded with sugar, butter, eggs, orange zest, and vanilla. It was a nice change and a nice bread, if a bit blander than I expected.

As for the lovely dinner rolls in *The Last Supper,* painted five centuries after the Catholic Church decreed that bread eaten at the Last Supper was unleavened, what was Leonardo up to there? While searching for an answer, I read some silly theory that if you view these dinner rolls as musical notes on a staff, they form a vaguely Gregorian-chant-like tune — or is it the Beatles' "Yesterday"? In any event, that doesn't explain why Leonardo chose to depict leavened bread. I think we can be fairly certain it wasn't a blunder on the part of the genius scientist, mathematician, engineer, inventor, anatomist, painter, sculptor, architect, botanist, musician, and writer. Was it, then, a slap in the face to the pope? A nod to the Eastern Orthodox Church? I have no idea. I do have a great idea for a novel, however.

Steamed

In the end we will listen to the voice of the machines.
We will have to. There is no choice. We will not go back to tallow
dips while the great shining wheels are there to bring us light.
— Mary Heaton Vorse (1874 – 1966), U.S. journalist and labor activist

Steam — it's not just for irons! It's the miracle vapor that's indispensable in bread making from start to finish! Steam powers the locomotives that carry the wheat from the fields of South Dakota to the mills of Minneapolis, drives the rollers that crush the grain into flour, and lastly, in your own oven, provides the crispy-chewy crust that turns good bread into great bread!

Clearly I missed my calling as a nineteenth-century ad man.

The ad would be a little dated today, except for the last part: there is still no substitute for steam when it comes to the final stage of wheat processing, baking a loaf of bread. I was looking forward to spending a calm day in the kitchen after a second consecutive week fighting a bizarre series of mechanical breakdowns that I'd taken to calling the Revenge of the Machines. The initial skirmish with technology had come when, merging onto the highway on the way home from work, I'd seen a huge plume of black smoke in my rearview mirror. "Wow, where's that coming from?" I said out loud before I realized it was coming from me.

The smoke was so thick, so black, that the headlights of the car behind me vanished in the dusk.

The exhaust end of my car looked like one of those Kuwaiti oil wells that were set on fire after the first (the "good") Gulf War. I made it home, but the car ended up in the shop for several days with a blown gasket somewhere or other. Within a week our other car downshifted into second gear all by itself at 60 miles an hour while we were on a 150-mile highway trip. That car ended up in the shop for two weeks while the dealer installed the new transmission required by yet another blown gasket somewhere or other.

All of this attention to cars apparently made the oil burner jealous, for *it* decided to spew a black, oily smoke remarkably similar to the car's oily exhaust, making the house smell like a Kuwaiti oil well during . . . you know. The cause? Yep, a leaky gasket. Then the connections on the stovetop sparked and turned black and the dishwasher sent water cascading onto the kitchen floor (gasket again), and a week later (I swear, I'm not making this up) the washing machine sent water cascading onto the laundry room floor (also known, unfortunately, as the kitchen ceiling). The Revenge of the Machines was taking no prisoners, giving me, I was told, the perpetual, hollow-eyed look of a hunted man.

At least, this morning, I could escape all that and immerse myself in the ancient tradition of bread baking, temporarily escaping the industrial age and all that it has wrought. All I had to worry about this week was getting some steam into my oven.

Most bread books explain why steam is important. It keeps the crust pliable and soft so the bread can continue to rise in the oven as the intense heat fuels the yeast into one last breath of furious metabolism, a dramatic process called oven spring. Less known, however (I found this in Harold McGee's technical book on food and cooking called *On Food and Cooking*), is the fact that steam also hastens heat transfer to the bread during those first few critical minutes in the oven. Steam is a great conductor of heat; that's why you can sit in a 212-degree dry sauna but not a 212-degree steam bath.

Commercial bread ovens have steam injectors built in, but the home baker has to improvise. I'd tried various systems over the years. First I put a rimmed baking sheet on the bottom shelf and poured in a cup of water just before loading the bread. This made steam, but it also made red-hot spittle and noises that scared the bejesus out of me as it buckled like a '57 Chevy hitting a telephone pole. Still, I kept using it, for a while substituting ice cubes for water, which was less traumatic but also made less steam and no doubt lowered the oven temperature as well. After a while I grew weary of the sight of this rusty, warped pan and threw it out.

Next I tried a technique recommended in some books: splashing water directly onto the oven floor. Anne caught me doing this and threatened to revoke my baking license if I didn't cease immediately. "What, a little water is going to hurt the oven?" I'd said defensively, yet I stopped nevertheless, switching to one of those squeeze-operated plant misters you can buy for a couple of bucks. But using that required an anaerobic workout to get a decent amount of mist into the oven — squeeze, squeeze, squeeze, huff, huff, puff — while the oven door was wide open, allowing all that precious heat to flow out.

Following the centuries-old tradition of bakers everywhere, I hopped onto the Internet, where I soon learned I wasn't the only one trying to make steam. Some entrepreneur, taking advantage of desperate home bakers like myself, was offering a $250 device that consisted of a stainless steel chafing dish cover (the kind you see at buffet tables) with a hole drilled in the side, a baking stone, and a handheld clothes steamer.

I'd almost given up hope of finding anything better than my squeeze bottle when, browsing in a garden shop, I happened upon a small pressurized sprayer intended for houseplants. After a few easy pumps to build pressure, this little device really sent out the mist, and much faster than my squeeze-trigger plant mister. The best feature was the sprayer's long, narrow neck, which would allow me to mist deep into the oven by opening the oven door just a crack, keeping heat loss to a minimum.

I slid my latest loaf onto the stone, stuck in the gooseneck, closed the oven door over it, and pressed the trigger. *Psssssssssst!* Steam poured out the oven door! This was fantastic, this was Old Faithful, this was the Union Pacific steaming into San Francisco! I sprayed some more. *Psssssssst!* This was — crack, snapple, pop, *shatter*!

"What was that?" Anne wondered out loud.

I opened the oven door to investigate. "I don't see anything unusual."

Anne peered over my shoulder. "I don't see *anything*."

The oven was dark inside. The light had blown out. And then some. When I pulled the loaf out an hour later, shards of glass from the heavy protective lens that covers — make that *covered* — the lightbulb littered the baking stone and the oven floor. Nothing was left of the bulb itself but the metal base and two insect-antennae filaments that waved, taunting me, at the slightest vibration. Apparently I had misted a little too deep into the oven, scoring a direct hit on the bulb on the back wall.

"Do you think any of the glass got into the bread?" Anne asked.

Oh, yikes. I stared at my loaf; I stared at my oven, the latest casualty of the Revenge of the Machines. Was there no end? Although I have to confess, revenge was justified in this case, for I had abused the machine, forgetting that cold mist plus 450-degree glass equals shattering. Still, I was more than a little unsettled by the fact that even bread baking had not given me refuge from humankind's fragile coexistence with the machines we depend upon so heavily. Bread baking is as homey, as removed from technology, factories, and engines, as you can get.

Or is it? As I picked glass out of the oven, I realized that this seemingly simple, earthy, non-factory-made loaf of bread could not in fact have been made without dozens of complex, sophisticated machines, from the combines that reap the wheat, isolate the kernels, and strip off the chaff; the trucks and trains that transport it; the computer-controlled factories that make the yeast; the mills that grind the flour; and the car in which I drove to the store to buy the flour, all the way down to the stand mixer I used for kneading and the electric oven that baked the bread.

What, then, is so basic, so supposedly back-to-nature, about baking bread? It seems it's really anything *but*. My loaf of "rustic" bread is so far down the supply chain that I can't see the beginning of it. Was the Revenge of the Machines simply an inevitable result of our being heavily dependent on machinery? Deep inside (I consider myself a man of science, not of mysticism; in my day job I'm the director of technology at a research institution), I knew it wasn't a personal affront, yet I couldn't help thinking that these breakdowns were sending me a message. It would take several months to fully reveal itself, but a new goal was fermenting, slowly forming in my mind: to actually bake a loaf of bread from scratch, out of reach of the Revenge of the Machines. Growing my own wheat was a start, but I wanted to do more. I wanted not just to say it, but to really, truly bake like an Egyptian.

Old Believer

> Isn't an agnostic just an atheist without balls?
> — Stephen Colbert

"Would you call yourself an atheist, Dad?"

"Not as long as Grandma's alive," I'd told Katie one Sunday morning as I kneaded dough.

Sunday bread making had progressed from an event to a habit to, within a surprisingly short time, a ritual. This of course meant that I wasn't participating in that other ritual more commonly associated with Sunday mornings, going to church — perhaps bringing to an end a family tradition that began, in this country at least, with my great-grandfather, a Russian priest who immigrated to establish the very first Old Believers church in America.

The Old Believers broke off from the Russian Orthodox Church in the seventeenth century after the Russian Orthodox Church introduced reforms, mainly related to ritual, intended to bring uniformity to practices in the Russian and Greek Orthodox churches. Some of these reforms, such as changing the direction of procession around the church (Orthodox services include a lot of circling around) from clockwise to counterclockwise, proved too radical for the faithful, who broke away and formed their own church, for which they were heavily and sometimes violently persecuted. Which is how great-grandpa ended up in America in

1908, founding the Old Believers church (still active to this day) in Marianna, Pennsylvania, where many Russian immigrants had settled to work in the coal mines.

For years, Anne and I had dutifully dragged the kids to church and Sunday school, weathering protests and temper tantrums, because Christianity was an important part of both our families' cultures — I was raised an Episcopalian, Anne a Roman Catholic — and we thought the kids should at the very least be exposed to that heritage. They could make their own choices later, as adults, as to whether they wanted Christianity to be a part of their own lives.

I had already made my own decision, even as I continued going, week after week, becoming increasingly sympathetic to the childish behavior in the backseat. Once in a while I even begged off myself, professing urgent work in the garden or the workshop, guiltily letting Anne do the dirty work of lugging the kids to church. Finally I stopped going except for Christmas and Easter; then I stopped attending altogether. I blamed the endless potluck suppers and uninspiring sermons, but these petty complaints mainly made it easier to come to grips with the fact that I had simply lost my faith.

This is not to say that I am antichurch or against organized religion in general. I am neither for nor against. I know a great many people whose faith brings them irreplaceable comfort and meaning — I suspect my great-grandfather found few atheists in the Pennsylvania coal mines — and the church has through the centuries provided a moral beacon and filled important social gaps left by secular society. For me, however, attendance at church felt like a charade, an increasingly uncomfortable one at that, once I had come to grips with the fact that I was no longer buying any of it. I was willing to leave open the possibility of some kind of higher being who created the universe (although that made me feel uneasily like the proverbial goldfish who is sure there is a God, because who else changes the water twice a week?), but surely not the God of the Old and New Testaments, an omnipresent, personal God who listens to our prayers and takes an interest in our lives. In truth, I wasn't sure if I was an atheist, an agnostic, a deist, or something else. I know I didn't believe in any kind of heavenly afterlife, although I found myself forced to reevaluate this certainty after my father (himself a religious man) died suddenly and prematurely over twenty-five years ago. Shortly afterward, he'd visited me in my sleep on a couple of occasions — his appearances more vivid than any dream, so real, in fact, that they could only be described as visions — to let me know he was still there if I needed him and, most importantly, to comfort me in my grief. I had just turned thirty, the age when I think adulthood really begins, when we are finally ready to leave the extended adolescence of college behind. These visitations by my father were disquieting because if I accepted that I had been visited by a spirit, I must therefore accept that spirits, and an afterlife, exist. After a while I concluded that these apparitions were more likely a cheap parlor trick of my mind than a proof of God's existence, but then, sadly, Dad, as if in rebuke, stopped coming around. In retrospect I wish I'd suspended judgment a bit longer.

In truth, the kids weren't the only reason I had attended church. I liked the ritual and the tradition. I found repose in repetition, in reciting prayers and singing hymns that I'd known for nearly half a century, in sitting in the same pew each week. Fortunately I found that my new Sunday morning ritual — baking — took me out of myself in the same way.

I had come to love my early mornings alone in the kitchen, the silence and the stillness broken only by the chirping of waking birds in summer and the hiss of the steam radiators in winter. All week I'd look forward to sliding across the wood floor, bowling-

alley slippery from flour dust, in my socks, as I skidded around
the kitchen. I'd come to cherish the feel of the dough in my hands
at that magical point where it passes from sticky to smooth and
elastic. In the same way that I used to take pride in not opening
the prayer book to recite that one last prayer after Communion,
I tried to bake without looking at the recipe: 2⅓ cups all-purpose
flour, 1 cup bread flour, ⅓ cup each rye and whole wheat — I
knew it, you might say, like I knew the Lord's Prayer.

This particular morning, as I watched the *poolish* gently bubble while upstairs everyone else slept, I couldn't escape the fact
that, having given up searching for God, I had started searching
for perfection on earth. I wasn't merely baking bread; I was on a
pilgrimage for *heavenly* bread. What's more, I was seeking perfection in the food most associated with Christianity.

The symbol of Christ's body. The staff of life. Why had I chosen bread? I didn't know the answer, but suddenly I was troubled
by the question. Might this quest be about more than crust and
crumb after all? And if so, why should that be upsetting? There
must be something else going on, I told myself, and just like that,
this Sunday morning deflated on me like so many of my loaves,
crushing me underneath a great sadness, a grief, a longing I hadn't
felt in many years.

What was I trying to connect to with this ritual, this almost
spiritual quest for perfection? Or should the question be, not
what, but *who*? No, no, no; the notion seemed absurd, too pat,
and way, *way* too Freudian. I wanted badly to dismiss it, but I was
shaking now, overcome with loss. As I sat over my bowl of *poolish,* full of life, life that would be extinguished within hours for
the benefit of my family, I inhaled deeply, filling my lungs with
its yeasty aroma. I ached for the release of tears, but all I could
coax from my hardened, nonbelieving soul was a single teardrop,
which I let fall, unceremoniously, into my bread.

"The Rest of the World Will Be Dead"

*Ownership of a good milch cow is a valuable means of . . . preventing
pellagra, and should be encouraged to the utmost.*
— Dr. Joseph Goldberger

"You want me to fly to South Carolina to talk to a book club?
Come on, Michael, I'm trying to bake bread here." Not to mention hang on to my day job, from which I'd have to take two
days off for this event. I had never turned down a request from
my publicist, but this one seemed a little unreasonable (nearly as
unreasonable as my excuse).

Until he explained that it wasn't just *a* book club. It was *all*
of the book clubs in the Charleston area, some seven hundred
readers, and the event was their annual luncheon, the literary/
social event of the year. They needed a last-minute replacement
for Khaled Hosseini, whose novel *The Kite Runner* had earned
more than the gross national product of his native Afghanistan
and was about to be released as a movie. Talk about a drop in
marquee value!

"No one will even know who I am," I protested.*

"They will when you're done." Spoken like a true publicist.

---

*That being that case, I guess I need to mention that my first book, an
irreverent gardening memoir titled *The $64 Tomato,* had come out the previ-
ous year.

Which is how I found myself, seminauseous with stage fright, sitting at a long table with three best-selling authors, all of whom had shared the experience of looking down from the lofty perch of the top — the very top, number one — of the *New York Times* best-seller list. How to open this fifteen-minute talk had been weighing on me for the entire week. I'd arrived in Charleston the day before and spent hours walking around the beautiful city, admiring its architecture, its gardens and old churches, and its waterfront but not enjoying any of it, owing both to nerves and to the fact that I didn't have an opening for my talk. As for the gardens, I'd never seen private gardens like these. Everyone in this city was a gardener, and a damned good one at that. What could I (an interloper from New York, no less) tell this southern audience about gardening?

Although my public speaking to date had been limited to places like Florida, New York (which is a town, not a typographical error), in front of barely enough people to field a baseball team, I had learned the importance of grabbing the audience in the first thirty seconds, or you're toast.

The problem was, I didn't want to talk about growing tomatoes; my mind was occupied with something else entirely. And it had to do with a slip of paper I had tucked away and recently found in my desk. A single word was written on it: "pellagra."

I wanted to tell the Charleston gentry how fortunate they were to be here at all; how as recently as seventy years ago, the bread that the people of South Carolina were eating was responsible for skin lesions, insanity, and death. That people with full stomachs were mysteriously dying of malnutrition. That governors of this proud state were both the fiercest critics of the New Yorker who saved thousands of South Carolinians' lives and the first to adopt his cure. This event had brought me to ground zero of one of the most fascinating epidemiological stories in our nation's history. I hadn't figured all of it out yet myself — especially the bread part — but I was starting to put the pieces together.

If you've ever been in the American South, one of the first things you notice is that people are big. Traveling through Alabama, South Carolina, Georgia, Mississippi, the places where most of college football's offensive linemen seem to come from, you don't see a lot of people, black or white, rich or poor, who seem malnourished. Yet many of these people are the grandchildren and great-grandchildren of the tenant farmers and mill workers who died by the thousands of malnutrition in the richest nation in the world in the first quarter of the twentieth century.

The disease they were dying from was pellagra. This was the reason, remember, cited by the King Arthur Flour Baker's Hotline for the presence of niacin in every bag of flour and every loaf of bread sold in the United States. Although seen occasionally in Italy for centuries, pellagra was relatively unknown in the United States until about 1908 and even then was largely confined to the South, where it was known as the disease of the four Ds: dermatitis, diarrhea, dementia, and death. Much like AIDS in the 1980s, it arrived on the scene as a mystery disease. There seemed to be no rhyme or reason to why one neighbor caught it and another did not. If contracted, it was horrifying. The first symptoms were often a severe dermatitis — a rash on the face, arms, and hands — which was followed by diarrhea and, when the illness progressed, severe dementia. The lucky ones reached the fourth D and died.

Because pellagra was most frequently found among poor Italian peasants who subsisted mainly on polenta and, in this country, among poor Southerners who consumed large amounts of corn in the form of grits, corn bread, and mush, it was widely believed to be caused by ingesting an unidentified fungus that grows on corn. This seemed reasonable because another fungus, called ergot, which grows on rye and other grains, was known to cause similar skin and psychological symptoms (later in the century, chemists would isolate LSD from ergot).

By 1914, pellagra, almost unknown in America five years earlier, was the second-leading cause of death in South Carolina. In just five southern states, the mystery disease was killing some four thousand people a year and infecting hundreds of thousands more. The government convened a blue-ribbon panel of scientists that discounted the corn connection, concluding that pellagra was caused by an infectious disease carried by a microorganism. Their reasoning? In the southern United States, pellagra was a common condition in prisons, insane asylums, and orphanages, whose residents lived in close quarters, often without proper sanitation. But which microorganism, and how to fight it, they couldn't say, so the U.S. Public Health Service, initially slow to wake to the worsening epidemic, put their best man on the job.

That would be Dr. Joseph Goldberger, a Jewish immigrant from Hungary raised on New York's Lower East Side. Goldberger had built a reputation for himself in combating the infectious diseases of the day — yellow fever, dengue, typhus, diphtheria — yet he was shocked by what he saw in the Carolinas, Mississippi, Alabama, Georgia, and Kentucky: orphans with cracked, hardened skin covered with lesions so severe they could not use their hands; asylums filled with skeletal figures staring through hollow eyes, disfigured, without bowel control, and insane.

Something else struck Goldberger. Wherever he saw pellagra, he saw cotton. As far as the eye could see, cotton, growing right up to the front steps of the wretched shacks of their sharecropper owners. The South was a cotton economy. If you didn't grow it, you worked with it in the mill. Sharecropper or miller, you barely made a living, and you spent what little money you made on the overpriced food at the company store. Under pressure to increase production, every available square foot of land was planted with cotton, as home vegetable plots were squeezed out and orchards cleared.

Goldberger also noticed that pellagra struck in clusters. At one Jackson, Mississippi, orphanage that Goldberger visited, he found that 168 of the 211 children had the disease. It was like the plague. Except for one troubling detail: all of the staff, many of whom spent up to fourteen hours a day with their patients — even sleeping in the same dormitory — were healthy. Odd, this didn't act like the plague.

Goldberger became convinced that a dietary deficiency, not infection, was the culprit. He tested his theory by performing an experiment at two orphanages in Mississippi, adding a daily ration of fourteen ounces of milk to each child's diet.* Within weeks, the telltale rashes started to fade.

Anticipating that skeptics would claim that some other unknown factor might have been responsible for the apparent cure, Goldberger designed another experiment, the converse of the orphanage trial. To absolutely prove that pellagra was a nutritional deficiency, he devised an experiment to *induce* pellagra by putting volunteers on a deficient diet. Goldberger's first challenge in conducting this clinical trial, which would be nearly impossible to replicate in our current age of institutional review boards and federal guidelines, was finding recruits. Imagine trying to sign up volunteers today for a study in which you attempt to induce AIDS; pellagra had the same social stigma in 1915.

Goldberger found his volunteers at Rankin State Prison Farm, eight miles east of Jackson, Mississippi, where the governor's

---

*Milk was a luxury food; the experiment became possible only when Goldberger obtained federal funding for the extra milk.

promise of parole at the conclusion of the six-month experiment was enough incentive for twelve inmates — half of them convicted murderers serving life sentences — to accept the risk. The political risk for Governor Earl Brewer was almost as great. Releasing a half-dozen murderers to the streets was as unpopular then as now, but Brewer knew his state was in trouble: the incidence of pellagra was up 50 percent over the previous year, with no end in sight.

On April 19, 1915, Goldberger put the twelve inmates on a diet similar to that which he'd seen at the orphanages: biscuits, grits, gravy, corn bread, coffee, and fried mush made from cornmeal. The only vegetable was cabbage, most likely included to prevent scurvy. Within weeks, the inmates reported feeling listless, but there was no trace of pellagra. Four months passed — still no pellagra. Goldberger was growing despondent. The trial was nearing its end, and he was only six weeks away from going home disgraced, when pellagra appeared in one of the prisoners. Then another, and another. Goldberger brought in independent doctors to confirm the diagnosis: half of the inmates had pellagra.

It was a complete triumph for Goldberger, yet the essential question still remained: What vitamin (the term was just coming into vogue) were these pellagrins lacking? Or put another way, what vitamin in a healthy diet (including milk and fresh vegetables) was the pellagra preventative (what Goldberger called the PP factor)? Other mysteries swirled. Why had pellagra increased in incidence so much in recent years? And why in particular was it hitting cotton workers so hard? Much work remained to be done, and Goldberger was ready to dig in, but unbelievably, the debate over pellagra's cause was not yet over.

The "infectionists," the infectious disease proponents, were not giving in. They conceded that the test diet was deficient but argued that it had simply weakened the inmates to such an extent that it made them susceptible to contracting pellagra from whatever microorganism carries it. Why were scientists and politicians so determined to cling to the infectious disease theory? Historians have speculated that to acknowledge that the pellagra epidemic was caused by malnutrition was to admit that the South couldn't feed its people. Only fifty years removed from slavery, the New South, driven by leaders like Huey Long and culturally active cities like Charleston, was trying to rebuild its image, to gain the respect of not only the North but the rest of the world. The embarrassing fact that malnutrition was indirectly the second-leading cause of death of South Carolinians was not the story they wanted to tell the world or even themselves. And they certainly did not want to hear it from a New York Jew, particularly one who was becoming increasingly vocal about the social causes of the disease, indicting the sharecropper system and the monoculture of King Cotton, which had pushed out local vegetable farms. The angry citizenry of one Georgia city telegraphed their senator: WHEN THIS PART OF GEORGIA SUFFERS FROM A FAMINE THE REST OF THE WORLD WILL BE DEAD.

They were confusing famine with malnutrition.

Goldberger had had enough of these attacks. He devised a desperate experiment to shut up these "blind, selfish, jealous, prejudiced asses," as he described them, once and for all. If pellagra was infectious, then he would do everything in his power to contract it. First he gave himself a blood transfusion from a pellagrin. Then he ingested scrapings taken from several victims' open sores. Not dead yet, he and fourteen other volunteers (including his wife, who insisted on joining him) made up dough "capsules," flour balls mixed with festering skin lesions, nasal secretions, blood, and even diarrhea from active pellagrins — worse, even, than eating at, say, your local fast food joint — and washed it all down with bicarbonate of soda. Goldberger hosted five of what they called their "filth parties" (what else they did at these parties was not documented).

This is beyond remarkable — even putting aside the volunteers' enormous faith in Goldberger's pellagra theory, consider the diseases they *could* have contracted from these weakened, immune-suppressed pellagrins! Yet not one of the sixteen partygoers displayed any pellagra symptoms. After the final gathering, Goldberger wrote in his journal, "Never again."

The experiment had its intended effect. The infectionists were quelled (for the most part; some clung to their beliefs into the late 1930s). Now Goldberger could turn his attention to the real mystery: What substance — vitamin or mineral — was lacking in the pellagrins' diet? What was the elusive PP factor? More dietary experiments determined it was present in great quantities in dried yeast, a food that could be manufactured cheaply, and by persuading the Red Cross to distribute yeast as a food supplement after a 1927 flood devastated impoverished areas of coastal Mississippi, a tragic pellagra epidemic was avoided.

Still, even though a preventative was known, the disease continued its rampage, peaking in the Depression years of 1929 and 1930, when pellagra, no longer confined to the rural South, claimed two hundred thousand victims. Unfortunately, Goldberger would never live to learn the identity of his PP factor, for he died young, not of typhus or diphtheria or yellow fever or dengue or any of the other dangerous tropical diseases he exposed himself to in the service of this nation's health, but of cancer, at the age of fifty-four. Precisely my age as I faced this group of South Carolinians. And like Goldberger, a New Yorker among Southerners.

I was still working out the connection between pellagra and bread, but I would've loved to tell this story of an unsung American hero to the seven hundred people seated in front of me. Some of them might well have had living relatives who remembered when South Carolina became the first state in the nation to mandate the enrichment of bread and flour, but I knew this group was hoping for a lighthearted talk on gardening. I heard my name spoken, followed by polite applause (naturally — Charleston has been named the most polite city in the United States), and I walked to the lectern. I had never found a satisfactory opening, so I decided to just speak the truth and tell them what had been troubling me about the talk I had to give.

"Yesterday I had a chance to walk through your beautiful city for a few hours," I began nervously, my New York accent hanging heavy over the enormous hall. "And do you know, I counted *approximately* one thousand three hundred and thirty-seven gardens?" I paused. "Each one nicer than mine."

They roared in appreciation. The rest was easy.

WEEK

9

Gute Recipes

When asked, "What does it take to be a good baker?" Brother Boniface
has a ready answer: "You've godt to have *gute* recipes."
— *Baking with Brother Boniface*, 1997

A twentieth-century American monastery ranks, on my own list of 1,000 Places to See Before I Croak, somewhere in the high nine hundreds, nestled between Graceland and the World's

Largest Ball of Twine, but the cover of the book in my hands was about to challenge that prejudice.

The book in question, a slim paperback titled *Baking with Brother Boniface*, had arrived in the mail while I was in Charleston. Monasteries have a long tradition of bread making, and I thought this book, written by a ninety-year-old monk, might have some traditional recipes for honest bread. I had trouble, however, getting past its cover, dominated by an arresting black-and-white photograph. Brother Boniface stands to one side in the foreground, stooped over, smiling benevolently, his arthritic hands clasped together, but ceding the stage to an enormous twisting tree behind him. The tree is thrusting from the ground, spiraling heavenward in great agony, trying to loose the bonds of earth.

I opened the book tentatively, expecting recipes accompanied by spiritual inspiration and biblical allusions, but this paperback was all business. Just "gute recipes." Plus one biographical detail that caught my attention: Boniface had not started baking until he was fifty, just about the age I was when I'd baked my first loaf of bread. I felt a weird connection to the tree and the baker and suddenly wanted to meet both. Now, where was Mepkin Abbey?

South Carolina. An hour from Charleston. Next time I mail-order a book, I'll spring for first-class postage. Although it turns out that even if I'd known about the abbey a week earlier, I wouldn't have met the baker. Brother Boniface Schnitzbauer had recently passed away at the age of ninety-six. The tree, presumably, lives on.

Born to Run

You got to make it by yourself.
— The 1970s pop band Bread

It was a matter of life and death, and every second counted. Having planned my steps beforehand with the precision of an organ transplant team, I moved quickly and efficiently, racing to the car, gingerly placing the parcel in the waiting cooler, and surrounding it with towels and ice packs.

Securing the ice chest next to me with a seat belt, I pulled out of the driveway, leaving pebbles and dust flying in my wake. If traffic was light, I figured I could make the trip in just under an hour. But if it took much longer — well, I didn't want to think about that. The living, breathing organ in my cooler was a kilogram of peasant bread dough. The recipient was a ten-ton wood-fired brick oven located at Bobolink Dairy, a New Jersey dairy farm and bakery.

I was on my way to test a new theory: that the solution to my missing gas hole problem (if a hole can be missing) lay in baking my bread in a wood-fired brick oven. I had stumbled across this suggestion when, while flipping through a book called *The Bread Builders,* I was struck by a grainy photograph of a slice of bread. One look, and I knew this was it: the perfect slice from the perfect loaf, full of irregular cells and possessing such an open crumb that the sunlight behind the slice streamed through in biblical fashion, revealing the rich, netted structure of the bread.

How could I create this slice of bread? Easy. All I had to do was build a twenty-thousand-pound wood-fired brick oven in my backyard. I liked the concept in an abstract fashion, and it did fit into my notion of baking a loaf of bread from scratch, removed from the industrial supply chain, but this seemed a little extreme, the lunatic fringe of home bread making. Still, I didn't want to dismiss it out of hand, so I figured I'd let Anne veto the project for me. I told her of my findings.

"We can do pizza!" she squealed. "And chicken! Where are you going to put it?"

That was unexpected.

"I don't know. It's ten tons. I put that much mass in one spot, I may affect the rotation of the earth. I can just see the headline now: BACKYARD BAKER THROWS EARTH OFF AXIS."

"Actually," Anne mused, "I'd rather have a hearth in the kitchen," reviving an old fantasy we had dismissed years ago as too impractical and expensive.

I tried not to show my alarm. Things were escalating rapidly. Anne was supposed to be my brake, reining in my harebrained schemes, not feeding them! Of course, the idea of a kitchen hearth, a waist-height wood-fired oven, was appealing. We love our living room fireplace but hardly get to use it, since, like most Americans, we practically live in the kitchen. As she dreamily spoke of a hearth, its glowing embers warming a chill snowy morning, I searched hard for an antidote.

"I think those are more for pizza than bread."

Anne frowned.

"And I don't think our hundred-year-old house can handle a ten-ton oven."

Truth was, neither could my half-century-old body, but it

seemed that the project was now on the table. Before I laid the first brick, however, I figured I'd better try one out first, and a little digging had uncovered the fact that one of the coauthors of *The Bread Builders,* Alan Scott, who was also considered the nation's premier outdoor wood-fired masonry bread oven expert, proselytizer, and apostle for baking bread in outdoor wood-fired masonry ovens, had built one at a farm less than a dough-proofing away.

The oven's owner was at first understandably cautious upon hearing my request. After all, she was running a production bakery.

"How many loaves do you want to bake?" Nina asked.

"Oh, just one two-pound loaf. I'm baking a loaf a week for a year."

I heard her giggle through the phone.

"You're only baking one loaf at a time?" She could barely contain herself. "How cute."

Cute? I was having an existential crisis a week over this single loaf. Producing each loaf was like giving birth, every weekend, over and over, except that Mama was disappointed with every newborn, and Nina was treating this as if it were a mere dalliance, a trifle!

"You can bake five or six loaves and freeze them, you know."

What did she think I had at home — a commercial Hobart mixer? I was having a hard enough time with one loaf, thank you very much. Plus, we could barely consume the bread I was baking now. If I baked a half-dozen loaves every weekend, we'd each be eating nearly a loaf of bread a day, like medieval monks.

In any event, once she stopped laughing, she agreed to let me bring my dough to her oven — and, by extension, her baker — the following week. I prepared for the big day by doing an overnight *poolish* in the refrigerator, then taking it out at six o'clock the next morning and letting it ferment a few more hours at room temperature. At ten thirty I kneaded and started the first rise. I was aiming for the loaf to go into the oven around two o'clock, with the second rise taking place at the bakery. After an hour of driving, though, I seemed to be lost. I had expected to be in the country, but this was new, dreary suburbia, sixty miles from the nearest city, a hodgepodge of luxury homes built on dead-end streets without sidewalks, all with names ending in *Lane* or *Court*. Where in this neighborhood could there possibly be a two-hundred-acre dairy farm?

I dialed the farm's number on my cell phone. No answer. As I was considering turning back and abandoning the mission, I rounded a corner, and looming before me, as incongruous as a skyscraper, rose a single silo, filling the windshield with its silent majesty, its strength, its courage standing tall in the midst of development, taking my breath away.

I had arrived.

I'd been looking forward to meeting the baker as much as meeting the oven. This would be my first encounter with a professional baker, and what better way to start than with an old-world, wood-fired hearth-oven baker, someone whom I imagined to be a heavyset man in a soiled, sweat-stained T-shirt, cigarette dangling out of his mouth, a real veteran of the flour wars. Or perhaps Nicolas Cage. As we'd be spending several hours together, I anticipated being regaled with tales of his baker's life and pumping him for information. I'd even rehearsed how to ask him to be my teacher, my mentor, my very savior.

Nina led me into the bakery. "This is our baker," she said cheerfully.

Where? The only person here was a wisp of a girl with a

smudge of flour on her nose, a twenty-two-year-old whose face radiated the earnest openness and innocence of a farm girl from Indiana. Which is exactly what she was. Surely she wasn't the only baker.

"Oh, no," the young woman, whose name was Lindsay, said when I asked if she worked alone. She introduced me to another woman of about the same age, an intern, who was loading the oven. Their combined ages were a decade less than mine. Lindsay had been an intern herself until four weeks earlier, when the baker quit and she inherited the job. She'd been baking for all of a month. "Let's see how it looks," she said, taking my loaf into the proofing room, a chilled room full of trays of dough, buckets of sourdough, and racks of proofing loaves.

I shivered. "I didn't know to bring a sweater." Like most home bakers, I'd been following the conventional wisdom by proofing in a warm area (the classic instruction is to proof in an oven with the pilot light on).

"It's actually a little warm in here today," Lindsay said, looking at the thermometer, which read sixty-seven. "We like to keep the temperature in the low sixties so we can do a long, slow fermentation and proofing. It gives you more flavor." She poked my dough. "I think you can form the loaf now."

Swallowing my pride and putting aside the thought that I'd been married longer than she'd been alive, I asked her to watch and critique. She wasn't impressed with my *boule*-forming technique.

"I usually do this," she said, half dragging, half rolling the dough across the table in a circular motion to develop surface tension and keep the loaf together. Her hands moved naturally and skillfully across the table. My dough was a little dry, she noted politely, but it was too late to do anything about it.

I dropped the *boule* into my colander and watched Lindsay

work, struggling to stay out of her way in the tight quarters. Whatever disappointment I'd initially felt at the fact that my tutor wasn't a seasoned baker melted away as I watched this kid moving confidently and quickly through the trays of dough, all in different stages of development, dividing, weighing, forming loaves, and loading the oven, keeping up a line of chatter and cheerfully answering my dopey questions all the while. I asked her about a couple of techniques I'd read about. One, known by its French name, *autolyse,* involves resting the dough for anywhere from ten to thirty minutes before kneading it. This method, developed a quarter century ago by the French bread scientist Raymond Calvel, was reputed to produce a superior crumb and better flavor by essentially "conditioning" the gluten before kneading. Such a dough requires less kneading, which results in less oxygen being incorporated, which makes better bread, say proponents.

"It works," she said, "but I don't know why." Interesting. I had tried it once and couldn't see any difference whatsoever in the bread.

How had Lindsay picked up more baking expertise in a month than I had in five years? Perhaps part of the answer lay in the math. She was baking twenty-five hundred loaves of bread a week. Was I wasting my time on books, theory, farming, and research, when I should just be baking bread, lots of it, every day? I had some thinking to do. But first I had a single loaf of bread to bake in a wood-fired masonry oven.

I was eager to start, but we had to wait both for my bread and for the oven to be ready. Lindsay checked the digital thermocouple. "Six eighty," she said. "Still a little hot for a *boule.*"

I couldn't believe my ears. It was three o'clock in the afternoon; Lindsay had been baking bread in the oven all day, opening the door frequently, mopping out the hearth, moving loaves in and out, and the oven, which had not received a lick of fuel since the previous night's fire, was still nearly 700 degrees. Clearly the ten tons of masonry was doing the job. Unlike conventional ovens, which heat the food, a wood-fired masonry oven heats the masonry — the brick — and it is this heat, slowly released from the huge mass of masonry long after the fire is out, that bakes the bread.* As loaves went in and came out — the narrow baguette-shaped loaves can be baked at higher temperatures than *boules* — the oven gradually cooled to about 640 degrees at the flue, meaning the temperature at the base, where the bread sits, was about 540 degrees. If I baked a loaf of bread with my home oven that hot, I'd end up with a charred round of raw dough, but Lindsay pronounced the oven ready.

She loaded in her own *boules,* letting me handle a couple. She even offered to let me slash them, which I declined, as I didn't want to render any of her bread unmarketable with my clumsy slashes. Slashing the loaf with a sharp knife or razor just moments before it goes into the oven produces those lovely *grignes* — the cuts in a loaf that can vary from a decorative pattern to cresting waves of crust — that open up in the oven. Baguettes tradition-ally have overlapping diagonal slashes, while many *boules,* includ-ing mine, receive a crosshatch, like a tic-tac-toe grid. The loaves that come from the famous Poilâne Bakery in Paris are carved with their signature script *P.* These cuts aren't just decorative, however. A loaf that is not slashed (and I speak from experience) will burst open at the weakest point. Slashing allows for con-trolled expansion during the oven-spring phase, when the gases produced by the yeast are expanding rapidly.

*I was simulating this action at home in a minor way by baking the loaves directly on a preheated pizza stone, which provided some thermal mass and conducted heat to the loaf more efficiently and evenly than would a baking sheet.

Back in my kitchen, I had what I thought was a professional *lame* — a ten-dollar model consisting of a razor blade permanently molded (read "nonreplaceable") into a plastic handle — but Lindsay handed me her truly professional *lame,* a cheap, replaceable double-edged razor blade threaded onto a flimsy strip of metal, and following her advice to slash quickly, without hesitation or too much thought, I made four cuts across my own loaf, which I slipped into the oven. Lindsay grabbed a ninety-nine-cent plant mister — the very one I'd rejected as being ineffective — and gave the oven walls a quick spritz.

The baking day was winding down, with only one batch of bread left after this, and I could sense the atmosphere changing, the pace slowing, as weary smiles started to appear on the tired faces of the bakers. A steady rain fell on the tin roof above our heads, making conversation almost impossible. Lindsay stepped out into the downpour and reappeared a few minutes later with a wheelbarrow full of firewood. She was soaking wet, the rain on her floury skin giving her the look of a loaf that had just been spritzed in the oven.

Lindsay weighed out the wood needed for that night's fire — exactly 175 pounds' worth (bakers weigh everything, I noticed) — which would bake tomorrow's bread. The last baking task of her long day would be to start the fire before leaving the bakery.

Now, for the first time in the entire afternoon, there really was nothing to do but wait for the loaves. The rain continued to fall as the light faded from the room. When the intern materialized with a wine bottle, my own fatigue suddenly evaporated. A glass of wine sounded lovely. Except that the bottle held olive oil. Lindsay poured some into a bowl and grabbed a bread knife and a small loaf made with leftover dough. A stick of homemade butter came out of the fridge. Good, fresh unsalted butter has a clean taste that enhances the flavor of bread, and this butter, spread on the slightly warm bread, was extraordinary. I actually felt a little drunk as I let the bread and butter play on my tongue, trying to absorb every bit of flavor before swallowing.

A few slices later, Lindsay took my loaf out of the oven. "It's singing!" she said, her eyes lighting up. "Listen!"

Sure enough, the bread was crackling, as the hot crust, a beautiful dark brown with shades of caramel and molasses, came into contact with the cooler air.

"Is that a good thing?"

"Oh, yes, that's a very good thing," she said, laughing.

No doubt about it, this was the most beautiful loaf I'd ever baked. It had sprung like never before in the oven; even my slashes, usually disastrous, had come out perfectly. I could hardly wait for it to cool to slice it open and see if the crumb matched the promise of the crust.

I thanked Lindsay and stepped out into a beautiful late afternoon, washed of dust and doubt, full of hope and optimism, as a wisp of a rainbow appeared in the east, exactly in the direction I was driving.

I followed it home, smiling the entire time.

III.

Terce

A Latin term for third hour. One prays
for light and strength as the day waxes strong
and one's work begins.

Goddisgoode

I beg you . . . to bear in mind that my observations and opinions
are only the result of my own impulse and curiosity and that there
are in this town no amateurs who, like me, dabble in this art.
— Antoni van Leeuwenhoek, letter to the Royal Society, 1673

Weight: 199 pounds
Bread bookshelf weight: 18 pounds

"Anne, can you bring home your microscope for the weekend?"

She just stared at me, unblinking.

"What's the problem?" I asked. "I'll be careful with it." Anne
is a physician of the old-fashioned sort who still looks at slides
(of what, I'd rather not know) under a microscope and has a nice
one in her office.

"It's not that. What do you want to look at?"

What was this all about? Oh, right, the last time I had borrowed her microscope was twenty years earlier. Exactly. How
do I know that? Because Zach was now nineteen. In the second
year of our marriage, after having unprotected sex, oh, five or
six times with no results of the reproductive variety, I was posi-
tive I was sterile. Perhaps it was my concern about the really hot
baths I love to take or some painful but temporary sports inju-
ries *down there,* but I think my hypochondria was mainly the
result of having had it drummed into my head since junior high

school health class that only two things can happen when you have intercourse: pregnancy and disease. The third possibility, that most of the time you'd simply have some fun, was somehow never mentioned.

Thus when I spilled a little of my seed onto a microscope slide, my stomach was tied up in a knot. I really, really wanted kids. I wanted to coach Little League teams; I wanted Kennedy-style touch football games on the lawn. Yet as I peered through the lens and twisted the focus knob forward, then backward, I saw... nothing. My worst fears were confirmed: I was sterile. "I knew it," I groused as I slumped into a chair. "Now what are we going to do?"

Anne peered through the microscope as she fiddled with the knobs. "Come take a look," she said. I gloomily dragged myself back to the instrument.

Holy smokes! There were dozens, no, hundreds, no, zillions, of my little guys swimming around like mad. It looked just like the health class movies. "Let's go!" I yelled, dragging Anne out of the kitchen and toward the bedroom. "We're celebrating. I can make babies!"

And not long afterward, I did. Twice. (For the record, I never coached Little League and couldn't ever interest anyone in touch football, but we had fun all the same.) This time around, once I'd explained that I simply wanted to play voyeur to a little yeast sex, Anne was relieved. The fact that I had in my lifetime asked to borrow her microscope, though, on exactly two occasions, both times involving reproduction, did not escape her attention.

Why pull out the microscope? Well, the bread baked last week in Bobolink's brick oven had, I am sorry to report, the same lousy, dense crumb under the gorgeous (and delicious) crust. In previous weeks, the water business had been a red herring; I had decreased the amount of yeast, changed the steam, changed the oven, and changed the flour, yet my loaves were still moist and devoid of holes. Frankly I was running out of ideas.

But not curiosity. I like science and had in fact wanted to be a doctor back in the day, but a C– in organic chemistry and a major in English literature from a state university didn't have medical schools fighting over me. According to Anne and the kids, this is the best thing that ever happened to me (and my community), and I have to concede that Anne, as an internist, speaks with some credibility on the matter.

"You would've hated medicine," she reminds me every time I bring it up, careful not to say that I would've been a terrible doctor, though I'm sure she believes that as well.

"I can just hear you, Dad," Zach adds. " 'Suck it up and stop whining! Next!' "

"You have no patience," Katie invariably chimes in. "And you don't like talking to people."

No patience? Well, I'd show her. We were going to do a little patient science in our own kitchen laboratory this morning. "Come on, Katie," I said in my most enthusiastic let's-go-out-and-play voice. "We're going to watch a little yeast sex!"

"Cool."

"Really, dear . . ."

Since none of the previous experiments had produced gas holes, I decided to look to the yeast. After all, it's the yeast that produces the gas that makes the holes, but that was about where my knowledge ended. I wanted to know more and even see the process in action.

I wasn't alone in not knowing much about yeast. For roughly fifty-nine of the sixty or so centuries that bakers have been making bread, they did so without knowing what yeast even was — not just how it worked, but even what it *was*. It wasn't until the eve of the Civil War, after the invention of the steam engine, photography, and even vaccination, nearly a full century after the discovery that plants convert carbon dioxide into oxygen, that we figured out what makes bread rise. For much of that time, baking was an act of faith — faith that the dough would rise, provided you added a little of yesterday's dough to today's.

The word *yeast* first appears in Middle English before the year 1000 and is derived, suitably enough, from the German word for foam (a vestige, no doubt, of Oktoberfests of yore). But no one really knew what yeast was, and certainly no one had a clue as to why it made beer and wine ferment and bread rise, let alone suspected it was a microorganism (naturally; the very concept of microorganisms hadn't been discovered yet). To some, the action of yeast seemed downright mystical, even proof of the divine. The 1468 *Brewers Book of Norwich* refers to yeast as "goddisgoode" because it was made by the blessing of God.

That wasn't good enough for Antoni van Leeuwenhoek, one of those wonderfully eccentric figures who thankfully pop up throughout history to enliven dull science texts. A Dutch draper from Delft (which sounds like the opening of a limerick), Leeuwenhoek was born in the same city and year as the artist Jan Vermeer. In fact, their baptisms are recorded on the same page in the Delft baptismal register, surely making it one of the most valuable register pages in the world. Leeuwenhoek became enamored — one might say obsessed — with microscopes and the invisible world after coming across a hot new best seller that was sweeping Europe in 1665, Robert Hooke's *Micrographia*. Filled with spectacular copper engravings made from Hooke's own drawings of the miniature world as seen through his microscope, the book enthralled Europe with its details of a fly's eye, a plant cell, and, most famously, a foldout of a louse that was four times the size of the book itself. (Contemporary Playmates can only blush with envy.)

Inspired by Hooke's best seller, Leeuwenhoek set about making his own microscopes, even grinding his own lenses, while his drapery business seemingly ran itself. But unlike Hooke's compound microscope, with its familiar lens tube holding an eyepiece and a second lens close to the object, Leeuwenhoek's microscope was remarkably simple: a single lens only about a half inch in diameter, held in place by two metal plates. In appearance it resembled the magnifying glass he used to examine his draper's cloth far more than it did a microscope. The whole thing could be concealed in the palm of his hand, yet he saw objects that were hidden to every other microscope in the world. Leeuwenhoek had an extraordinary talent for grinding lenses. In fact, his pocket microscopes — he made dozens, only a handful of which survive — with a magnification of up to 266 times, are superior to most microscopes used in university classrooms today. What other instrument from the seventeenth century can you say that about?

Leeuwenhoek (he added the "van" as an affectation at the age of fifty-two) had no scientific training whatsoever, but he was blessed with boundless curiosity and started looking at everything from rainwater to mouth scrapings under his microscopes. One of his first investigations has become a ritual experienced by millions of elementary school children: bringing pond water to the classroom and examining it under a microscope. Leeuwenhoek coined the delightful term *animalcules* (meaning "little animals") for the single-celled creatures — protozoa and the like — that he discovered in the water, swimming "upwards, downwards, and round about."

He sent colorful letters in layman's language describing his observations of these sightless, wriggling microbes, "the most wretched creatures that I have ever seen," to the Royal Society of London for the Improvement of Natural Knowledge (more commonly called simply the Royal Society), which is like my sending doodles of my garden to *Scientific American*. One can imagine the initial reception his letters must have received: a Dutch cloth merchant telling the London intelligentsia that he had discovered microorganisms and bacteria under a microscope he made in his kitchen. Leeuwenhoek might have vanished into obscurity had not Hooke, after initially failing to substantiate the draper's wild claims of microscopic life, gone back and built a better microscope, thus becoming the second man in history to view microorganisms.

Eventually, Leeuwenhoek got around to looking at a little brewer's yeast under his microscope.* He described seeing clusters of "globules," as he called them, and went so far as to make a wax model to play with. He squished it with his hands, tugged it, and twisted it, trying to understand the meaning and purpose behind the structure. His letter to the Royal Academy describing his findings included these sketches:

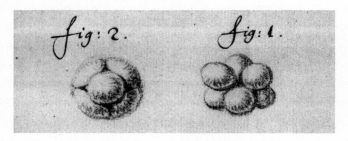

Most likely, Leeuwenhoek's globules were yeast cells in the process of "budding." Yeast reproduces asexually by growing a small bud that forms into a new yeast organism before breaking off, the process of cell division called mitosis.

*But not before making another observation startlingly similar to one of my own. Producing a sperm sample, however, was a more delicate matter in seventeenth-century Holland than in twentieth-century New York, so Leeuwenhoek was careful to note that he had obtained his "without sinfully defiling myself" (I confess I had no such compunction myself), rushing his sample to the microscope "before six beats of the pulse had intervened," leaving his wife no doubt unsatisfied, but giving the world its first valuable clue about the mysterious reproductive process.

I figured I should be able to easily observe yeast cells in the act, and I wondered if I would see anything close to what Leeuwenhoek drew three hundred years before. With the microscope set up in the kitchen, I smeared a drop of this week's *poolish* onto a glass slide and called Katie into our impromptu kitchen laboratory. Silly me. All we could see were huge particles of flour obscuring the microscopic yeast. So we stirred about a teaspoon of instant yeast into warm water to which we'd added a pinch of sugar as a nutrient. Fifteen minutes later, the mixture had turned almost creamy, frothing as small bubbles rose to the surface, and we prepared a new slide. Under the microscope, the drop of water seemed to contain a host of yeast cells, many clustered together, but at this magnification it was hard to see any detail. Yet when I moved to the highest power of the microscope, the field was too dark to see anything. I moaned to Katie.

"Let me see," she said, nudging me out of the chair to take over the microscope just as her mother had done twenty years earlier. Katie reached under the microscope stage and turned a diaphragm I hadn't seen, letting in more light and revealing the yeast. At high power now, several of the clusters looked similar to Leeuwenhoek's sketches, but I couldn't see anything that I could conclusively say was budding yeast. This was confusing. We should be seeing reproducing yeast in various forms of development. I kept searching across the field of view, moving the slide up, down, left, and right, and then I saw what I was looking for: budding yeast.

There was, however, surprisingly little of this budding going on. We prepared a few more slides but still couldn't find much evidence. This bothered me. Had I overestimated the amount of reproduction taking place? But if the yeast wasn't reproducing all that much, then where did all the gas that makes the dough swell come from? Just that tiny bit of yeast originally added? And I had another question: Carbon dioxide is odorless, but there were some strong, pungent smells coming out of that bubbling yeast. I wondered exactly what was going on in there.

As did Leeuwenhoek. Aside from the budding, something else puzzled him: "I saw a great number of gaseous bubbles rising from a blackish particle which was a thousand times smaller than a grain of sand," he wrote, "but in spite of all my pains I was unable to arrive at their cause."

In fact, it would be nearly two centuries before anyone would "arrive at their cause," and it would happen almost by accident. In 1854 a young chemist named Louis Pasteur took a position at the new Faculty of Sciences in Lille, in northern France. This industrial city, home to a number of sugar beet distilleries, had recently underwritten the school in hopes of training its young men in practical industrial applications of science. Pasteur, though, seemed ill suited for that role, needing to be reminded by his dean to make sure his "applications adapt themselves to the real needs of the country."

Pasteur griped about this privately but descended from his ivory tower long enough to help the father of one of his students, a distiller who was having a problem. A number of M. Bigo's sugar beet vats were sick; rather than fermenting into alcohol, they were going sour. When Pasteur examined the contents of the healthy vats under his microscope, he saw, as expected, many yeast cells. But in the sick vats, the yeast was being crowded out by something else — microorganisms far smaller than yeast cells and shaped like long rods.

Bacteria.

WEEK
12

Choreography

Chance favors the prepared mind.
— Louis Pasteur

Louis Pasteur claimed credit for being the first person to observe bacteria, but this life form had in fact been observed and described in some detail by that draper from Delft two hundred years earlier. Pasteur, equipped with knowledge and tools that Leeuwenhoek could only dream of, set about understanding the chemistry and biology of what was happening in both the sick and the healthy yeasty vats. One of his contemporaries, the famous German scientist Justus von Liebig, had for years loudly insisted that it was chemical decomposition of the yeast cells, not a living process, that was responsible for the bubbles in beer and dough and for the change that yeast brought to beer and wine. How could it be otherwise? Everyone knew that life required oxygen and could not possibly exist in the bottom of a beer vat.

Pasteur, however, didn't "know." Instead, he performed experiments in the laboratory, proving beyond a doubt that the bubbles in the vats and the dough — the bubbles Leeuwenhoek had seen — were due to a living process: *Yeast, in the absence of oxygen, converts sugar into alcohol and carbon dioxide.* As for the bacteria, it was also feeding on the sugar but producing lactic acid, not alcohol, causing the vats to sour.

We have no record of what became of M. Bigo's distillery business, but today, Lesaffre, the largest yeast producer in the world, has a state-of-the-art plant in Lille, where sugar beets still go to be fermented. As for Pasteur, he was off and running on a career in practical science. He would continue to study bacteria and, after proving conclusively that microorganisms were not created through spontaneous generation (a fact Leeuwenhoek had pretty much established), go on to save the French silkworm industry, return to studying yeast in a patriotic mission to make French beer the equal of German (most would say he failed), and develop vaccinations for smallpox and rabies. Not to mention that, finally, Pasteur had discovered the secret of what makes bread rise, this action called fermentation, which he defined simply as "la vie sans air" — life without air — living yeast cells feeding on sugar and producing, as waste products, carbon dioxide and alcohol. Chemically speaking,

$$C_6H_{12}O_6 \quad \Rightarrow \quad CO_2 + CO_2 \quad + \quad C_2H_5OH + C_2H_5OH$$

1 molecule sugar	2 molecules carbon dioxide	2 molecules ethyl alcohol

How simple and elegant. Notice how all the numbers add up on both sides of the equation, those six carbon, twelve hydrogen, and six oxygen atoms of a molecule of sugar rearranging almost in a divine plan to form two new, quite different substances.

This formula explained more than what makes dough rise. That pungent smell I'd detected in my fermenting *poolish*? Alcohol. But the left side of the equation still bothered me. Sugar is obviously present in a vat of sugar beets, but where was the sugar in the dough coming from? My bread contained only flour, yeast, water, and salt.

I found the answer in "my Pyler," as I'd started calling my two-volume reference book. Some of the starch granules in flour are inevitably damaged in the milling process. And it so happens that flour contains enzymes that, in the presence of water, convert these "broken" starch granules into the sugars glucose, fructose, and maltose. Not much of the flour is damaged (maybe 5 percent on average), but it's enough to feed the yeast and to fuel fermentation, aided by a tiny amount of malt flour that is added at the mill to each bag.

What wonderful choreography of nature and man. Subtract any one dancer — the miller, for example, whose mill inadvertently damages the starch — and the ballet falls apart. Aesthetics aside, I felt I now had the full picture of what was happening with my bread. It wasn't just rising; it was literally *fermenting* on the countertop, like wine and beer. Quite literally, in fact. A fully fermented *poolish* has an alcohol content of 3 percent — nearly the equivalent of a bottle of light beer.

Could understanding this process be key to baking exceptional bread? Surely fermentation must be as important to bread as it is to its alcoholic cousins, beer and wine. At dinner, eating another unsatisfactory loaf of peasant bread (made with a *poolish* that I'd fermented overnight, hoping to extract more flavor), I mentioned that I needed to know more about yeast.

"But why?" Katie asked. "How is this going to help you make the perfect loaf?"

"You never know where basic science is going to lead. Look at Pasteur." I pushed the gallon jug of milk across the table. "Read the label."

"Pasteurized."

After dinner, surprised at how little of the bread we'd eaten, I put the remainder of the loaf in the refrigerator, since it looked as if it was going to be around for a while.

WEEK

13

Note to Self

Dear Heloise,*

Recently I put the remains of a loaf of peasant bread (against my wife's better judgment) in the refrigerator. Afterward, it seemed more stale than if I'd just left it out. What gives?

— Intrepid Baker

Dear Intrepid,

Your wife, as usual, is right. Refrigerating bread actually hastens staling. To see why this is, let's back up to examine what happens when bread bakes. As the dough warms, starch granules absorb moisture from the gluten, swelling and giving bread its structure. This is what keeps the loaf from deflating after it comes out of the oven. After the bread cools, the action begins to reverse: water gradually moves from the starchy walls back into the gluten, leaving the crumb dry and crumbly. This process

*No, not *that* Heloise! I mean Heloise Ledbedder down the street, our neighborhood busybody (and my alter ego). This question was actually asked of Heloise the syndicated columnist (March 7, 1990), but to print it I'd have to pay a fee, and frankly, I've given her enough money (see *The $64 Tomato*, p. 96). Besides, all she said in her answer to this question was to freeze the bread. You want the science, you come to me.

is highly temperature-dependent, occurring much faster at 34 degrees Fahrenheit than at 70 degrees, so keep bread out of the fridge! And out of plastic.

The best way to store fresh bread is on a breadboard, cut side down. A whole loaf can be stored in a paper or cloth bag, or frozen in a plastic bag and thawed in the oven or on the bread-board. And remember that stale peasant bread makes great french toast.

WEEK
14

Metric Madness

The metric system is the tool of the devil!
My car gets forty rods to the hogshead, and that's the way I like it!
— Grandpa Simpson, *The Simpsons*

Water: 1 lb. 9.6 oz.
Salt: 0.3 oz.

I looked from the recipe to my digital kitchen scale and back again. The scale had two modes: imperial, which displayed pounds and ounces in increments of one-eighth of an ounce; and metric, which was calibrated to the nearest gram. But 0.3 ounces salt? How many eighths was that? I started scribbling on paper... ¼ was 0.25 ... too little ... and ⅜ was ... let's see ... 3 divided by 8 ... 30 divided by 8 is 3, leaving 60 divided by 8 ...

This was insane. What would possess Jeffrey Hamelman, King Arthur Flour's head baker and one of the most respected baking

instructors in the country, who undoubtedly uses metric measurements in his bakery and his teaching, to give measurements
in *tenths of an ounce,* in essence mixing the metric and imperial
systems? In fact, what would possess him to give measurements
in ounces at all? Probably his editor, who properly pointed out
that he was publishing *Bread: A Baker's Book of Techniques and
Recipes* in the United States, not the United Kingdom.

Memo to the United States of America: CAN WE PLEASE,
EVERYONE, JUST GO TO THE METRIC SYSTEM AND BE DONE
WITH IT?

Weren't we supposed to do this, like, forty years ago? I remember being prepared for this earth-shattering change when I was
in high school, where the metric system was and still is used in
science labs. Since virtually all Americans have attended at least
some high school, we've all been exposed to kilograms by now,
and we all know what a two-liter bottle of soda looks like, so what
are we waiting for? The Metric Conversion Act of 1975 stated, "It
is therefore declared that the policy of the United States shall be
to coordinate and plan the increasing use of the metric system in
the United States and to establish a United States Metric Board
to coordinate the voluntary conversion to the metric system."
The operative word there is *voluntary.* Americans didn't want to
hear weather forecasts in degrees Celsius or buy gas by the liter.
So we simply volunteered not to. President Ronald Reagan, who
was probably convinced this was yet another Communist plot
to destroy the American way of life, abolished the Metric Board
in 1982, leaving the United States standing alone with the super-
powers Liberia and Burma as the only nations in the world that
haven't adopted the metric system. Even Canada converted, letting pounds, ounces, and miles go the way of the cubit. Anne
was in the country as an exchange student at the time (Why go
to, say, Paris or London when you can be an exchange student in

Saskatchewan? must have been her thinking) and tells me they did it cold turkey. One day the meteorologists started giving the temperature in both Celsius and Fahrenheit, and then one day they simply stopped giving the Fahrenheit, at which point you stopped doing conversions in your head and just started to understand what 21 degrees Celsius felt like.

Meanwhile, here, south of the border, every time I need to tighten a nut, I have to fumble through two sets of nearly identical wrenches — the ones in fractions of an inch, and the ones in millimeters — not knowing which system the hardware was made to. Every time I want to halve or double a recipe, I struggle with fractions and conversions between pounds and ounces. Well, damn it, this week I was adapting the metric system in my own kitchen! Not only that, I was going to start measuring by weight, not volume. After watching Lindsay weigh everything that went into Bobolink's bread, from the yeast to the firewood, I'd finally seen the light and, heeding the advice of numerous authors and bakers, purchased an inexpensive digital kitchen scale.

The "scoop and sweep" method of measuring flour is at best an estimate, affected by how tightly the flour is packed in the measuring cup and even how much it has settled in the bag. It would turn out that weighing is also easier than measuring. Rather than dipping the measuring cup repeatedly into the canister, leveling off the top with the back of a knife, and switching between different measuring cups to achieve 4⅓ cups flour, it is far quicker simply to place the mixing bowl on the scale, press the Zero (or Tare) button, and pour out flour till it reaches, say, 500 grams. This is especially true with water. Instead of waiting for the liquid to settle, then bending over and peering at the side of the measuring cup, trying to locate the meniscus — the curvature of the water surface caused by attraction of water to the container — just pour out 215 grams.

I had purchased Hamelman's book after reading on an on-line bread forum, "I finally got holes!! I used Jeffrey Hamelman's technique of folding!" As for those pesky fractions of an ounce, I converted Hamelman's peasant bread recipe to grams and was soon ready to fold some dough and make some holes. Not every-one shares my passion for these gas holes, by the way. Some prefer a more even crumb, and I'll be the first to admit the difficulty of making a tuna fish sandwich on a slice of bread with a gas hole the size of a Buick. Still, some holes would be nice, and not just for texture; I'd read that holes play an important role in drying out the bread by giving the moisture a path out of the loaf. This was good news, for it meant that my two problems — moisture and tight crumb — were intertwined. Solving one would also fix the other.

Hamelman's folding technique involves *gently* flattening the dough, then folding the sides into the center a couple of times during the first rise, gingerly pressing out the dough to degas it some, but not too much. This represents a departure from tra-ditional bread making, in which we are instructed to leave the dough in a warm, draft-free area for several hours and not touch it, not jostle it, not even breathe on it (until you slam a fist into it just before forming the loaves). The rationale behind folding is that the accumulation of carbon dioxide in the dough suppresses yeast activity; folding both releases some of the gas and exposes the yeast to fresh flour. As for punching down the dough, it seems the last person who'd done that was Julia Child. Bakers today are gentle with their dough, working to redistribute the yeast but not push out all that hard-earned gas.

These explanations made sense, and I'd bounded into the kitchen this Sunday morning with new energy. Energy that it turned out I would need, for this was one exhausting loaf of bread, demanding more attention than a newborn. To follow

Hamelman's recipe, I'd had to start the day before, letting some dough ferment for sixteen hours on the countertop. Now, on Sunday, after kneading, the folding started. Every fifty minutes. It was like changing diapers.

"Want to go grocery shopping with me?" Anne asked mid-morning.

"Sorry, can't leave the house."

Nor did I want to tackle that leaky faucet or start mowing the lawn. I was a prisoner of my kitchen, a hostage to my dough. Eventually I made it to forming the loaf and had a window of seventy-five to ninety minutes before it had to go into the oven, so for the first time all day I could leave the house.

Or have sex. Which is what was on my mind. Makeup sex, specifically. Anne and I had had a fight. The usual thing. I'd been moody all week and giving out the leave-me-be vibe, she was leaving me be, and I was resenting the lack of affection. So she was leaving me *more* be. And so on.

Except this time I'd added a new twist. The episode had started with my saying, "I just want you to know that if Naomi Watts ever offers to marry me, I'm leaving you." I'd just watched *King Kong* in high def, and if there was an ape in the movie, the one drooling on the sofa didn't notice.

Anne's face darkened. "Why do you feel it necessary to tell me this?"

"Why are you upset? I'm joking."

"No, you're not."

Hmm. Her accusation made me a touch uneasy. Had I, like Jimmy Carter, just committed adultery in my heart? Regardless, I have to be careful what I say to Anne. If I comment on something I'm reading in a magazine, say, "Wow, it says that only twenty-seven percent of married people have fantasized about being with someone other than their partner during sex — can you believe it's that low?"* this starts a wholly unintended cycle of, not exactly suspicion, but upsetting curiosity. Who is Billy thinking of? A co-worker? My sister? My mother? You'd think she'd welcome Naomi Watts in lieu of any of those alternatives.

I should've just apologized. I'll be the first to admit that the comment was dopey and unnecessary (let's face it, there was no need to forewarn Anne of an event that had no chance of happening), but instead I dug myself in a little deeper.

"Who would *you* run off with?"

"No one."

"Come on, there must be someone."

In retrospect, who was she going to say? She wouldn't know a Brad Pitt from a grapefruit pit. Cary Grant? Rock Hudson? All of the real male heartthrobs of Hollywood are either dead or gay. Or both. Anyway, this was all a few days earlier. I'd since climbed out of the hole (we sensibly agreed to cross the Naomi bridge when we came to it), and Anne had called a truce: "The battle of the sexes is over," she declared. "Sex wins."

Sounded like it was time for makeup sex (the best kind of sex, as Seinfeld fans know), *afternoon* makeup sex, which is the best kind of makeup sex.

As soon as Katie left the house for drama club rehearsal.

"We have forty-five minutes," I said to Anne, checking my loaves and the kitchen timer as Katie closed the door behind her.

Plenty of time. We raced upstairs. Anne got paged and had to handle a hospital admission over the phone. Beep-beep! Another admission. Finally Anne jumped back into bed and wrapped her arms around me. I could feel her tense, then release. Something was wrong.

*An actual statistic, by the way — can you believe it's that low?

"Are you looking at the clock?" she asked.

It was almost time to put the loaf in the oven, to steam, and to watch. If I went downstairs, I wouldn't be coming back anytime soon.

I looked at my wife, looking lovely on the bed.

I imagined my dough, rising in the kitchen.

Dough that had been started over twenty-four hours ago and into which I'd invested hours watching, folding, caressing. If I let it sit too long, there'd be no yeast left for the oven spring, and the bread would be dense and heavy.

Kind of like my marriage at the moment. Argghhh! What to do? Sex or bread? Bread or sex?

Who am I kidding? This was a no-brainer.

WEEK

15

We Make Biomass

While the dough is rising, life goes on.
— Peter Reinhart, *Brother Juniper's Bread Book,* 1991

"We make biomass," Gary Edwards, president of the American Yeast Division of Lallemand, declared, as if no other explanation were required.

Within the hour I would learn that this was a little like Noah saying, "I'm building a rowboat," but for the moment, as I sipped coffee in a comfortable conference room a few blocks from downtown

Montreal, I was oblivious to the hundreds of tons of biomass feeding, growing, and doubling in quantity every four hours under my seat. If I'd known, I might have been a bit nervous.

Lallemand, though not a household name like Red Star or Fleischmann's, is one of the major yeast producers in North America, supplying the yeast for Wonder bread and other large commercial bakeries as well as countless corner bakeries and wineries and even the home baking enthusiast (a *real* enthusiast — their smallest package of dried yeast is a one-pound bag). My microscopic exploration of yeast had left me wanting to know more about this mysterious substance, so I'd come to Lallemand to see firsthand how yeast is made. Or rather, since we technically don't *make* living things, farmed.

Hairnet and hard hat in place, I was distinctly underwhelmed by my first sight of a yeast production factory. Two young lab technicians in white coats were bent over a lab bench, scraping a trace of yeast from a "slant" — a small tube in which the pure strain of yeast is stored in agar — onto a wire loop to be transferred to a garden-variety test tube. A few previously inoculated test tubes sat nearby in a rack. On another table sat six five-gallon jugs with hoses coming out the top, filled with a wicked-looking brew that resembled Guinness stout. The place seemed eerily familiar. I'd been here before, but when? Slowly it dawned on me. This was a small (very small) version of my high school chemistry lab. "This is your research laboratory?" I asked Gary.

"Oh, no!" he said, nearly taking offense. "This is the beginning of a production batch."

This little room? He pointed to the row of test tubes. "This is the first stage. Each batch begins in a test tube with a sterile growth medium we inoculate from the slants. That's what we're doing right now." None of the techs took their eyes off their work as we talked about them. "Now, over there" — Gary gestured to-ward a table of conical flasks directly behind me — "is the next stage." As I swung around, my arm nearly struck a flask that was sitting out in the open. "After about twenty-four hours in the test tube, the yeast is transferred to Erlenmeyer flasks."

I took a step back so as to not destroy an entire production cycle of yeast with my clumsiness. And just how much yeast would that have been?

"In six days each of these test tubes will become six hundred thousand pounds of wet yeast, if everything goes according to plan." Disbelieving, I made him repeat the figure. "Six hundred thousand pounds, *if* all goes well," he repeated. "You can also end up with six hundred thousand pounds of crap."

And what can go wrong? Aside from an errant visitor knock-ing over a flask, there's M. Bigo's problem (namely, bacterial in-fection), improper growth of the yeast, or infection by the wild yeast that is always present in the air. But barring problems, less than a week from now, the scrapings of a few yeast cells from a slant into those six test tubes would multiply into, altogether, a mind-boggling 3.6 million pounds of yeast!

We make biomass.

Looking into the Erlenmeyer flask, that familiar conical flask with the narrow cylindrical throat,* commercial yeast seemed an impossibly long way off. But the distance would be covered quickly. After spending a day in the flask, the yeast is transferred into a five-gallon sterile glass bottle called a carboy. The glass car-boys resembled nothing so much as a science fair exhibit, with hoses coming out the top, air bubbling through the thick brown

---

*Kids, don't try this at home. Mere possession of an Erlenmeyer flask is a drug offense in some states.

molasses, and — get this — aluminum foil topping the whole assembly. The only thing missing was the poster listing your hypothesis and homeroom.

"This is the first time that oxygen is introduced," Gary said, explaining the hoses. I was surprised to hear the reference to oxygen. Everything I'd read about yeast referred to it as anaerobic, living only in the *absence* of oxygen. "Yeast is an interesting critter," he explained. "It can live with or without air. And it's brilliant in its simplicity. When air and sugar are present, the yeast says, 'Times are good. I've got air to breath, sugar to eat; I'm going to make some more yeast cells!' This tendency of yeast to grow and reproduce when large amounts of oxygen is present is called the Pasteur effect.

"But when it has sugar but no air," Gary continued, "the yeast says, 'I've got to convert this sugar into something that will help preserve me. If I don't, the bacteria are going to come in and crowd me out.'" So it switches over to anaerobic fermentation, producing carbon dioxide and alcohol. This is the fermentation we are interested in, the process that bakers and brewers utilize to make the bread rise and the beer brew. Anaerobic fermentation has another advantage for the yeast: if times get hard and all the sugar is used up, the yeast can dine on the very alcohol it produced. Most bacteria cannot, so this serves as yet another defense mechanism against bacteria, in addition to being a third way that this simple, one-celled organism can feed. Yeast, by the way, can only tolerate alcohol up to a point — about 14 or 15 percent. This is why wine always has an alcohol content of roughly 11 to 13 percent. You can't make yeast produce more alcohol than that, or the yeast itself will die.

The fact that yeast has these distinct aerobic and anaerobic lifestyles explained why I hadn't seen much budding going on in my microscopic experiment. If I was going to see budding, I'd have to force in air with the sugar, as Lallemand was doing, to get the yeast to metabolize *aerobically* and reproduce. But even then I wouldn't have seen all that much in a few minutes under the microscope. Gary told me that yeast reproduces only about every four hours. Leeuwenhoek and I were lucky to have seen any budding at all.* As for the bubbles Leeuwenhoek had seen, and the doubling of the volume of dough in a few hours that all bakers witness? Both are due primarily to the anaerobic respiration of the original yeast, not an increase in the colony size. In other words, bubbles, not budding. We moved onto the production floor to see the fermenters. This was the part I'd been looking forward to. I expected we'd step onto a long stretch of white tile floor so clean you could eat off it, with gleaming stainless steel vats lined up on either side, accompanied by the warm hum of bubbling yeast and perhaps a slight bakery smell. The reality was more like stepping onto the deck of an aircraft carrier while jets were landing and taking off. The noise was deafening, the reek of molasses overpowering. And eating off the floor? Not recommended. True, I was in a food factory, but the entire milieu suggested more "factory" than "food."

"This is the next stage," Gary yelled over the din as we stood in front of the first fermenter, a stainless steel tank not much larger than a bathtub, into which a technician had emptied the contents of two carboys a few hours earlier. I could barely make

---

*So how does Lallemand go from almost nothing to 3.5 million pounds of yeast in six days? Because the growth is exponential. For example, start with a mere hundredth of an ounce of yeast. In four hours it doubles to 0.02 oz.; after eight hours it doubles again to 0.04 oz. At the end of the first day, it's doubled six times to yield a modest 0.64 oz. After another day, though, you're up to 40 oz. Now the numbers start rising fast: day three yields 164 pounds; day four, 10,000 pounds; and by the beginning of day six, when the yeast has doubled thirty-one times, that original hundredth of an ounce has grown to over *1 million* pounds.

out his words as he yelled over the roar of the huge blowers that force air into the fermenters. Because yeast needs oxygen, and lots of it, in order to be induced to undergo reproduction, huge quantities of air were being drawn in from the skies over Montreal. After being passed through a HEPA filter to remove, among other things, any wild yeast that might be present in it, the air is bubbled up through the yeast and molasses broth in very fine bubbles. This takes a lot of pressure — and electricity — as the volume of air in the tanks is replaced every minute.

I had envisioned yeast production as a low-energy, environmentally friendly process, but I'd had it completely wrong. It takes a tremendous amount of electricity to make lots of yeast in this short a time: power to blow in the air, heat exchangers to draw off the excess heat generated by the yeast. I mentioned to Gary that it was as energy-intensive as any other factory farm.

"We *are* farmers," he said. "With a much shorter growing season."

Gary took me through the next several steps of making yeast, the first- through fifth-stage fermenters, full of bubbling molasses, until we finally reached a huge rotating drum. Something that was now recognizable as yeast was coming off it as it turned. I caught some in my hand. It had a consistency remarkably similar to Play-Doh. This was fresh crumbled yeast, about 30 percent solid, ready to be packaged into fifty-pound poly-lined bags and sent out on refrigerated trucks to commercial bakeries. Or pressed into five-pound blocks of compressed yeast. Or dried further into instant dry yeast, the kind of yeast that home bakers use. This is what I wanted to see.

Next we came to an extruder, essentially a giant cookie press fitted with an extrusion die, which is a steel plate with hundreds of tiny holes. I held my hand under it as little squiggles of yeast — drier than what had come off the drum but still pliable — collected in my palm. The yeast had a surprisingly satisfying feel in my hand, not wet, but not dry, either, and when I brushed it off my hands, it left behind a pleasant dryness and yeasty aroma, a persisting reminder that I would savor for hours afterward, like the faint, lingering memory of a woman's perfume.

The final drying takes place in a large cylindrical tank in which the yeast flies around in a vortex of warm air for about twenty minutes, until the solid content is up to 96 percent, putting the yeast into a dormant stage, ready to be siphoned off into vacuum-sealed bags for shipping.

The yeast Lallemand was making was *instant* dry yeast, different from the *active* dry yeast that was developed during World War II (so that, according to Fleischmann's, our boys could have fresh bread abroad). Active dry yeast quickly replaced fresh yeast in American home kitchens, where it reigned for some fifty years before instant yeast (variously labeled instant, fast-acting, bread-machine, or RapidRise) joined it on the shelves. Active and instant dried yeast look similar, but active dry has to be rehydrated before use to bring the yeast out of dormancy and make the cell walls permeable again. This is why many cookbooks call for "proofing" the yeast (not to be confused with proofing the dough, another name for the second rise), mixing it with a little warm water and a pinch of sugar before adding it to the dry ingredients.*

The instant dried yeast I was holding was developed in the 1980s from a different strain than active dry (but the same species — all commercial yeast sold for fermentation belongs to the species *Saccharomyces cerevisiae*) and, dried at a lower temperature in the vortex, doesn't have to be rehydrated or proofed (in fact, Gary told me it's better *not* to rehydrate), doesn't have

---

*The other reason for proofing dry active yeast is to "prove" it is still active and not just dry.

to be refrigerated, and has a room-temperature shelf life in its vacuum-packed bag of two years. Once opened, it is susceptible to oxidation and needs to be stored in an airtight container if not used within a few weeks.

I was leaving the factory floor with my one-pound bag of instant yeast, which would last me an entire year (and then some), when I noticed a wall with sacks of yeast stacked to the ceiling.

"That's for corn," Gary explained.

"Corn bread?" I didn't understand.

"Ethanol. It's becoming a big market."

Of course — how do you turn corn into alcohol? You ferment it. I would find myself thinking of that wall of yeast six months later, as corn and wheat prices soared, sowing hunger and threatening civil unrest in Africa and the Middle East, but for now, it was just a curiosity. I was getting ready to leave for the long drive back home when I remembered why I was here: my lousy bread.

I described the problem I was having with my dense crumb and lack of holes, hoping for the little nugget, the missing link, that would give me the perfect loaf. Gary was impressed that, as a home baker, I was "running sponge and dough," as he called my *poolish*. He confirmed my instinct that the long fermentation in the sponge produces some complex and sophisticated flavors that you don't find in a straight dough loaf. And as a bonus, thanks to the compounds formed during a preferment, the resulting bread stales less quickly. "The other thing that does for you is it's actually giving you a different crumb structure, a different texture and feel in your mouth."

So the yeast, in addition to supplying the gas for rising and the compounds for flavor, has an effect on the crumb! This was something I'd not heard before; I'd thought the crumb was determined solely by the other factors I'd been playing with: the gluten and protein levels of the flour, the kneading, resting, and rising processes. There seemed to be no end to yeast's influence on bread, and more and more, it was becoming apparent that making the dough rise was the least of its roles.

I left with a new respect for yeast and felt I was on the right track with sponge and dough methods, but how to get rid of that dense crumb? How to make some air holes?

"You need to ask a baker," Gary suggested. "An authority."

WEEK
16

A Chill in the Air

Bread is relief for all kinds of grief.
— Spanish proverb

"I'm turning the heat on," Anne said, wrapping her hands around a mug of coffee.

"But it's May."

"I'm freezing."

"I'm fine," I lied through chattering teeth. "What's the temperature in here?"

"Sixty." Fahrenheit, that is.

Outside, it was thirty-eight on this chilly spring morning.

"Once the sun hits the side of the house, it'll warm up." With a gallon of heating oil costing more than a gallon of milk, the oil bills for our rambling, nominally insulated old house were enough to support a modest Arab emirate, despite the fortune we'd spent on new, energy-efficient windows, and I was eager to end the heating season. I knew the house would be up to sixty-eight degrees by noontime and didn't see the point of wasting oil to simply get it up there a few hours earlier. Let the woman wear a sweater. Or three.

Anne went upstairs to put on a second sweater, get under a down comforter, or both, and I returned to my loaf. That's when I realized that my bread wasn't going to rise much in a sixty-degree kitchen, considerably colder even than Bobolink's proofing room. I turned the heat up, hoping that Anne wouldn't guess why, especially given my recent *coitus interruptus sourdoughus.* All that coddling I did with the dough that day, my incessant gentle folding and turning? There had been no discernible change in the bread whatsoever. My attentions would've been better spent on my wife.

WEEK
17

The Short, Unhappy Life of
an Assistant Baker

In Turkey in the 18th century . . . it was common to hang
a baker or two. This was common enough that it was the custom
of master bakers to keep an assistant who, in return for
slightly higher wages, was willing to appear before
the courts in case a victim were needed.
— Halvor Moorshead

We bakers have never had it easy. I suppose the more society depends on you, the more society is going to scrutinize you. Bakers were so mistrusted in the Middle Ages, a time when a slice of bread could mean the difference between salvation and starvation, that thirteen years before the Magna Carta, English magistrates felt it necessary to write into law severe penalties for bakers who committed fraud by selling underweight or substandard loaves.* This isn't to say that the bakers were always innocent victims. Oftentimes, if the millers weren't adulterating the flour with sawdust, the bakers were. Bread tensions in jolly old England came to a head in the 1266 "bread trials," which resulted in a new regulation: each baker was required to mark his loaf with a distinctive mark — perhaps the world's first commercial trademark — to make offending loaves easier to trace.

Why do I bring all this up? To be sure, I was in no danger of being hanged (my kids belonging more to the tar-and-feather crowd), but I was starting to sense a level of discontent with the all-peasant-bread-all-the-time menu. I couldn't be sure, but I thought I'd even heard the words "Groundhog Day" whispered. And we were only in week 17, just a third of the way through the year.

Perhaps it was time for a new recipe. I'd been reading James Beard's *Beard on Bread* and noticed he had a free-form loaf made from a *poolish,* using a long fermentation. I've always been a fan of James Beard's, and not only because the dust jacket of *Beard on Bread* has my all-time-favorite author photo: here's the old man, bald as a cue ball, dressed in his tweed jacket and bow tie, looking every bit the aging, uncomfortable, closeted gay man that he was, stiffly holding at arm's length an enormous, misshapen loaf of bread that more resembles a giant wild mushroom than a *miche* (an imprecise word for a large, flattened loaf).

It's absolutely marvelous. Thus I was distraught when I'd

---

*That other stuff, like specifying the rights of the king's subjects and the writ of habeas corpus, could wait until 1215.

lost it. I'd been reading outdoors on this pleasant, breezy day and had put Beard down to retrieve the mail. And predictably forgot all about him. "Predictably" because my memory lapses and confusion were becoming more frequent and disturbing. I'd been forgetting to pay bills and giving contradicting instructions at work, and most upsetting, I had recently spent a good five minutes looking for sunglasses that were perched atop my head.

Anne handed me the naked book. "Where's the jacket?" I asked.

"I didn't see a jacket on it."

Didn't see a . . . I ran out and started searching the yard, then the neighborhood, studying the wind and trying to calculate how far the jacket might have traveled, all the while wondering how the wind could've stripped a dust jacket off a closed book. Regardless, I had to find dear old Jim. After a fruitless search, though, I dejectedly headed back to the house. There, patiently waiting at the front door, on my welcome mat, was James Beard, offering up that huge loaf of bread to me.

Wow. Relief was followed by a deep chill that stayed with me for days. If I saw this scene in a movie,* I'd say, "Oh, please, that's a bit of a stretch, don't you think?" But there it was. No, there *he* was, having returned home after his tour of my neighborhood. And what did that ugly, misshapen loaf being passed to me by a dead American culinary giant represent?

I wasn't sure, but I knew I had to bake his peasant loaf (he calls it a "white free-form loaf") this week. There was only one small problem. It included oil and buttermilk.

Adulterated bread. Okay, so it wasn't sawdust (or chalk, pea,

---

*Or [cough] read it in a memoir.

bean, or potato flour, alum, sulfate of zinc, subcarbonate of magnesia, subcarbonate of ammonia, sulfate of copper, or plaster of paris, to name a few of the additives that have been snuck into bread to cut costs or improve poor flour), but I was a charter subscriber to the school of thought that "true" bread, the stuff of peasants, has only four ingredients — flour, water, yeast, and salt — and with the single exception of my rich Easter bread, I'd stuck to my guns. Oil and buttermilk? I'd as soon add plaster of paris.

To be fair to Beard, it is not unusual to find bread (especially white sandwich bread) that includes some milk and fat in the form of oil or butter. Both milk and fat add flavor and are dough conditioners. Fat coats the gluten strands, making the bread more tender and increasing its shelf life. Additionally, the sugar (lactose) found in milk caramelizes during baking, producing a golden crust.

I followed Beard's recipe to the letter, with the exception of substituting a little whole wheat flour for some of the white. The result?

"This is better than your bread, Dad," Katie said. Zach agreed.

"Enjoy it today, then," I said, the sharpness of my voice surprising me. "You're not going to have it again. It's not eligible for the perfect loaf. It has milk and oil in it."

"Guess that means you won't be making croissants, either," Katie groaned.

"Just bread with four ingredients, kids."

"So why'd you make *this*?" Zach asked.

I just shrugged. They wouldn't have believed me, anyway.

Waffling

> When I was a boy of fourteen, my father was so ignorant I could
> hardly stand to have the old man around. But when I got to be twenty-
> one, I was astonished at how much he had learned in seven years.
> — Mark Twain

It was Father's Day, so I was having a special Father's Day breakfast. That I made by myself. And ate by myself. While Anne was
weeding in the garden and Zach and Katie were sound asleep.

It felt kind of weird. I'd told everyone that I didn't need anything for Father's Day and, for that matter, that we didn't even
need to observe Father's Day — a holiday for my father, not
me — but when my kids actually took me up on the offer, I found
myself unexpectedly disappointed. Not even a "Happy Father's
Day" from anyone.

Serves me right.

For my special Father's Day breakfast, I made a special bread,
a delightful quick bread with egg and butter and baking powder,
cooked in only three minutes between two hot metal grids. In
other words, a waffle. Yes, a waffle is bread, and an interesting
bread at that.* Most commonly, a waffle is made as a quick bread,

---

*Lest I be accused of cheating, let me point out that I also made a loaf of
peasant bread this week, although the less said about it the better.

meaning it is leavened with baking powder and baking soda, but waffles can be leavened with yeast. If, that is, you have the foresight to begin preparing your breakfast while still digesting your dinner.

The word *waffle* has the same origin as *wafer,* and in fact they are quite similar, each a flour-water mixture cooked between two hot, embossed metal plates. When the plates are close together and nearly flat, except for the etching of, say, a cross, the result is a Communion wafer. Change the etching from a religious symbol to a shallow grid, add some sugar, and your wafer takes the form of an ice cream cone. Now make the indentations on the iron much deeper, add some leavening, and your wafer becomes a waffle.

Breakfast waffles can be challenging to make at home, because a good waffle is crisp on the outside and soft and airy on the inside (not unlike a good loaf of bread). The indentations of the waffle iron, by increasing the surface area, contribute greatly to the crispness. So does the addition of more fat (I prefer melted butter to vegetable oil); by substituting fat for some of the water, the waffle steams less inside the iron, allowing it to crisp up. There are a number of other tricks various cooks employ for crispness, from adding more eggs to slipping in a little corn meal, but the waffles I was making this morning were in my opinion the best in the world and represented the realization of another earlier bread obsession of sorts, dating back to the mid-1980s, when we were on a family beach vacation in North Carolina.

At a local breakfast/lunch spot, the kind of place where the waitresses call you "hon" and your bone-colored coffee mug gets refilled whenever it falls below the three-quarter mark, we'd breakfasted on the best waffles we'd ever eaten. A card on the table boasted that they were something called Carbon's Golden Malted waffles. A commercial mix, not a homemade recipe. This was great news. It meant I could make these at home. It took some work to track the company down in the pre-Internet age, but I eventually talked to someone at Carbon's in South Bend, Indiana, and was directed to a distributor in Cincinnati, from whom I tried to order some mix.

"Our smallest quantity is fifty pounds," I was told. I was fond of their waffles, but not fifty pounds fond. I turned to making my own but had no success whatsoever in duplicating Carbon's 1937 "secret mix" of wheat and corn flour, malt, and unspecified flavorings. A full decade passed, and I'd despaired of ever having such a good waffle again, when I saw a squat circular can of "malted waffle mix" at our local market. The brand wasn't Carbon's, but the flavor was unmistakably Carbon. Even ten years later, I could tell. Turns out they sell it today under several brand names, including their own, all in the same circular cardboard container.

I took two lessons away from this experience. Homemade isn't always better, and sometimes I get to win one. I learned one more thing that evening at dinner, when Katie discovered the leftover waffles in the refrigerator.

"You made waffles this morning?"

"For Father's Day," I said pointedly.

There — it was out! How would they react? Katie looked at Zach, and they both looked at Anne, and finally Zach cleared his throat nervously and said, "Uh, Dad?"

I waited for the apology.

"Father's Day is *next* Sunday."

And I wouldn't be making my own breakfast.

Playing the Percentages

Alcohol and calculus don't mix. Never drink and derive.
— Anonymous

Katie had a question.

"Dad, why do I need to know calculus? When am I ever going to use that?"

Good question, Katie. Thirty years ago, during the three years I spent teaching high school math, I heard this question from students a lot (without, ahem, the "Dad"), and my answer hadn't improved any. The truth was, Katie was never going to use calculus unless she went into a hard-core engineering or scientific field, and even then it was doubtful. Statistics, trigonometry — that was cool and useful stuff. But calculus?

"Because it helps you to understand the world. And it makes you smart, that's why."

Maybe even smart enough to understand the baker's percentage, which is a secret code that bakers use to describe the proportions of ingredients in dough. Every serious bread book touches on it, some books even giving the recipes in percentages in a sidebar or something similar. The baker's percentage is — oh, let's have a professional clearly explain how it's used:

In the case at hand, I have 4,200 grams of leaven sponge, which consists of 2,100 grams of water and 2,100 grams of flour. I subtract 2,100 from 6,402 and I find that I must add 4,302 grams of "flour" (approximately) when I make my dough. This will reduce the amount of white flour I add to 2,380 grams. Similarly, 4,097 minus 2,100 means that I add about 1,997 grams of water. I will still add 128 grams of salt (2 percent times 64).

Any questions, class?

You can see why I was avoiding the baker's percentage — more than avoiding it; I was deriding it every time I came across yet another reference to it. It seemed both unnecessary and unintelligible, at least until this note arrived:

> Bill, certain ratios in your recipe stand out. Your total flour weight is 595 grams, so if you were to hydrate that weight to 68% your water weight would be 404.6 (405) grams. This would be the standard percentage.

Meaning the standard baker's percentage.

Oh, damn. It was time to learn baker's calculus. This e-mail from a professional baker had dropped "baker's percentage" into the conversation as naturally as a baseball manager might drop the phrase "batting average." I couldn't avoid it any longer.

I had taken to heart the advice of Lallemand's Gary Edwards — "You need to ask a baker. An authority" — realizing that even though my bread-making books were stacking up faster than pancakes (a bread, by the way, technically a griddle-baked quick bread) at IHOP, they didn't seem to be taking me any closer to my goal. But who could help me with this quest? I wasn't about to just start knocking on bakery doors.

As I was pondering this, I happened upon an article featuring Steven Kaplan, an American professor of history who, remarkably enough, is respected (if not celebrated) in Paris as an expert on French bread, having written several books in French on the subject.

I found his e-mail address on the Cornell University Web site and sent a note asking if he knew of a baker who might be able and willing to help with my quest for the perfect peasant bread. I foolishly suggested a bilingual baker in France might be acceptable, giving me a good excuse to run over there for a few weeks or months, but his reply, which came from the southwest coast of France, splashed cold Evian on that prospect:

> I salute you from Biarritz, where there is an acute dearth of good bread, despite my most evangelical actions.
>
> I am dubious about finding a solution to your quest for a baker-mentor, especially on the French side. There are two structural barriers. The first, your apparent lack of mastery of spoken French. I know hundreds of French bakers, only a small handful of whom have some English. The second is more forbidding: active bakers have an acute, chronic penury of free time. I just cannot imagine anyone who actively works in the fournil taking you on. Probably a retired baker is a better prospect.
>
> On the American side—especially for home-baking protocols—you might consult Charles van Over.

Who? Charles van Over? Never heard of him. The contact info that followed indicated that he lived in neighboring Connecticut. I did some scholarly research* and found that, like both Lallemand and Professor Kaplan, Charles van Over, while not a household name, is apparently well known in the field. His 1997 book, *The Best Bread Ever* (bakers are not generally known for their modesty), won a James Beard Foundation Award.

I contacted van Over, who responded amenably to my e-mail, in which I detailed my problem with the crumb. He asked for the

---

*I googled him.

recipe I was using, and a few days later, his reply, with its casual reference to the baker's percentage, came back.

Sitting down with a calculator and studying van Over's comment, "Your total flour weight is 595 grams, so if you were to hydrate that weight to 68% your water weight would be 404.6 (405) grams," I saw that he simply arrived at 404.6 by multiplying the flour weight by 68 percent. That's all there was to it?

It turns out the baker's percentage is actually relatively simple and is used universally in the baking world. It is the ratio of any ingredient in the dough to the total flour, expressed as a percentage. So if you are making a loaf with 100 grams of flour and you use 50 grams of water, the baker's percentage of water is 50 percent. In the case of water, another way to state this is that the dough has 50 percent hydration.

What's confusing to those of us who remember any high school science is that, in my example, the water represents *one-third* of the total weight of the dough (which weighs 150 grams, once you add the water), not one-half, so intuitively it seems that the hydration should be 33, not 50, percent. But the baker's percentage expresses all the ingredients relative *only to the flour,* not to the total, so 50 percent is correct.

This is actually a lot easier than computing percentages of the total, because in that case you'd always have to account for how much the ingredient you're adding is going to affect the new total, which is the kind of thing that saddled me with a C– in undergraduate organic chemistry and is yet another reason why Anne is the doctor in the family, not me. But we needn't dredge all that up again. Simple as it is, the baker's percentage can be perplexing when you encounter percentages of over 100 percent (which means there is more water than flour), or when you use it to figure out how much flour to add to a *poolish,* which itself contains both water and flour.

I understood enough to know that my dough was seriously underwatered. The "standard" 68 percent called for 405 grams of water, and I was only using 345 grams, which gave me a hydration of just 58 percent!

A number of artisan bakers have written that they are making bread with much wetter dough than in the past, and when I mixed up a batch at 68 percent hydration, I could see they weren't kidding. The dough started out wet and sticky, but after kneading, it started to come together. Still, it was far less firm than my usual dough and would take a bit of practice to get used to.

To be honest, I didn't see a huge difference in the final loaf, but I was going to get a hands-on lesson. Charlie had invited Anne and me to spend the weekend baking at his home on the Connecticut River. It wasn't exactly the Seine, but at least the baker and I would be speaking the same language.

À bientôt!

WEEK
20

Feed It or It Dies

"Feed the bitch!" said the voice on the phone.
"Feed the bitch or she'll die!"
— Anthony Bourdain, *Kitchen Confidential*, 2000

I was as nervous as a sinner in the first pew, which may have partly explained the undersized, dense, and misshapen loaf I'd just baked, the least attractive one I'd made in months of bread making.

Zach took one look at it and winced. "Ooh. Doorstop."

Even worse, one of the four crosshatch slashes had blown out as if a hand grenade had gone off inside, leaving a large tumor on that side of the loaf, while the other three cuts were mere scratches that hadn't opened up at all. This had happened because my fancy ten-dollar *lame* was already dull and ready to be tossed in the garbage. If ever I wanted a loaf to turn out well, it was this one, for I was on my way to a weekend with Charles van Over, bread authority and author. I was hoping that van Over could diagnose my airless and tight-crumbed peasant loaf.

I kissed Katie good-bye.

"Dad, what if he tells you your 'lousy' bread is great? That'd be pretty embarrassing. What do you say then?"

"I guess I'd feel pretty foolish." But the odds of that happening were about nil. I eyed the loaf, so sorry-looking I had seriously considered "forgetting" it to save face. But, I reasoned, if you're going to the proctologist, you'd better be prepared to drop your pants, so, loaf and overnighter in hand, Anne and I headed out to van Over's home overlooking the Connecticut River.

Charlie greeted us warmly and went right for the bread knife.

"This is very good bread," he said, chewing on a lopsided slice. "Better than what you'll get in most bakeries."

Huh?

"But there are no air holes," I protested.

He held it up to the window to better see the texture. "Nice. You don't want air holes in bread like this. A peasant loaf is sandwich bread."

Oh. I hadn't known that.

"But it's too moist inside," I protested again.

"Leave it in the oven a half hour after baking. It'll dry out. Bill, I'm serious, this is really good bread."

I could see Katie smirking in our kitchen a hundred miles away.

"I'm not happy with the spongy texture. I want a much more open, webbed crumb, an *alveolar* crumb," I argued, using the wonderfully evocative word I'd swiped from Steven Kaplan — "the Professor" (as Charlie called him) — who'd hooked us up.

"You're not going to get that with this bread. You've gone about as far with this bread as you can go, but now you need to go to the next level. Have you ever used a starter?"

Oh, jeez, a starter. No way.

A starter is a batter or dough of flour, water, wild yeast, and bacteria (in other words, a sourdough, or in French a *levain**) that you maintain with regular "feedings" of flour and water for years or even generations. It can be used either in place of or with commercial yeast. I had thought about it a couple of times but had been frightened off by the demands of caring for it. The celebrity chef Anthony Bourdain described his baker's *levain* this way:

> A massive, foaming, barely contained heap . . . which even now was pushing up the weighted-down lid of a 35-gallon Lexan container and spilling over the work table where it was stored.

Then there were worried posts like this to a professional bakers' Internet forum:

> I am wondering what one does during holidays to feed their
> levain—besides the obvious going in to feed it. We feed ours

---

*Although the terms are synonymous, bakers tend to stay away from the term *sourdough* because of its connotation of San Francisco sourdough, which is a unique, rather sour variety of sourdough and is not representative of most starters.

2 times a day. The levain is going to miss 2 feedings. I will be
sleeping and it can die before I go in to feed it.

Feed it twice a day, every day, or it *dies*? I don't always manage
to feed my kids twice a day! Who needed this hassle?

"I don't know, Charlie. It seems like a lot of work."

"Not if you keep it in the refrigerator." He pulled a one-gallon
recycled plastic container marked "Crème Fraîche" out of his
fridge.

"You only have to feed it once a week. I got this from a friend
in Alaska who asked me to take care of it while he did some
traveling."

He opened it up. It had an acrid, but not particularly unpleas-
ant or sour, smell.

"How long ago was that?"

"Twelve years."

I gulped. My neighbors wouldn't trust me to water their houseplants for a week while they're away. "I don't know . . ."

"I'll give you some to take home. It's the only way you're going
to bake the kind of bread you're after." We had a delicious lunch
on Charlie's patio and returned to the kitchen to make bread
(using Charlie's twelve-year-old *levain,* of course) in, of all things,
a food processor.

"You ever make bread in a food processor?" Charlie asked.

I was tempted to answer in my W. C. Fields voice, "No, and if
I did, I wouldn't admit it." Food processor? What kind of baker
was this?

———————

"What exactly does he do?" I asked Charlie's baker, Skip, at
five o'clock the next morning while he formed baguettes in the
kitchen of the Copper Beech Inn in Ivoryton. In the early morn-

ings the inn's kitchen became, under Charlie's auspices, a small commercial bakery, doing one thing but doing it extremely well, baking a single type of bread (baguettes) for a single client (the inn). Having spent a full day with Charlie, I still couldn't quite figure out exactly who he was or what he did. Former restaurateur and baker, occasional food industry consultant, author, inventor of the folding bread knife and the HearthKit oven insert (a three-sided baking stone meant to simulate baking in a brick oven), proselytizer, bon vivant, chef, bread authority, tinkerer, Jacques Pépin's *boules* partner — none of these really captured the essence of this youthful seventy-year-old who, above all, was passionate about bread.

"Charlie's a concept person," Skip said, a smile crossing his face. "He likes ideas. Big ideas."

His biggest idea to date is that the best way to knead bread, whether at home or in a bakery, is in a food processor, a method he discovered practically by accident when asked to prepare bread for a party honoring the president of Cuisinart. Van Over was so impressed with the result — and the ease of preparation — that he patented the process for commercial bakeries. One would not expect dough subjected to a razor-sharp metal blade whirring at over 1,300 rpm to make good bread or anything else, but I had sampled a baguette the previous night at dinner and thought it among the best I'd ever eaten.

Charlie attributes the technique's success partly to the fact that the kneading time is short — forty-five seconds — and does not whip air into the dough the way a commercial dough hook does as it lifts and stretches — and aerates — the dough over a ten- or fifteen-minute kneading.

"I thought flour needed oxygen," I'd asked in his kitchen. "Isn't that why it has to age for several weeks after milling?"

True, but once the flour is mixed with water and becomes

dough, oxygenation destroys the beta-carotenes in flour and can cause the flour to break down, Charlie had said. His explanation echoed the words of the French bread authority Raymond Calvel, the scientist who'd come up with the technique he dubbed *autolyse,* letting the dough rest and condition before kneading.

In the kitchen, Skip now added instant yeast, water, and salt to the flour and processed it for just forty-five seconds, then went home to have breakfast while the dough fermented. He'd return at eight to make the bread. Later that morning, the baking finished, Charlie came in with a tub of starter for me. He mentioned that he and his wife, Priscilla, were on their way to France in a few weeks.

"Oh, really?" I said. "You wouldn't happen to know of any ancient monasteries over there that still bake bread, would you?" Brother Boniface, the ancient baker at Mepkin Abbey, might be deceased, but the appeal of his ancientness had stayed with me. "I like old things," I explained as we stood in the inn's gleaming, modern stainless steel kitchen. "I think it'd be neat to make bread in a place where they've been baking for a really long time, you know, to get in touch with the tradition."

"I suspect you'll have a hard time finding one," Charlie said, adding that, as an atheist, he wasn't really in touch with that world. "That's a dying tradition. But I'll ask around. Do you know Peter Reinhart? He's written a couple of books on bread, and he's a former monk or something. He might know."

Charlie handed over the *levain.* "Just feed it at least once a week with equal parts flour and water." By weight, he meant. "Leave it out for a few hours after each feeding, then keep it in the fridge. It's like having an undemanding pet."

During the long drive home, Anne kept glancing nervously into the backseat at the starter. I asked her what she was so jittery about.

"Remember friendship bread?"
I almost drove off the road.

WEEK
21

With Friendships Like This ...

Friendship is not so simple.
— Albert Camus

"Eeek!" Anne had screamed that fateful day as she opened the refrigerator door. She jumped clear across the room, fulfilling the foreboding I always have upon returning home after a vacation. As I approach our street, I often think I smell smoke, confirming the vague dread I've had all week that the electrical wiring I did without a permit in 1992 has shorted and the house is now a charred wreck. Or the water pipes have burst. Or I left the back door wide open and a family of deer has taken possession of our living room. Not that my neurosis is totally unfounded. We have in fact returned after a week away to find the unreliable front door blown wide open (but no deer or burglars present — the house was apparently too cold for either) and water dripping from the light fixtures. But none of my worries had ever included the refrigerator.

"Calm down," I said, assuming that the milk jug had leaked again. I have an amazing skill for buying the one jug out of sixty that has a pinhole leak in the bottom. I opened the refrigerator.

"Yow!" I cried, jumping backward and slamming the door. "What is that?"

"I don't know," Anne said, "but we're going to need a bigger boat."

"Or Steve McQueen. It looks like the Blob."

Having exhausted our Hollywood analogies, we cautiously approached the refrigerator like a couple of timid explorers entering a cave.

"You go first," Anne said.

I cracked open the door. Slime rolled out onto the floor. What a mess. A glutinous, beige gook was draped over everything on the top two shelves and the inside of the door. Some of it had hardened onto the walls of the refrigerator, creeping into every crevice, coating every surface. In other places it was still fresh and very much alive. Anne spotted the culprit — a one-quart plastic container with the words "Friendship Bread" written on it. The lid had blown off and was nowhere in sight. Anne gingerly picked up the container even as ooze continued to flow over the top, like an active volcano, and dropped it into the garbage.

"Martha's friendship bread," she muttered with disgust as we started mopping up the mess. Several weeks earlier, our babysitter had given us this mysterious container of friendship bread starter, onto which was taped an index card with the recipe for baking friendship bread, plus instructions on passing the starter along.

Apparently it was a well-established tradition in town. Of Amish origin (so the story goes), the idea is to pass this container of bread starter from neighbor to neighbor. If you're lucky enough to have it find you, the instructions call for letting this yeast culture ferment at room temperature for four days before adding equal parts flour, sugar(!), and milk(!!). After letting it sit another five days at room temperature(!!!), you use one-third of it to make your "bread" and pass on the other two-thirds, along with feeding instructions and the bread recipe, to not one but two unsuspecting neighbors.

Rather than being appreciative of this gift, we found ourselves faced with an unplanned project that we had to deal with, ready or not. "My people," Anne noted dryly—meaning the Irish—"bake the bread before giving it away."

"Sounds like a gastronomic chain letter," I mused, rather wary of ingesting this substance that had been sitting on countless countertops around town for who knows how many weeks, months, or even years. What really caught my attention was the warning, "DO NOT USE METAL SPOON OR BOWL!" Why? Was it corrosive?

"We're terrible people, aren't we?" Anne said. "It *is* a nice way for a community to bond."

"That's what Jim Jones said as he was serving up the Kool-Aid. Look at this recipe. A cup of oil, a cup of sugar, and . . . vanilla pudding? This isn't bread, it's a Twinkie." Still, we couldn't very well just throw it out. So until we could figure out exactly what to do with it, we stuck it in the fridge. And promptly forgot about it and went on vacation. But it didn't forget about us. While we were lounging on a North Carolina beach, growing fat on Carbon's Golden Malted waffles, the Blob was growing fat on sugar and spoiled milk, growing and growing and growing and finally bursting from the confines of its plastic Chinese-soup-container prison.

"I'm never going to get this refrigerator clean," Anne muttered as we mopped, wiped, scraped, and rinsed for the next hour. This wasn't mere hyperbole. The hardened slime was more difficult to remove than old paint, and we would ultimately end up throwing out the refrigerator. It was due to be replaced soon, anyway.

In truth, friendship bread did sound like a nice tradition, and this is how bread had been sustained for thousands of years. The

Egyptians, you'll recall, didn't use yeast from a foil packet in the refrigerator; they saved a bit of the dough as a starter from each day's kneading to kick off the next day's bread. And I'm sure they passed a little starter along to family members and neighbors, though probably absent the warning about metal utensils.

———

Now, with Charlie's twelve-year-old starter from Alaska in the refrigerator, I had joined that tradition, and I was secretly rather happy and proud about it. Twelve years old. But would it give me the alveolar, netted crumb that Charlie had promised? I just hoped that I could keep the beast alive long enough to find out.

The next weekend I baked my first loaf of peasant bread using Charlie's *levain*. I was hooked. The naturally leavened dough rose slowly (even with the dash of instant yeast Charlie recommended to give the *levain* a little boost) and not as high as a commercial-yeast-risen dough — in fact, it hardly rose at all — but making bread this way felt pure and was immensely satisfying. The question was, how would it taste, and, more to the point, would the *levain* give me my gas holes?

At dinner, I sliced off the end piece and held it up for everyone to see.

"Holes!" Katie cried.

"Holes!" Anne yelled.

"Holy sh . . . ," I started to yell.

Charlie had been right. Switching to a *levain* was the key — but not to *every* door. The second slice had fewer holes than the first, and the one after that had none. In fact, the middle 80 percent of the *boule* was too dense and too moist. Still, it was the best loaf of bread I'd ever baked, and I was elated.

The crumb had a rich, natural flavor, a bit tangy but not nearly as strong as a San Francisco sourdough, a result not only of the

wild yeast and bacteria in the *levain,* but of the long, cool fermentation, which allowed time for the production of various organic
compounds such as alcohols, esters, ketones, and aldehydes —
scientists have identified over two hundred such compounds in a
fermented dough — which even in their minuscule amounts provide the signature taste and smell that we associate with freshly
baked artisan bread.

The real treat, however, was the crust, extraordinarily sweet
and bursting with flavor, and for once not rock-hard. If I could
get the entire loaf to taste like the crust, I'd have the best bread
on the planet. Of course, to make the crumb taste like the crust is
physically impossible, for the crust — both its brown color and its
unique, sweet flavor — is formed by a complex chemical process
known as the Maillard reaction, which begins to take place at
about 300 degrees Fahrenheit, a temperature that the surface of
the bread can easily reach, but not the moist interior, which never
rises above 212 degrees, the boiling point of water.

During the Maillard reaction, proteins under high heat break
down (or "denature") and recombine with sugar molecules and
all those wonderful products of fermentation to form dozens of
new flavor compounds, which in turn break down to form even
more compounds, hundreds in all, giving the crust a flavor as different from the crumb as toast (also a Maillard-reaction product)
is to bread.

For the first time, I had baked a loaf of bread that I didn't feel
I needed to apologize for. As I placed the replenished *levain* in
the fridge, though, Anne pointedly asked, "What are you doing
with that?"

"I'm putting it in the refrigerator. What does it look like I'm
doing with it?"

"I mean next week. When we go on vacation. You're not leaving it here, are you?"

So it could creep out of the container and destroy another refrigerator?

"Of course not," I improvised, thinking this *was* like having a pet. "I'm bringing it with us. Got to make the bread."

Even on vacation.

WEEK
22

Kneadin' in Skowhegan

It is all mossy and moosey.
— Henry David Thoreau, *The Maine Woods,* 1864

Any event with the word *conference* in its name is an event to be avoided, as far as I'm concerned. Even if the preceding word is *kneading.* Even if it's in Maine in August, when the blueberries are piling up faster than Bangor snow in January. This one in particular, the First Annual (that's got to be an oxymoron, no?) Bread Kneading Conference, promised to be an avoid-at-all-costs Birkenstock-shod whole-grain brown-bread affair, with seminars called "Whole Wheat Pastry Workshop" (ever munch on a whole wheat croissant? — that would cure Katie of her passion for them) and "Build a Clay Oven with Kiko Denzer."

Wait a second — Kiko Denzer, the high priest of backyard bread-oven building, was going to be there? Denzer is the everyman's Alan Scott. While Scott's ovens, such as the one I'd baked in at Bobolink's bakery, cost thousands of dollars and weigh tens of thousands of pounds, Denzer's message is that you can build a perfectly good wood-fired oven in a weekend from earth, sand, and water found, if not in your backyard, then not far from it.

Ever since baking in Bobolink's brick oven, I'd had a growing urge to make bread in a wood-fired oven again, so, pushing my conference misgivings aside, I told Anne, "Pack your pie tins and flatten your *a*'s, honey — we're going to Maine!"

———

As Anne made blueberry pies back at the cottage, I pulled into the parking lot behind the Federated Church in Skowhegan to find my worst fears about the conference seemingly confirmed. The very first, and I mean the absolute very first, person I saw was a gangly hillbilly type who looked to be sixty-five, wearing a beard that looked to be seventy-five, over a linen shirt and jeans held up by suspenders. But the attendees, about seventy in all, turned out to be much more diverse than I'd expected. True, I saw more pigtails and ponytails than I'd seen since third grade, and it was oddly reassuring to see that kerchiefs haven't gone out of style, but the group was a mix of young and old, professional and amateur, rural and urban. There were small farmers and potters, professional bakers and home bakers, dabblers, retirees, and babies. Not to mention a statistically improbable proportion of writers.

When I heard one gentleman saying he only bakes "authentic French artisan bread," I inquired where his bakery was.

"I'm not a baker, I'm a *writer*," he snapped, insulted at the insinuation that he might be a mere baker. I should've known from his pressed khakis and long-sleeved checked shirt on this ninety-degree day, but caught off-guard, I did a really dumb thing.

"What a coincidence," I said. "So am I."

A pair of close-set eyes over a sharp nose gave him the look of an aggrieved eagle. He glared at me, I stared back, and we stood there for a moment like a couple of bandits who'd arrived simultaneously to knock off the same bank. Two writers at an obscure gathering of seventy people?

This other writer, whom I'll refer to only as "this other writer," was clearly not happy with my presence. He expressed his displeasure by saying one thing semipolitely, while above his head hovered a word balloon, clear as could be, with the words he was really thinking. The effect was dizzying.

"What brings you here? [How dare you cover the same event I'm covering! I'm a much more important writer than you!]"

"I'm trying to bake the perfect loaf of peasant bread."

"What do you mean by 'peasant bread'? You mean, a *pain de campagne*? [You don't know what you're talking about, do you?]"

I explained, realizing how stupid it sounded when I verbalized my quest aloud, that I was trying to perfect just one type of bread. Although it did sound slightly better in French; *pain de campagne* means, literally, "country bread."

"Do you know the origin of peasant bread? [My right pinky knows more about bread than you'll ever know, punk.]"

I admitted I didn't.

"World War Two. [Bet you thought it was a lot older, didn't you?]"

I mentioned that I was hoping to bake bread in a very old place, perhaps a monastery somewhere. That seemed to pique his interest.

"Do you know Paris? [You wouldn't know Paris, of course, because unlike me, you don't have a flat there.]"

"Not really."

He drew close. "There's a monastery off the rue de Rivoli," he whispered, as if letting me in on a secret. "Take the Métro to Rivoli, then go behind l'Église Saint-Paul, down the steps toward the Seine."

His eagle eyes darted around nervously, either to make sure no one was listening or to watch for an unsuspecting mouse.

"You'll find a street vendor who sells wares made in the monastery. It's the most odd church. Catholic, yet they pray holding icons.* You may find bread there."

I furiously scribbled down notes, feeling as if I'd stepped onto the set of *The Da Vinci Code*. This time I couldn't read the balloon above his head. Was this guy giving me a valuable lead or putting me on?

Regardless, it was about the tenth time that day that the words "France" or "Paris" had been uttered, usually in response to the question, "Where'd you learn to bake?" or "What got you interested in bread?" Everyone but me seemed to be going to France to taste the bread or learn to make the bread.

The raptor and I avoided each other the rest of the day, and I focused on why I had come — to learn to build an earth oven. On the way through the parking lot, I'd wondered if the suspender-clad man with the ZZ Top beard was Kiko Denzer, for he'd fit my image of the evangelist of earth ovens, this creature who looked as if he'd risen (and not all that completely, to be honest) from the earth itself. So when I met Denzer, I was almost a little disappointed. He was a youngish-looking forty-eight, clean shaven, with curly blond hair peeking out from under a straw hat,

---

*Veneration of icons is a practice strongly associated with the Eastern Orthodox church and rarely found in Catholicism.

his only other concession to my notion of him being his sandals, which, it turned out, he wore for practical reasons.

"Everyone, take off your shoes," were his opening words to his class. "We're going to mix some mud."

You never saw so many pairs of shoes come off so quickly. This was a crowd that didn't need to be encouraged to get barefoot, and in a moment, eighteen pairs of shoes littered the grass. Except there were nineteen of us.

"Your shoes are still on," Kiko said to me, smiling.

I winced. The idea of sticking my clean feet into a mound of dirty clay along with thirty-six other feet was about as appealing as the Egyptian custom of kneading dough by foot. "Uh, I'm going to be visiting some other seminars this morning, and that clay looks pretty messy."

Kiko was clearly disappointed with me but didn't press it. I watched, took notes, and, with the clay oven steadily taking shape, occasionally wandered off to hear other talks. In the afternoon, I sat in on a lecture on raising grain, which I thought might be useful, as my own wheat was ripening back home. The speaker was the parking-lot longbeard. I strained to hear his unamplified words in the church community room, my mind drifting off, and I reflected on the fact that this bread conference was being held in and outside a church hall. It seemed fitting, as the event felt like a church community supper, full of optimism and the conviction that somehow we were saving the world from its path of white bread and factory farming. Throughout the day, I'd heard people wax optimistic about the rise in the state's organic farming acreage; the recovery of wheat, once widely grown in Maine but now a niche crop; the dramatic comeback of small farming; and the growing demand for whole-grain, locally milled products.

Needing air, I went back outside to see what else was going on. Somehow a white-flour baker had slipped into this whole-grain program. This guy knew his craft. In fact, all of the bakers working here knew their craft, all baking in portable, unfamiliar wood-fired ovens that had been brought in on trailers, working, not in their climate-controlled kitchens, but outdoors in the ninety-degree heat, and producing beautiful breads. The white-flour baker was taking questions as his session wound down. I couldn't resist.

"How do you get those much-desired, irregular air holes in bread?"

He misunderstood my question and started to tell me how to *eliminate* air holes. Jeez. How could anyone have *that* problem?

"I'm sorry, I wasn't clear. I have the opposite problem. My bread is like a kitchen sponge. I'm trying to *get* some air holes into it."

"You're probably overkneading or not using enough water. How long are you kneading at second speed?"

"Twelve minutes in my KitchenAid," I said. "Less if I *autolyse*," I added so he wouldn't think I was a dumb novice. He let his mouth drop open.

"Twelve minutes?! In a KitchenAid?" Everybody turned around in their seats to look at the dumb novice.

"A KitchenAid beats the hell out of the dough," he lectured, "unless you have a new model with the different dough hook, but even then, three minutes is plenty. If you *autolyse*, you probably need only a minute. Every turn of that dough hook whips oxygen into the dough."

A minute? Hardly seemed worthwhile to drag the thing out. In fact, I didn't know it then, but I had used my KitchenAid for the last time.

Powerless

> Necessity may be the mother of invention,
> but play is certainly the father.
> — Roger von Oech, *A Whack on the Side
> of the Head,* 1983

Somehow my KitchenAid mixer hadn't made it into our over-flowing baggage of fishing gear, kayaks, bicycles, board games, and books. Any more stuff, and we would've needed to bring along some Sherpas. My *levain,* naturally, did make the trip to Maine, and with company expected tonight for dinner in our rented cottage, I was ready to make some bread. Even if it meant — ugh! — kneading by hand. The last time I'd done this, it had taken a good twenty minutes and my arms and back had ached afterward. As they were already aching from the previous day's kayaking with Zach, I wasn't looking forward to the chore. How could I make this easier?

The baker who'd ridiculed me at the Kneading Conference had said that only a minute of kneading with the stand mixer was sufficient if preceded by an *autolyse.* It stood to reason that *autolyse* should reduce the hand-kneading time as well, so after mixing all the ingredients, I gave the dough a twenty-five-minute rest before kneading. Any longer than that, and

I feared the dough would start to rise before I'd even started kneading.*

The difference was astounding. The dough, which started out feeling gritty and sticky, became smooth and elastic with just the first couple of turns. I had tried *autolyse* once before, with no discernable change, so what was different? First, I was using, on Charlie van Over's advice, a much wetter (68 percent hydration) dough; second, about a third of it came from the *levain,* which already had well-developed gluten; and third — and most importantly — I was kneading by hand, not with a machine.

The function of kneading, of course, is to develop the gluten in the dough. Among the largest protein molecules found in nature, gluten consists of long, tangled chains lying about in a haphazard arrangement. Kneading stretches the coils out, aligning them side by side so that they can bond with one another, forming the strong elastic network that enables the dough to stretch and capture the carbon dioxide gases emitted by the yeast.

I discovered that I actually liked kneading by hand, feeling the dough transform under my hands from a gooey, thick batter into smooth dough with each push, turn, and fold. A quick and enjoyable seven minutes later, my dough felt ready, elastic and supple. And there was no equipment — no machinery — to clean up.

Two weeks on the Maine coast sent me home with a bellyful of lobster and a determination to redouble my efforts. My peasant bread, a yeasty *pain de campagne,* made with a wild yeast

*Technically, the *autolyse* is done before yeast and salt are added, so the resting time isn't critical (unless you're baking for Passover), but since my dough had plenty of *levain,* with its active yeast cultures, I figured I might as well add the remaining ingredients before the *autolyse.* At the least, I wouldn't forget to add them later.

levain, was vastly improved over the bread of twenty-two weeks ago. The texture and gas holes I so desperately desired seemed as elusive as ever, but I wasn't ready to give up. Before summer was over, I'd be harvesting and grinding my own wheat and baking in an earth oven. Give up? I was just getting *warmed* up.

IV.

Sext

Sext takes place at midday when the sun
is at its apex and one has become a bit weary
and mindfulness is all but impossible.

White-Bread Diet

> A dog fed on fine white bread flour and water does not live
> beyond the 50th day. A dog fed on the coarse bread of the military
> lives and keeps his health.
> — François Magendie, writing in the *Lancet,* 1826

Weight: 205 pounds
Bread bookshelf weight: 33 pounds

Anne looked uncommonly grim as she appeared for breakfast in the kitchen, where I was munching on a slice of *pain de campagne* toast.

"How many weeks are left?" She didn't have to specify how many weeks of *what.*

"I don't know. A lot. Why?

"I'm getting fat."

"You're blaming the bread? I don't think so. Look at me."

"Have you weighed yourself lately?"

"Ninety-three kilograms."

"Two hundred and five pounds? You're getting fat."

I'd forgotten that as a doctor (and a former resident of Canada), she knew the metric system.

It was true that we'd been eating a lot of bread lately, having toast for breakfast and slathering butter over peasant bread at dinner, and when I wasn't making my own, I was coming home with armfuls of bakery bread to compare with mine. The Atkins diet this wasn't. Yet my bread felt so . . . healthy. Made from my own hand, eaten fresh, with a little whole wheat and rye, and now wild yeast — it looked and tasted wholesome.

Still, it was essentially white bread, that little bit of added whole wheat and rye notwithstanding. Let's be honest, I was on a *white-bread diet*. I couldn't even bring myself to say it out loud, these code words for bland, nonnutritious, boring. It's easy to confuse white bread with Wonder bread and view it as a twentieth-century corporate evil. However, while whipping chemicals and air into bread and wrapping it, presliced, in cellophane may be a recent innovation, as long as there has been flour, millers have been sifting out the coarse bran to make white flour, which has long been a symbol of purity and refinement. In fact, the English word *flour* comes from the French *fleur de farine,* literally, the "flower of the flour," or the best of the flour, meaning the refined flour left after the bran is sifted off. In ancient Rome and Greece, white bread was prized, though even the "bread and circuses" Romans knew that whole wheat bread was healthier. Which is why their wrestlers were forbidden to eat white bread while training for their circuses.

Yet the fact remains that bread made from sifted flour has sustained a good portion of mankind for thousands of years. So what happened? When did a food that was basically healthy come to stand for blandness and nutritional emptiness? And was that reputation justified?

Certainly it was in 1937, nearly a decade after Dr. Joseph Goldberger's death, when the vitamin that could prevent pellagra, Goldberger's elusive PP factor, was finally isolated by an agricultural scientist at the University of Wisconsin. Oddly enough, this compound was extracted from a plant that was almost as common in the South as cotton, a crop that also grew up to the front steps of the shacks, with a leaf that on a windy day gave the air the heady smell of an old pipe: tobacco.

The cure for pellagra was right under their noses. Although

chewing or smoking tobacco did not supply the essential vitamin, the nicotine in tobacco leaves could easily be oxidized to make what was named nicotinic acid, the preventative and cure for pellagra. Recognized as an essential nutrient, nicotinic acid was added to the vitamin B family of water-soluble vitamins — that is, vitamins that are not stored in body fat and so must be consumed regularly — as vitamin B_3.

Finally, a pellagra preventative was available as an inexpensive vitamin that could be synthesized in the laboratory. Thiamine, another vitamin in which Americans were deficient, had just been synthesized the previous year. But how to get these critical vitamins and others into the American diet? Well, what was the one food that everyone ate? Spurred by concern about public health and the readiness of the nation's boys to go to war, action was taken, not by the government, but by millers and bakers who voluntarily started adding vitamin supplements to their flour and bread in 1938. Two years later, an American Medical Association panel recommended restoring riboflavin, thiamine, iron, and nicotinic acid to white flour to the levels in which they are naturally present in whole wheat flour. In the case of nicotinic acid, this would turn out to be sufficient to prevent pellagra. The word the AMA came up with for restoring nutrients lost in processing (after rejecting *restorative*) was *enriched*.*

By 1942, without a single piece of federal legislation having been passed, millers and bakers had embraced the enrichment movement so thoroughly that over 75 percent of all flour and bread products sold in the United States were enriched. A year later, the War Food Administration required that all flour and

---

*Fortified refers to the addition of nutrients in levels higher than found in the unprocessed, natural form of the food. Thus milk is "fortified" with vitamin D, while flour is "enriched."

bread sold to the government be enriched for the duration of the war, and that took care of the remaining 25 percent. Pellagra was all but wiped out. You won't see the words *nicotinic acid* on the side of your bag of flour, however. Bakers, uneasy with a name that evoked tobacco, successfully lobbied for a new term, which we still use today: *niacin.*

Following the war, the federal government, seeing the success of the program, naturally ended it, and enrichment was returned to voluntary status. The millers and bakers wisely ignored the government, and it became a de facto requirement: American flour would forever after be enriched. Even today the Food and Drug Administration only specifies what constitutes "enriched" flour (adding folic acid in 1996); it does not mandate its use.

The enrichment of flour, and eventually cornmeal as well, was so successful that few contemporary Americans have even heard of pellagra. Of course, no Americans had heard of it in 1900, either. I still wondered why pellagra suddenly appeared in the United States in the early twentieth century.

I brought the librarian at the research institute where I work a loaf of bread and a long list of interlibrary loan requests, and a few days later I learned that the conventional explanation involves corn. This didn't take a lot of research, to be honest, as one oft-cited book on the subject is titled *A Plague of Corn.* Corn is high in niacin, but most of it is bound and cannot be metabolized in humans. Unless, that is, you first treat it by soaking the corn overnight in a limewater bath, which happens to be the first step in making tortillas. For centuries, Native Americans had been soaking their corn overnight in water to which either mineral lime (calcium carbonate) or wood ash had been added in order to soften the dried kernels and make it easier to remove their thick, tough hull (think of popcorn).

Was it just the Native Americans' good fortune that this chemical softening treatment happened to release the niacin in maize, or did they also learn over the generations that families who ate treated maize were healthier? My reading suggests that the answer depends on how you view the Native Americans. What is certain is that their knowledge of the need for liming the corn was lost to the conquerors who defeated them. Corn was still soaked (or "tempered") before grinding, whether stone-ground or crushed by industrial roller mills, but the lime was omitted; thus much of the niacin remained unavailable. This became a moot point around 1905 because a new invention, the Beall degerminator, was selling like hotcakes. Millers loved it because it greatly increased the shelf life of cornmeal and corn flour by stripping the fatty germ and outer bran from the kernel. Unfortunately, as with wheat, those were also the very parts of the seed where most of the vitamins and minerals were concentrated.

Corn was now nutritionally bankrupt, and this "plague of corn" is the conventional reason given for the rise of pellagra in the United States. As I read Goldberger's original papers, however, something bothered me, something that is virtually unmentioned in the literature. Goldberger kept meticulous notes, down to the weight (in grams, bless his heart!) of all the food his subjects were eating, and I noticed his pellagrins were eating a lot of bread, largely in the form of biscuits made with self-rising white flour (which is leavened with baking powder), denying themselves even the niacin present in yeast.

At the time that pellagra started appearing in the United States, corn consumption was on the decline and wheat flour consumption was on the rise, the completion of the railroads having resulted in the flow of inexpensive wheat from the Midwest. In 1931, during the peak of the pellagra epidemic, a survey of South Carolina farm families affected with pellagra found that corn was providing only 16 to 20 percent of their caloric intake.

I wondered, had corn gotten a bum rap? The scientific literature on pellagra nearly unanimously cited corn, ignoring wheat flour, but it seemed to me it might well have been bread, my beloved bread, that was primarily responsible for pellagra in the United States. Scientists, historians, and the government credited enriched wheat flour and bread with *preventing* new outbreaks of pellagra, but they did not connect changes in those same foods with the *cause*.

Which brought me right back to my original question: What had happened to white bread? When did this sustenance food become unhealthy, and why? I pondered this as I made another piece of toast.

WEEK
25

Sweeney Todd

The Gillette safety razor became an object for heightening sexual pleasure when it received the "united thanks of two fond hearts" by allowing the honeymooner to shave off a 3-day beard. Underarm deodorant, toothpaste, mouth wash, Wonder Bread . . . and a host of other products were advertised as . . . ensuring the attentions of a new lover.*
— Joel Spring, *Educating the Consumer-Citizen,* 2003

Here's why I'm still a working man: Back in 1952, if Floyd Paxton of Yakima, Washington, had offered me an opportunity

---

*Yes, that says "Wonder Bread" for assuring sexual satisfaction.

to invest in his new invention, little plastic clips to close bread bags, I'd have said — well, I'd have to have said, "I can't. I won't be born for another year yet." But even if I'd been fifty at the time, I'd have said, "No thanks, Floyd. You can only charge a fraction of a cent for them. Do you know how many of those you'd have to sell to make any money?"

A hundred billion Kwik Lok tabs later, Floyd presumably knows, while I'm clipping coupons. The Kwik Lok Corporation sells over five billion bread tabs annually. Most of these wind up in landfills, but a handful end up in human intestines, which isn't a bad percentage, all things considered. Unless you happen to be one of the unlucky ones. As foreign objects go, this is one you really don't want to swallow. Kwik Lok tabs have been found to cause, in the words of one medical journal, "small bowel perforation, obstruction, dysphagia, gastrointestinal bleeding and colonic impaction." It seems that the same tenacious qualities that make these clips so effective at staying attached to plastic bags make them equally effective at staying attached to your small intestine.

Still, there are worse things to swallow in a loaf of bread — for example, a double-edged razor blade. Like the one on the end of my *lame* right now. Yes, I finally had a real, professional *lame*. Well, almost. Charlie van Over had sent me home with one, which I'd promptly misplaced before I could use it. So I'd made my own from something I'd inexplicably found in my desk at work — an unapologetically nerdy little metal ruler, a quarter-inch wide, with engraved rule markings and a clip for your chest pocket.

Figuring I'd have less need to whip a ruler out of my shirt pocket for an impromptu measurement than I'd have for scoring dough, I removed the clip and ground one end of the ruler to make it narrow enough to fit into the slots of a double-edged razor blade. Surprisingly, I found double-edged razor blades near the checkout counter at Kmart. This bothered me for days. Finally I asked Anne for a consult.

"What are they doing at the checkout counter? For that matter, why are they even still manufactured? I can't believe anyone shaves with these anymore."

She patiently listened to my diatribe about how the double-edged safety razor was good in its heyday, especially compared to its early predecessor — the jawbone of an ox — but the decades since have seen the introduction of the twin-bladed Trac II, the triple-bladed Mach3, the four-bladed Quattro, and, most improbable and redundant of all, the five-bladed Fusion, which we can only hope represents the end of this artificially extended evolutionary line. Choose your favorite weapon and number of blades, but any of these razors shave closer and nick less than the so-called safety razor invented in the late eighteenth century.

"How do they sell any?" I concluded. "Name me one person who even uses a double-edged razor."

"My dad."

By the way, if you'll pardon one more digression — this one is worth it, trust me — I have it from an extremely reliable source who works in market research that when a razor company introduces a new razor, which they do every few years whether there is a consumer need for one or not, they intentionally dull the replacement blades of their existing razors to make the new one feel superior. So, caveat emptor. (That's Latin for "the bastards!")

In any event, I had no sooner thrown away my ten-dollar mail-order *lame*, with its nonreplaceable blade embedded in a stick of green plastic, and loaded up my homemade French-style *lame* with a fresh double-edged razor blade when I came across the following piece of information, staggering in its magnitude: My "authentic" French *lame* had recently been outlawed in France. *Boulangers* giving up their metal *lames*? Unthinkable! As was the replacement: the fixed blade on a plastic stick I'd just thrown away. Indeed, "fixed" was just what *le docteur* ordered; the reason for this blasphemous law was that while Americans were merely digesting Kwik Lok tabs, the French were swallowing double-edged razor blades that had fallen off bakers' *lames* and ended up in loaves of bread!

Now, consider this for a second. Imagine you're a baker in a large bakery, maybe even a production bakery. And granted, you're slashing hundreds of loaves, quickly, rushing to load them into the oven, just as I always find myself doing, even with a single loaf. You suddenly realize that your *lame* is missing its blade. Do you stop and look for it, to determine whether it's on the floor or in a baguette, or do you yell, "Merde!" then pop on a fresh blade and just keep going?

Apparently, French *boulangers* have been doing the latter. Well, I wasn't going back to that ten-dollar *lame* with its non-replaceable blade for anything (presumably they're considerably cheaper in bulk, in France), but I'd make damned sure my metal ruler still had a blade attached when I was done.

I was determined to slash like Scaramouche today, having been inspired at the kneading conference in Maine, where I'd seen what a *lame* in the right hands could do. The very same professional baker who'd embarrassed me with his cutting remarks about my kneading did have a redeeming quality: he was an artist, I mean a veritable Rembrandt, with a razor, a regular Sweeney Todd. In less time than it takes me to make a simple crosshatch on my loaf, he'd scored a butterfly into his *boule*. And I don't mean merely scratched into the surface. This butterfly opened up in bas-relief as the loaf baked! This is even more difficult than it sounds, for not only do the cuts in the wet dough have to be done in the right shape, but they have to be made at a consistent depth and at the correct angle. This was something I was having difficulty doing even with my simple crosshatch. The lopsided loaf I'd baked for Charlie van Over was a fairly typical case.

Still, my makeshift *lame* was working far better than the single-edged razors I'd also tried for a while. One thing I'd learned from Lindsay at Bobolink's bakery is that you have to slash almost with abandon, that is, with confidence and without hesitation, and on an angle, not perpendicular to the loaf. A slow, careful cut will invariably catch and drag in the dough, while a quick, bold slash will slice through cleanly.

Slash with confidence and abandon. As the Katha Upanishad exhorts, "Arise! Awake! Approach the great and learn. The sharp edge of a razor is difficult to pass over; thus the wise say the path to salvation is hard."*

And not about to get any easier.

WEEK

26

Pane Toscano

You shall find out how salt is the taste of another man's bread, and how
hard is the way up and down another man's stairs.
— Dante

One bite, and I desperately wanted to spit it out. Fortunately it wasn't my bread. Unfortunately we were in a fancy restaurant

---

*The passage from this ancient Hindu scripture is said to have been the inspiration for the title of W. Somerset Maugham's novel *The Razor's Edge*.

known for this very bread, according to the review we'd read, so I couldn't just cough it up or pocket it in my napkin.

The bread, baked on the premises, was flat, tasteless, and heavy. This was, in fact, some of the worst bread I had ever eaten. I looked around at my fellow diners to see if anyone else was pointing to it and gesticulating like me. Clearly the baker had screwed up tonight.

"I think he forgot the salt. I should let someone know, shouldn't I?"

"You absolutely should not!" Anne pleaded. "Why would you want to do that?"

"If I were the baker, I'd want to know my bread was terrible."

But to my utter astonishment, we seemed to be the only ones in the packed restaurant who felt that way. Everyone else was enjoying the stuff, tearing off chucks and dunking them in olive oil. The only way I could eat the doughy, tasteless stuff was to add salt and pepper to the olive oil before dipping.

I was *sooo* glad I listened to Anne and kept my mouth shut. As we left the restaurant, we stopped to read a framed magazine article hanging near the doorway, and the mystery was solved. The inedible bread the restaurant is known for is their faithful reproduction of the traditional salt-free Tuscan bread, *pane Toscano*. According to legend, the recipe evolved centuries ago during a dispute over a salt tax, when the locals simply refused to buy salt rather than pay the tax. Although the bread was born of necessity, the Tuscans, who are famed for their gastronomic prowess (and whose restaurants are spreading through America faster than Fascism spread through Italy), inexplicably developed a taste for it; thus the bread continues to be popular there to this day. With all due respect, my advice to Tuscany is, get over it. The evil salt-taxing king is long dead, and a few grams of salt would do wonders for your tasteless bread. With tourists flocking to

Tuscany — the new Provence — you really don't want their first taste of your region to be flavorless bread.

Salt. If Tuscany is the new Provence, then salt is the new olive oil, providing ample opportunity to spend major sums of money on something to which your mother never gave a second thought. "Blooming in summer, it develops a pink tinge and an aroma of violets." This has to be a critic's description of a bottle of wine, right? Wrong. Try French sea salt (fifteen dollars for ten ounces) from a mail-order catalog. Salt elitism first became trendy in a few high-end restaurants, then quickly caught on among foodies, leading some home chefs to discard their Diamond Crystal for twenty-dollar-a-pound *fleur de sel* from Brittany. Well, Thomas Keller and Jean-Georges wouldn't be caught dead using the same salt in their kitchens as you use in yours, so they had to up the ante, turning to such exotics as African clay salt and black lava salt from Hawaii. David Pasternack, the chef at the highly regarded Manhattan seafood restaurant Esca, keeps *several* types of sea salt on hand, matching the salt to the fish.

Whatever. In my bread, I simply use the coarse kosher salt I keep for my everyday cooking. I don't even have conventional table salt in the house, by the way. After you get used to coarse kosher salt, the traditional fine stuff becomes quite unappealing, a weak, chemical imitation of the real thing, as Cool Whip is to whipped cream. Now, have I done a blind taste test? No. Am I then as guilty of salt snobbery as David Pasternack? It's all about scale, I say. I just like using coarse kosher salt. Whatever it is the rabbi has done for it works for me.

Salt was very much on my mind as I chewed joylessly on my *pane Toscano* because I had just started following a recommendation from my latest bread book to withhold salt until the very end of kneading. Salt, the author said, interferes with gluten development. Frankly I couldn't say I had noticed any difference, but I continued holding the salt back anyway, out of equal parts superstition and reluctance to ignore a renowned baker, but also just in case it really was a critical step — one whose benefit was being masked by the other mistakes I was making.

It certainly isn't making the bread any worse, I figured, so what's the harm?

WEEK

27

The Sound of One Hand Kneading

MASTER: In clapping both hands a sound is heard: what is the sound of the one hand?
STUDENT: The pupil faces his master, takes a correct posture, and, without a word, thrusts one hand forward.
MASTER: It's said that if one hears the sound of the one hand, one becomes a Buddha. Well, then, how will you do it?
STUDENT: Without a word, the pupil thrusts one hand forward.

— Buddhist koan

"This is really good bread," Katie said as she buttered up another slice. "But the loaf seems smaller."

"That's because I didn't measure anything."

Her eyes grew wide. "Why?"

Because for the past week, during my commute I'd been listening to a recording of *Zen and the Art of Motorcycle Maintenance* — at least trying to listen to it. It wasn't going well. I hadn't read the book back when it was originally published; I was too cynical, too closed-minded to want to read such nonsense. The fastest way to get me out of a room back then was to say "Zen." (Saying "motorcycle" was a close second.) Now, thirtysome years later, my mind was open to the concepts expressed in the book (okay, more open, at least), and I popped in the CD with anticipation, only to find that the book had grown as stale as last week's bread.

Today the prose of *ZMM*, as fans call it, sounds (to my ear, at least) stilted, pedantic, and preachy. Maybe it always sounded that way. I wouldn't know, but it seemed now as if there never really was a good time for reading this book. When the book was ready, I was too young; when I was ready, the book had aged. Still, it seemed important, so I was determined to finish it, until, about a week into it, I realized with genuine horror that I was starting to write — even think out loud — in Pirsig's preachy prose. Somewhat shaken, and praying that my own voice would return, I slammed the lid on the CD case and returned it to the library. Maybe I'll read the *ZMM* Cliff's Notes — the quick path to enlightenment.

I'd heard enough *ZMM*, however, to understand that in Pirsig's way of looking at the world, the perfect loaf was not something I was going to create; it was something that I was going to *find*. It was already there, waiting to be discovered or baked, but I had to elevate myself to reach it. It would not reveal itself until I was ready.

I'd been coming around to this way of thinking of late, which is perhaps subconsciously what led me to this decades-old book, a book about another journey. Although the writing didn't impress me, I was struck by the relevance of its themes — the divide (bridgeable, in his view) between spirituality and technology, the attempt to define quality — to my own culinary undertaking. Is bread making art or science? Must we scorn technology and resort to wood-fired brick ovens and stone-ground flour in order to achieve truth in bread? Or could technology help me find the perfect loaf? And what, indeed, constitutes perfection? In any event, the book had inspired me to create a loaf of bread by feel, without measuring, trusting my instincts and whatever skills I'd developed over twenty-seven weeks.

I didn't know how to explain all of this to Katie over dinner, so I just mumbled something about wanting to get closer to the bread.

"But Dad, what if this had been the perfect loaf?" Implying, of course, that it wasn't. I let her continue. "You didn't measure. How would you ever make it again?"

Good question. How would Buddha respond? Perhaps with "I wouldn't have to."

Except that wasn't true. Reproducibility — consistency — was one of my primary goals. I needed another answer. But what? I suppose a true master might answer in that annoying Buddhist way by asking another question, and I considered, "How does the salmon find his spawning ground?" Not bad, but not wanting to mix foods, I instead replied to Katie, not in the manner of Buddha, but in the manner of the old Asian handyman in *The Karate Kid:* "Ah, my little seagull, you have so much to learn."

But not as much as I, for not only did I cheat (I'll explain in a moment), but my Zen experiment had nearly landed me with a loaf of pure *white* bread. Working without a recipe seemed wonderfully liberating until, as I started to leave the kitchen after kneading the dough, I realized that I'd forgotten to add the whole wheat and rye flours.

Zen dilemma. There was still time to adjust the bread, but . . . should I? I sat down and had a Platonic dialogue with myself in the kitchen. Possibly the whole-grain-flour omission was a sign that the bread was meant to be as white as I. On the other hand, it might merely be yet another indication that I was becoming an increasingly forgetful, middle-aged man who shouldn't be baking without a recipe. Now, the point of the experiment was to get closer to the art of bread making. But must one be totally spontaneous in order to be in touch with the bread? You don't go to the supermarket without a grocery list, merely picking items off the shelf that appeal at that moment in time. If you did that, you'd never have mayonnaise in the house.

While I was having this fascinating discourse, the gluten was setting up, so when I finally decided that, Zen or no Zen, I simply didn't *like* pure white bread, I had my hands full. It took several strenuous minutes of folding and twisting, but the whole wheat and rye flours eventually blended into a homogenous mix. More or less.

The most revealing part of this exercise was the discovery that making decent bread in this manner wasn't all that difficult. *Letting go was.* Even in the very first step, when I was ready to add water to a handful of flour to make the *poolish*. I knew I wouldn't have enough *control* (what a loaded word — no wonder I'm a Zen flunk-out) if I simply put the bowl under the running tap, so I looked for something to put the water into first — and instinctively grabbed a measuring cup.

Whoops. That clearly wouldn't do. I used a tall drinking glass instead, but I found myself thinking, It's about twelve ounces. Not fair. The clock was an even bigger problem. As much as I tried to ignore it, I couldn't. Anne and I went for a walk during the proofing, but I was distracted and not "in the moment" because I feared the yeast would be exhausted before we returned, as the bread had been rising for over two hours. I knew that because I'd sneaked a look at the clock when I set the dough aside to proof.

None of this should've been surprising to me. After all, I'm someone who weighs the water for coffee every morning — to the nearest gram. Need I say more? Zen Buddhism is about being in the here and now. For me, though, the clock on the kitchen wall was the whisperer in the concert, that tiny irritation that becomes so colossal it can drown out a symphony, taking you totally out of the experience. Just knowing it was something to avoid changed the experience from being about oneness with the dough to a test of self-control: *Don't peek!*

Yet by another measure, this exercise was a success. I had, after all, made bread without a recipe, by feel. And the bread?

"I think it's better than usual," Katie offered.

Certainly it was tasty, perhaps because of the longer rises, but I noted out loud that the crumb was the usual disappointment, soft and spongy as angel food cake, without any large air holes.

"What's with you and the air holes!" Katie yelled, exasperated and mystified at my obsession with this feature.

"It's not just the air holes, it's the texture. It's too soft and moist."

"I *like* it soft and moist. And I don't know what you're trying to improve on. I think it's great!"

I was so flustered that I forgot to thank her for the compliment.

A Mind Is a Terrible Thing to Waste

> What a waste it is to lose one's mind. Or not to have a mind
> is being very wasteful. How true that is.
> — Vice President Dan Quayle, speaking at a
> United Negro College Fund event

"What'd you forget?" Anne asked after biting into a slice of peasant bread.

"It's like eating air," Katie added.

"It tastes familiar," Anne said, taking another bite.

I'll say.

One often reads that bread made without salt is "insipid." Except, of course, when it's made in a renowned Tuscan restaurant using a traditional recipe. I was fairly distraught over my own insipid loaf. It didn't even make for edible toast, and almost *any* bread tastes good once you toast it, but Anne reassured me, "You're just off your game," as she placed my mangled reading glasses in front of me.

"Oh, you found them. Where were they?"

"The clothes dryer."

Off my game? More like off my rocker. Forgetting the salt was the culmination of a week during which I had experienced a series of mishaps worthy of Mr. Magoo, all of them due to forgetfulness or confusion. I'll spare you the details because I suspect that anyone over the age of fifty could supply his or her own version of them, but suffice it to say that the week's adventures included losing both pairs of prescription glasses plus my sunglasses, brewing coffee onto the kitchen floor (weighing the water doesn't help if you forget to replace the pot), deleting an important computer file at work, forgetting Anne's birthday for the first time in twenty-five years, and, most baffling of all, turning left when a sign displayed an arrow pointing right.

In that last instance, when I'd realized something was amiss and backtracked to the intersection, I couldn't believe my eyes. The left-pointing arrow now clearly pointed to the right! What was this, a Road Runner cartoon? Had Wile E. Coyote flipped the sign around on me? Forgetfulness was one thing, but confusion, lack of recognition, not being able to follow a clearly marked street sign, was something else.

Was I experiencing early dementia? (Or in retrospect, was I just obsessed with cartoon analogies?) "I think I need to see someone," I told Anne.

"You're just tired. Give it some time and see if it improves."

But now . . . I'd forgotten to add salt to the bread. Enough time.

"I'm going to say a letter, and I want you to say as many words as you can that begin with that letter — no proper names like Tom or Jane — as quickly as you can."

Once I'd decided to have my memory loss and confusion evaluated, I faced the problem of whom to see. I was doing this behind Anne's disapproving back, and I felt awkward going to my regular neurologist. Plus, he's the guy I see for my pinched nerve, and I didn't want him asking about my dementia every time I came in for a sore neck. Then I remembered (remarkably enough) that I work in a psychiatric research institute, where they know a thing or two about dementia, so I approached the head of the geriatrics division.

"Beeelll," he said in his elegant Italian accent, making my mundane name sound like a character in an Italian opera, "I don't-a-think you have anything to worry about. You know, we see an interesting thing. Patients who come in and think they have Alzheimer's almost never do." As he spoke, his hands waved through the air as if directing actors around a stage. "Yet the patients who do have Alzheimer's are in denial. They insist they are healthy."

Just like the mosquito, I said. I'd read once that only female mosquitoes bite (to obtain blood for their eggs), but only male mosquitoes buzz (it's a mating call). Thus, on a summer night, when you hear a mosquito buzzing, you needn't worry. It's when you don't hear *anything* that you should move indoors.

"Exactly," he said, his large hands going into motion again. He didn't think that leaving salt out of bread was such a big deal, explaining that memory requires attention and focus. In other words (I'm paraphrasing liberally here), you can simply be too busy to remember things. "From everything you've told me, you're probably just under stress. It sounds like you are very busy."

Stress? Busy? To be sure, I was no Leeuwenhoek, virtually ignoring my vocation while fiddling with my avocation in the kitchen all day, but I wondered if my determination to bake the perfect loaf had approached or even crossed the line from passion to, well, something less healthy. I thought of Katie yelling, "Dad, what's with you and the air holes!"

It looked as though we were done. I'd just get some rest and —
"You say you are making breads," he mused as I started to rise.

"*Bread*," I corrected him. "Just one kind." I was tempted to joke, "Two, now; peasant and *pane Toscano*," but thought better of it. He was, after all, Italian.

"Just one kind?" His words hung in the air as I eased back into my seat. "I would suggest," he continued, "if it would make you feel better, we can do an evaluation. Of course, everything is confidential."

That last part was important. Having this testing done at work violated my time-honored principle of not crapping where I nest. Did I really want my colleagues performing a psychiatric evaluation on me? But it was only a memory test, nothing to be ashamed of, and after all, these were the experts.

The next morning I reported to the lab at nine thirty. I was able to do reasonably well in the word-recall test, in which you are read a long list of words and asked to recall as many as you can. I thought I'd aced the cognitive tests, such as assembling colored blocks to match a drawing, and the motor-skills test, putting some pegs into a pegboard. I was, in fact, sailing along until we came to a new game: beat the clock. The research assistant explained that she would give me a letter, and I'd have to name, in a limited time, as many words as I could — but no proper names — that began with that letter.

The research assistant readied her stopwatch. "No proper names, remember. Ready? Letter *f.*"

"Frank."

She looked at me funny. Was I being a wise guy?

I wanted to say, "The adjective meaning 'honest,' not the common name," but that would've eaten up too much of my time. Still, I wondered if she was counting or discounting the word, while precious milliseconds flew (*flew* — hey, there's one I missed!) by. I moved on.

Inexplicably, the very next word that popped into my head was *fellatio.*

Well, I couldn't say that! Problem is, the word wouldn't budge. I tried to think of another word. *Fellatio.* No, go away! I pleaded silently, but it refused, standing erect and blocking every other word beginning with *f* in the dictionary. Why was this happening? Should I just say it and move on? It is, after all, a valid word, and it's not as if it's that *other f*-word, the four-letter one. And speaking of which, of all the letters in the alphabet, why did they have to choose the loaded letter *f*?

But guarantees of confidentiality notwithstanding, I feared that if I released it, within hours the entire institute would be hearing about the director of technology's dirty mind or, even worse — much, *much* worse — his sexual harassment of the young research assistant. This was becoming a nightmare. I had to come up with another word, but every time I tried, that damn *fellatio* reared its ugly head.

At this point, I imagine I may be raising some speculation as to why I became fixated — damn, that's another word I missed — on that particular word, so it's probably a good idea to pause and discuss this, and let's all be adults about this and do it without smirking, thank you. I don't think I got fixated on *fellatio* because I always have sex on my mind.* Nor was it because the test was being administered by a young woman. No, I think it's because Federico freakin' Fellini was sitting in the next room, no doubt waving his hands, and Italian was on my mind.

I've always admired the word *fellatio*. It sounds so Italian, full of vowels and soft consonants, so exotic and lyrical, suggestive of a Roman orgy. By contrast, the English word commonly used for the act sounds harsh and crude to the ear, ending in a hard,

---

*If the reader is wondering whether that sentence means that I don't always have sex on my mind, or means that the fact that I always have sex on my mind wasn't to blame — keep wondering.

clicking consonant. Why would anyone say "suck" when you can use the very same lovely four-syllable, vowel-dripping word that Julius Caesar himself used?

What can I say — I have a good vocabulary. Still, there was no way I was going to say that word to that woman. Especially since I was in a psychiatric research institution. Anything is possible here. What if this test was not really a memory test at all but a psychiatric evaluation in disguise? After all, she wasn't just counting the words I was saying; she was *writing them down*. Sounds a touch paranoid? Well, then, maybe the test was designed to induce paranoia! After all, I was in a psychiatric research institution (did I mention that already?).

As I was having this lengthy and fascinating (another *f*-word I missed) discussion with myself, precious seconds ticked by, and I realized I hadn't said a *f*— ing word in what seemed an eternity. The evaluator's gaze bore down on me as beads of sweat started popping on my forehead. I'd been warned by Fellini that subjects sometimes become upset and storm out of these tests; now I could see why. Meltdown approached. Sirens were whooping, red lights were flashing, I could feel my mouth moving, but nothing was coming out of it. Oh, *fudge*!

"Fudge," I croaked, barely audible, breaking the mental block.

"Foot. Find. Fred — no, forget Fred. Forget!"

"Time's up," she said, expressionless.

"Now tell me as many words as you can that begin with the letter *s*."

"Suicide."

Kneadless to Say

Why, a four-year-old child could understand this report. Run out and
find me a four-year-old child, I can't make head or tail out of it.
— Groucho Marx in *Duck Soup*

"Oh, jeez," I moaned to Anne when I came home from work.
"Connie's bringing in bread Monday. A" — I made quotation
marks with my fingers — "'fantastic new, easy-to-make' bread
she wants me to taste."

"Bittman's no-knead?"

"What else?"

"Oh, jeez."

I'd stopped telling people I was making bread, because the
next thing out of their mouths was invariably, "Have you tried
that no-knead bread?"

I told Anne I was going to tattoo the answer onto my forehead
(right under "No, kids, I am *not* making croissants") and save
them the trouble. Even when I wasn't talking bread, I couldn't
escape this glutinous tidal wave. Once, while we were looking
at Dutch ovens in a kitchen-supply store, a salesman wandered
over and offered, unsolicited, "They're great for making that
no-knead bread."

"That no-knead bread" was a reference to an article by the
New York Times food writer Mark Bittman, who'd breathlessly

described a "revolutionary" new method of baking bread that produced an "incredible, fine-bakery quality, European-style boule" that "a 4-year-old could master."

That assessment (Bittman raised the minimum age to eight) came from the recipe's creator, Jim Lahey of Manhattan's Sullivan Street Bakery. For home bakers, Lahey promised no less than the holy grail: easy-to-make bread that required almost no time and effort — and, most notably, no kneading — yet produced a fantastic crust and perfect crumb.

If a kitchen technique ever needed a good PR firm, it's kneading, with its reputation as an onerous, burdensome process to be avoided at all costs. Kneading *can* be tedious if done by hand, but most kitchens these days probably have either a food processor or a stand mixer, both of which do a perfectly fine job without effort, although by now I'd completely stopped using mine. Having been forced to knead by hand in our Maine rental cottage, I'd discovered how easy it was if preceded by a twenty- to thirty-minute *autolyse*. That resting period for the dough (combined with the already-developed gluten in the *levain*) does much of the preliminary work for you, greatly shortening the kneading time. Thus after returning from Maine I'd stuck with hand kneading, a seven-minute process I found relaxing and enjoyable. With each week I was becoming more familiar with the dough, able to tell by feel when it was ready and when it wasn't, a skill you never acquire when kneading by machine.

Still, after months of being asked about no-knead bread, I decided it was high time to find out what everyone else was talking about. I dug out the recipe and, to my surprise, immediately found something appealing about it that I had originally missed: the promise of a perfectly steamed crust. Like me, Bittman had struggled to make adequate steam in his home oven, even "filling a pot with stones and preheating it, then pouring boiling water over the stones to create a wet sauna (quite effective but dangerous)."

To say the least.

Lahey's recipe, though, required neither hot rocks nor kneading to produce a perfect artisan *boule*. What was his secret? A wet, wet dough; an eighteen-hour *autolyse* in place of kneading; and a heavy pot, covered for the first half hour of baking.

It all made perfect sense. If the dough was wet enough, the strands of gluten could move around and align themselves without being forced into place physically. The wet dough took care of the need for steam as well, for it steamed itself inside the pot. Not owning a Dutch oven (if the salesman's pitch had been, "They're great for roast chicken," I might've), I borrowed a wonderfully ancient oval one of cast aluminum, which Anne's brother had grabbed from their mother's kitchen before I could get my hands on it, and got to work. This really was a wet dough — the hydration was a dripping 75 percent or so. After letting the dough sit overnight on the countertop, I set out the next morning to form a *boule* as directed. Except it was impossible to form anything with this gloppy mess. "Put dough seam side down on towel," the recipe instructed. Seam? How could you possibly have a seam with this glop? It wasn't dough; it was thick batter. I wondered if I'd made my mixture too wet. If so, it wasn't my fault; the recipe gave all the ingredients in volume (grrrr!), using the unreliable "scoop and sweep" method for measuring flour, no doubt a concession to the home bakers without kitchen scales at whom the article was aimed.

Instead of using a towel to form the *boule*, I pulled out my linen *couche*, a heavy cloth used for proofing long loaves, floured it thoroughly, and put the gloppy mess on it in a shape as close to a ball as I could muster. Two hours later, the dough had risen and was ready to go into the preheated Dutch oven. Now, how to flop this wet mass of batter into a 450-degree pot without scorching myself? Bittman's suggestion was to "slide your hand under towel and turn dough over into pot." Which I did. Nothing happened. The dough hung upside down, clinging to the cloth like a sleeping bat. I pulled at it with my fingers, and it started to descend slowly, resembling some kind of otherworldly protoplasm.

Finally the slowly sagging goop reached the hot metal, where it sizzled and hissed and gave off a puff of steam, but the other end of it was still attached to my *couche,* stretching out like Silly Putty. What a mess! Using my metal bench scraper (a handy five-by-seven-inch metal blade in a wooden handle, used for dividing dough and scraping up flour), I skimmed off as much as I could from the *couche,* giving up the pretense that I was dealing with anything resembling a loaf, and got the damned thing in the oven before it finished frying.

I turned my attention to cleaning up. My new *couche* was virtually ruined, permeated with the batter, the kitchen littered everywhere with little globs of dough: clinging to the coffeemaker, dripping off the countertop, stuck to my jeans. An hour later, I flipped out the bread. To my surprise, it fell out cleanly. The crust — and there was a lot of it, because the dough had spread out to cover the bottom of the pot — was golden and shiny and covered with appealing blisters. It looked appetizing but more resembled pastry crust than bread crust.

The "*boule*" was all of two inches high. Rustic *boule?* Hardly. The crust was crispy and thin as promised, but without the sweetness and depth of my peasant bread crusts. The bread itself lacked flavor, which was surprising, given its eighteen-hour fermentation at room temperature. Yet it wasn't a total loss: when I sliced into this flat, oval loaf, my suspicions were confirmed: I had made a pretty good *ciabatta,* that flat Italian white bread with a delicate, crispy crust and an airy interior ideal for dipping into olive oil.

"Are you going to be working with this method again, Dad?" Zach asked, enjoying a slice. "Trying to make your perfect loaf?"

I thought about that for a moment. Making this bread had been about as much fun as doing the dishes. Bittman and Lahey truly seemed to think this method would spark a revolution, creating a nation of new home bread bakers, enabled by this easy, no-knead, no-steam method of baking bread. As with van Over's hope for a food-processor-bread revolution, I suspect they will be disappointed, for all have missed something essential: when it comes to bread, the end does not necessarily justify the means. Still, I was glad I had done the experiment. It reminded me that there's more to bread than bread. This isn't simply about lunch. The process needs to be rewarding.

"No, Zach, I have to give the Dutch oven back to Uncle John," I said, pulling a hunk of dough out of my hair. Then I went upstairs to take a shower, and as the water ran down my back, I thought about my answer. Why was I so quick to dismiss a promising if imperfect and unsatisfying method after only a single try? What was I in fact after? If I thought we made bread because it took us to another place, what *was* that place for me?

Why bread? Why me? Why now?

I needed a good shrink.

Bread Shrink

The reptilian always wins.
— Clotaire Rapaille

I'll say this: Clotaire Rapaille certainly knows how to make an entrance. After keeping me waiting for five minutes in his spacious study, long enough for the opulence of it to fully set in but not long enough to be rude, Dr. Rapaille, in a *très* French sports jacket, his wavy salt-and-pepper hair swept back with a certain je ne sais quoi, descended the sweeping marble staircase of his Tuxedo Park, New York, mansion, built in 1890 by the very architect (Rapaille was quick to point out) who designed Grand Central Station. I nearly had a case of the vapors.

I'd been nervous about this interview all morning, changing clothes twice, and then, when told by Dr. Rapaille's assistant to make myself comfortable anywhere (as if that were possible!), spending several minutes choosing the right seat.

Faced with over half a dozen options, this was no trifling matter. I didn't want my back to the entrance, which ruled out several seats. There was a chair facing his desk, but that seemed too formal an arrangement, forcing Rapaille to sit behind his desk, and besides, I didn't want to feel like a delinquent third grader waiting for the teacher to arrive. Other chairs in a grouping around the large fireplace were blocked in by the furniture arrangement, which would make getting up to shake hands awkward.

Hoping to dodge the issue entirely, I remained standing while I examined the paintings on the wall and the books on the table, so carefully arranged, his own book prominently displayed among the French-language classics that were stacked perfectly askew, each book rotated at a twenty-degree angle from the one below it, like the treads of a spiral staircase.

Finally I settled into a richly padded leather chair with a fur thrown over it. That is, a *mink* fur, thrown carelessly over the chair the way I throw my underwear onto the bed. I hoped I'd chosen the right chair. With a man who is a marketing psychologist (and from the looks of his digs, a fabulously successful one at that), who has made a career of picking up on people's subconscious actions and hidden codes, you can't be too careful.

Dr. Rapaille is known for taking a novel approach to market research, not listening to what focus groups *say*, but getting to what he calls the "structure" behind their words, the emotional connections to the object. A former clinical psychologist, Rapaille does this partly by wearing down his groups in lengthy, three-hour sessions, for the last hour putting his subjects on the floor with pillows, under dimmed lights, while subtly conducting a kind of group analysis session. The third hour is when the truth comes out. For example, Rapaille writes, when you ask people what they want in a car, they'll rattle off practical things like fuel efficiency, comfort, and safety. But that's the brain's cortex speaking, and the cortex doesn't buy the car. The brain stem does. Ask people about their fondest memory of a car when their guard is down, and you'll more likely hear about sex in the backseat or the freedom of the road or that family trip to Grandma's. Tap into these primitive, subconscious feelings — the reptilian brain, Rapaille calls it — and you'll sell the car. Which is why

Chrysler's "gangsta" PT Cruiser (Rapaille advised on it) was so successful that there was a long waiting list, despite its having been dismissed by reviewers as, technologically speaking, a piece of junk. Same with another Rapaille project, the resurrected Jeep Wrangler, whose round headlights subtly suggest a horse, an image Jeep played up in their Wild West advertising for a car more likely to be driven on the Jersey Turnpike than in a Texas cattle roundup.

"What is it about bread?" I asked Rapaille after he'd finished the theatrical descent down a staircase that made the one at Tara look like a fire escape. "Why do people have such strong emotional attachment to it? Why do the French line up every day to buy their baguettes? Why do we buy so much of the stuff, even when it's not very good?" I knew he had done market research into bread and had consulted for at least one commercial bakery. If anyone would know, Rapaille was the man.

"You have this smell," he began, in his seductive Yves Montand accent, "this very special smell that triggers a lot of references, like home and safety, and mother, and 'I'm going to be fed.' It's a very safe place."

That was precisely the kind of answer I might've expected from a psychologist — "mother" in the first sentence! Although his beginning with smell, not taste, was interesting and hinted at the very reason grocery chains often have in-store bakeries. The next sentence, though, surprised me. "If you have water and bread, then that's enough."

"Enough?"

"You know *The Count of Monte Cristo*? It is a novel. The *compte* was put in this fortress, a jail, for, like, fifteen years and given nothing but bread and water. For fifteen years. But he developed so much muscle that he was able to dig a tunnel to escape. Which means if you have the right water, and the right bread — the old-time bread — you have total survival. There is something very archetypal and basic in bread. It is the number one thing you need for survival. I was born during the war, you know, in France, and sometimes we had nothing else besides bread. And we were happy. The bread was good.

"There is a very special definition of bread in France," he continued. "You should have a crust, and it should be hard. And the center should be" — he groped for the word in English — "*molle.*"

"Soft?" I guessed.

"*Oui,* soft. So you need this opposition there. This is very important. When you have this opposition, this is a great bread. We don't say that about other foods, vegetables, whatever. Only about bread, which is a category of its own. Bread and water. If you have good bread and water, you can survive."

And the reptilian brain, at some level, knows that.

We talked a bit about the rituals surrounding bread, and Rapaille noted that in France, bread at the table is not sliced but broken, a powerful, communal act that begins a meal. (In America, of course, most of us would recoil if a dining partner handled food in such an intimate and unsanitary manner. We prefer our bread neatly sliced, ready to be plucked out of the basket with antiseptic hands.)

"When French people come to America, they say there is no bread," Rapaille mused. "There is no distinction between the crust and the center. It is all just like plastic. The symbolism is that you should ... *keech*" — he made a crackling sound to accompany his hand motion — "break the bread. When you cannot do that, this American bread is not really bread."

A knock at the door interrupted us. A young man — a servant, not an aide, not a secretary, but a real, live, honest-to-God servant — dressed in a tie and dark suit,* entered with a silver tray, on which sat a silver pot of coffee. I briefly wondered what country — and what century — I was in.

I took advantage of the distraction to reflect on what I really expected to learn from Rapaille, why I was even here. But I couldn't quite get it out.

"What type of bread are you making?" he asked after the servant had silently closed the door behind him. I explained my single-minded, year-long quest for the perfect *pain de campagne.* "Just one type?" he said, raising an eyebrow.

Here we go again. Why did everyone (especially shrinks) have such a problem with this? If I were baking a different kind of bread each week, no one would blink an eyelash, but somehow this pursuit of trying to do one thing very well made me eccentric.

Rapaille talked more about rituals, the difference between sharing a baguette and sharing a *boule* (with a baguette, someone always gets the end piece — the *croûton* — but with a round loaf, as with the Knights of the Round Table, all the slices are egalitarian). He displayed a surprising degree of bread knowledge when he discussed how the shape of the loaf also affects the ratio of crust to crumb, and therefore the flavor as well, and he kept returning to the smell.

And I kept returning to, "What is it about bread?" I'm not sure what I was looking for, but I didn't feel I was finding it. If the aroma was such an important factor, that made my obsession with bread all the more mysterious. I'm pretty sure that as a child, I never experienced the smell of fresh-baked bread in my house, not even once. Yet that could be important in itself. Was

---

*Disappointingly, not in a tux, as we were in Tuxedo Park, which actually is the source of the eponymous suit.

I subconsciously trying, not to re-create something primal from my childhood, but to create something that had been *missing*?

Finally, after more than three-quarters of an hour, a little worn down, slumped in my chair, the lights in my brain dimming a bit, my cortex relaxed and my brain stem blurted out the true, reptilian reason for my visit.

"Dr. Rapaille, why am *I* obsessed with bread?"

The doctor glanced at his watch. The fifty-minute hour was over. Our time was up.

WEEK
31

State Fair

This is Fair Week and everybody is going to enjoy it if
I have to follow them with a shotgun.
— Phil Stong, *State Fair,* 1932

Looking up at the dead-of-night sky, I was relieved to see stars. I was half-asleep, but at least I'd have good weather for my predawn, four-hour drive to Syracuse.

Thirty minutes later, still a good hour from daybreak — if day could break through at all — I found myself closed in by a fog so dense I could barely see the shoulder of the road. The speed limit was sixty-five; the sensible limit in these conditions, thirty. Yet I didn't know how long this fog would last, and if I drove all the way to Syracuse at thirty miles an hour, I'd miss the competition. I eased the cruise control back to sixty and hoped for the best, praying that this was a local phenomenon that would soon clear.

Two hours later, still in darkness, the fog had become so thick it was condensing on the windshield, requiring me to give the wipers a kick now and then, which mainly had the effect of smearing the accumulation of splattered bugs on the glass, further reducing my visibility and making the car feel small and isolated, with no signposts to follow and no reliable gauge of direction or progress.

In other words, the perfect metaphor for my journey to bread perfection. Just past the halfway point of my fifty-two-week odyssey, I needed a sign, a validation of the six months I'd devoted to this single-minded passion. Yes, it was high time for an independent evaluation of my bread, by people who weren't family or friends, who didn't know of me or my quest, and who would be totally objective and bluntly honest, no matter how much it hurt. We call such people judges, and within a few hours, a half dozen of them would be comparing my peasant loaf to the other entries in Category 02, the Yeast Breads class at the oldest state fair in the nation, the New York State Fair.

Although it wasn't warm in the car, I kept the windows closed and the air conditioner running the entire trip so that the crust wouldn't wilt in the endless cloud I was driving inside. Glancing at the loaf in the passenger seat from time to time, my only companion on this long, dark journey, I thought of Tom Hanks's volleyball in *Cast Away*.

Except this *boule* wasn't round. Hoping to impress the judges, I'd tried a variation on my peasant bread, making a large loaf leavened only with the wild yeast in the *levain,* which made it a true *pain au levain.* That meant using more *levain* to compensate for the absence of commercial yeast. Somehow I'd screwed up the baker's percentage (perhaps not correctly accounting for the water already in the *levain*), and the dough for this two-and-a-half-pound *boule* had come out way too wet. As a result, when I flipped it onto the baker's peel before sliding it into the oven, it flattened out almost into a pancake. I quickly slashed the moving target as best I could, then jammed it into the oven, where the hot baking stone stabilized the slithering mass into something resembling a flying saucer. I modified the label for the entry, turning my *pain au levain* into a *pain au levain miche,* hoping to salvage some of the 30 points awarded for appearance.

I had already written off the 20 points awarded for texture because the judges apparently had a strong, preconceived notion of what bread texture should be, the contest rules stating that "the texture should be moderately fine, even-grained." In other words, the very opposite of what I'd spent the past six months trying to achieve.

Zach came in a few minutes later, surprised to smell bread baking at ten o'clock at night. I explained that I wanted the loaf to be fresh for the fair tomorrow.

"Tomorrow's the fair?" Sensing my gloom, he broke into the theme song from the Rodgers and Hammerstein musical *State Fair,** cracking me up. "That's better," he said. "Be happy! You're going to the fair!"

After four hours of driving, I finally reached the fairgrounds, and after two wrong turns, followed by an illegal U-turn in front of a state trooper (who gave me a break when he saw the loaf riding in the passenger seat), I found the culinary arts competition

---

*Totally astounding to me until Zach explained he'd just seen a community production.

building and dropped the bread off a little after nine thirty. The woman who took it told me the judging would be completed by noon. I parked and, with several hours to kill, went to See the Fair, my first state fair ever. There was so much to see!

I saw lots of cows (spring calf, spring heifer, summer heifer, fall calf, winter yearling, spring yearling) being judged in a ring, teenagers leading the bovines around on a leash, which I found somehow touching and reassuring. They seemed like good kids, and I was thankful that there were still teenagers in this country, full of innocence and wonder, whose idea of a good time was leading a cow around a ring. Which made the following announcement all the more chilling.

"Attention: The ice man is here."

"The iceman cometh!" I exclaimed out loud. Two women sitting in the bleachers next to me turned and looked quizzically. I decided I'd seen enough cows and excused myself.

I headed back to the culinary arts building, hoping that I could discreetly observe the judges at work. They hadn't yet arrived, so I went back out to See the Fair.

I saw pigeons (archangel, parlor tumbler, American saddle muff tumbler, nun, jacobin, Lahore, frillback, Indian fantail, flying tippler, Chinese owl, American show racer, flying-type homer, show type king, damascene, swallow, Modena, English pouter, pigmy pouter, almond roller, bellneck roller, baldhead roller, show roller).

I saw geese (Toulouse, Emden, African, Sebastapol, American buff, pilgrim, Pomeranian, brown China, white China, Canada, and Egyptian, Roman tufted, African, Toulouse, and frizzle — "clean-legged only").

I saw Modern Game bantams (birchen, black, black-breasted red, blue, self blue, brown red, golden duckwing, lemon blue, red pyle, silver duckwing, wheaten, white, and AOV) and Old

English Game bantams (black, black-breasted red, blue, brassy back, brown red, crele, ginger red, mille fleur, and red pyle).

I saw rabbits that weighed fifty pounds, rabbits with erect ears, and rabbits with huge floppy ears; ducks (a chocolate Muscovy, which sounded as if it were already cooked); chickens (rosecomb, Japanese, American, Cornish, silkie, bearded, Brahma, Andalusian, and a category called "Other").

My favorite barn was the one with the sheep. The competition was about to begin, and everywhere you looked, sheep were being groomed and shaved, washed, vacuumed, and combed, giving the barn the expectant air of backstage at the Miss America pageant.

It was only eleven o'clock, but I was getting hungry (after all, I'd had breakfast at four thirty), so I headed for the food midway, hoping to find something interesting. I saw fried dough (more stands than I could count), fried curlicue fries, fried corn dogs, fried funnel cakes, fried onions, fried chicken, fried mushrooms, fried cauliflower, fried zucchini, and even fried pickles. Any food that wasn't fried was frozen. I saw Sno-Cones, Sno-Kones, and snow cones, plus their haute cuisine cousin, shaved ice. I saw smoothies, ice cream, the Colossal Sundae Center (where their slogan, I imagine, is "Quantity, not quality"), and something called Dippin' Dots ("ice cream of the future"). I hadn't even covered a quarter of the food court yet. There were rows and rows of trailers selling food. It seemed that half the fairgrounds was given over to food. Yet not a sandwich to be found anywhere.

After eventually succumbing to the siren call of the deep fryer and "authentic" Belgian *frites* (if only!), I headed back to the culinary arts building. It was almost high noon. The tables laid out to display the baked goods were empty. A sign greeted me: BREAD RESULTS WILL BE POSTED AT 3:00.

Three o'clock! I had hoped to be on the road by one. The

judges, all matronly-looking woman, were behind soundproof glass, tasting, drinking water, and scribbling notes. I went back to See the Fair.

I saw a log cabin, a luthier, a weaver, two youth dance troupes, and a man I judged to be eighty-five making natural brooms by hand, his head bouncing like a bobble-head doll as he worked the foot-powered mechanism. I bought a hand broom from him and wondered who would be doing this five years from now. Of course, I couldn't very well ask *him*.

I'd always associated the word *fairgrounds* with ground, so I had been surprised to see that this fair was set in concrete, concentrating and reflecting the searing ninety-three-degree heat. With more time to kill, I went to the super-air-conditioned New York State dairy-production pavilion, where I learned that fudge is a dairy food ("butter in every bite") and downed a refreshing cold milkshake while studying an impressive life-size sculpture, *in butter,* of two boys in overalls, leaning over a rail fence, looking at their cow.

Three o'clock. Finally. A small group had gathered in the culinary arts building, but the judges were still compiling their results behind the soundproof glass. I had expected that all the entries would be displayed, with ribbons on the winners, as the geese and jams had been, but that wasn't the case for the bread competition. Only the first-prize winners were on display, in a fogged refrigerated case, the kind where Greek diners keep their over-the-top-gorgeous but inedible deserts. My loaf was not in the case.

A judge emerged and I handed in my receipt. She couldn't even find my folder. This was getting humiliating. I was getting ready to leave when it turned up. "Here it is," she said, pulling out a red ribbon. "You won second place."

Holy smokes! I studied my scorecard. I'd received 25 out of a possible 30 points for appearance ("One side dropped"). They awarded me 15 out of 20 points for creativity, but only 20 of 30 points for flavor. This puzzled me, as flavor was the one thing I thought I had going for me, my long, room-temperature fermentations drawing out plenty of yeasty flavor. Perhaps they didn't care for the tangy taste of the *levain,* or like Katie they favored something lighter. Say, croissants.

The score that really had me upset, however, was for texture. I'd earned a perfect score, with the added note, "It's what it's supposed to be." No, it's not! It's too tight, too moist, even when I get some holes. How could they give me a perfect score on crumb! Several of the judges were still around, and I wanted to take issue with their verdict, but realizing the absurdity of such an argument, I took my red ribbon and drove home, having won second prize in the New York State Fair bread competition, Category 02, Yeast Breads.

It had been a good day. I had won a prize and Seen the Fair, but the strangest sight still awaited me, as I left Syracuse at seventy miles an hour.

I saw a pink high-heeled shoe flying across the road, bouncing crazily in the slipstream of the cars. I wanted to close my eyes and sleep. I'd seen enough for one day.

V.

None

None is a time to pray for perseverance,
to pray for the strength to continue bearing
fruit as one reaches one's prime and
needs to keep going.

Don't Fear the Reaper

Do not muzzle an ox while it is treading out the grain.
— Deuteronomy 25:4

Weight: 205 pounds
Bread bookshelf weight: 44 pounds

"Wheat-eater, wheat-eater, wheat-eater, *wheat!*"

I glanced at the numbers on the clock radio, glowing dimly in the dawn — 5:30 — pulled the pillow over my head, and tried to go back to sleep.

"Wheat-eater, wheat-eater, wheat-eater, *wheat!*"

"Tell that damned bird to pipe down," I moaned. Then I realized what its call — one I had never heard before — was saying.

"Wheat-eater, wheat-eater, wheat-eater, *wheat!*"

I bolted upright. Today was harvest day!

The previous October, Anne and I had planted four beds of winter wheat. For nine long months I had waited for this day, watching over my crop like a nervous mother-to-be, rejoicing at its germination when the first sprouts cautiously peeked through the soil, missing it in its childhood when it disappeared under a blanket of snow, then celebrating its return in the spring. For nine long months I'd protected it against the neighbor's cats, shooed away grasshoppers, and deterred greedy crows as it grew to maturity, turning from grassy green to bread-crust gold.

Growing winter wheat is a horticultural act of faith, if there ever was one. You'd think one ought to be able to grow a grain of wheat in less time than it takes to make a human baby, yet the gestation period is almost precisely the same. As is, remarkably, the number of chromosomes. Wheat contains one of the most complex genomic structures in the plant world, with forty-two chromosomes, only four fewer than humans.

The wheat had "died off" in the winter, going dormant. Then, in the first days of spring, despite looking deader than a bale of straw on a Halloween hayride, it had reawakened the very same week as its swanky suburban cousin ryegrass, and by late spring it had grown to a straight, strong, three-foot-high stalk.

Of grass, not grain. Even in May there was nothing to suggest that this stalk of grass might turn into something remotely edible. The wait for it to form seed heads and change from green to golden seemed endless. But three weeks ago, startling in its suddenness, it had almost magically become recognizable wheat. A week after that, the proud wheat heads bowed to the earth, each stalk curling over in a graceful arc, a biological mechanism that protects it from rain, for as the wheat approaches ripeness, a good soaking could cause it to sprout uselessly on the stalk rather than fall to the ground and sprout in the earth.

It was a touching gesture, the swollen, almost voluptuous seed head bending over to face the very earth it had sprung from, bowing as if offering its head in sacrifice to its master so that others might gain nourishment — and life.

I was only too happy to oblige. First I had to be sure it was ripe. I brought a seed head over to Erle Zuill, a local seventy-five-year-old farmer, for a look. The very first thing out of his mouth made my blood run cold.

"Are you sure this is wheat?"

He ran his fingers over the threads that were coming out of the seed head. "It looks more like barley. I've never seen threads like this on wheat."

Oh my God! What had I done? My mind started racing. I was sure the packet had said wheat — wasn't I? — but the seed company could've made a packing error.

"Of course, the last time I harvested wheat was fifty years ago," Erle added. Erle or anyone else in the county, I thought. Later on, I would learn that some classes of wheat, including the soft red winter wheat that he might have planted back then, are "beard-less," lacking those long threads.

I relaxed a bit as he rubbed his aged, coarse farmer's hands together vigorously, opened them, and blew. The chaff drifted away with his breath, leaving a small palmful of wheat berries, a little smaller than popcorn kernels, behind.

"It's ripe for sure."

That's what I was waiting to hear.

Harvesting grain, the act that turned *Homo sapiens* from no-madic hunters and gatherers to village, then town, and finally city dwellers. Once our ancestors had learned to cultivate grain some ten thousand years ago, they could put down their own roots and stay in one place. And create pottery. And houses. And societies and schools and arts and writing and buildings. Thus in a sense the grain I was about to harvest was a direct and necessary antecedent to the magnificent Empire State Build-ing, sixty miles to the south. As my knowledge of harvesting was based in whole on the same Flemish art that had filled my head when I planted the wheat, I had a similarly romantic vi-sion of how the process would go. Stooped over, grabbing hand-fuls of wheat in my left hand, I'd swing the curved sickle in a graceful arc with my right, cleanly cutting the stalks off a few inches above the earth. The Good Wife would follow behind, gathering the wheat into sheaves, tying them, and laying them in the field, where the Happy Children, laughing and making a game of the work, would gather them up and bring them to the barn.

In my memory I'll always believe I succeeded in living that painting, despite three facts: I didn't own a sickle, there seemed no reason beyond art to bind the wheat into sheaves, and the children were both at their summer jobs.

One thing I got right: me stooped over. But with a tool no peasant in a Flemish woodcut would've been caught dead with. After taking a few useless swings with my old, rusty scythe (essentially a sickle on a long pole), I went into the basement and emerged with my not-quite-as-rusty hedge shears. For this small crop, they were ideal.

For a larger crop, we would've wanted to use a mechanical reaper, and some of us may remember from school the story of the McCormick reaper. Picture a crude robot — or automaton, as it would have been called back then — that took the form of a human, bending at the waist, swinging a scythe. This fanciful machine, which McCormick abandoned after fifteen years, was, not surprisingly, an abject failure, taking more rolls in the hay than the proverbial farmer's daughter.

Huh? That's not the story we learned in school. Cyrus McCormick a failure? His reaper an automaton? Of course not; I'm talking about his father, Robert McCormick. The kid said, "Pop, I think you're taking the wrong approach to this," and devised a horse-drawn device that looked nothing like a human but effectively cut and gathered the straw. Other reapers were appearing on the market at this time, just before the Civil War, but McCormick, with his business acumen and aggressive legal tactics (he once hired a small-town lawyer named Abe Lincoln), drove the competition out of business and went on to found International Harvester.

Back to our little crop, Anne (playing the Good Wife) and I moved down each row with our hedge shears, Anne gathering handfuls of stalks, which I snipped off a few inches above the ground, very much aware that I was harvesting wheat more in the style of a twenty-first-century Mexican landscaper than a fifteenth-century Flemish peasant, but after all, it *was* the twenty-first century. The whole operation took less than half an hour, and when we were done, we'd filled two large garden carts with wheat. Of course, most of that was straw and would be discarded.

The burning question the entire time was, how much edible wheat would this crop actually yield? I was hoping to get the equivalent of a five-pound bag of flour out of my 150-square-foot plot, but my minimum requirement was to get at least enough for one loaf of bread — that is, about a pound. Seeing how few wheat berries came out of the seed heads I'd sampled thus far, though, I was worried about getting even that much.

With the wheat stalks all laid out in the same direction, it was time to thresh. The word is closely related to *thrash* for good reason. Threshing consists basically of beating the hell out of the wheat until the berries are battered loose from the seed heads that encase and protect them. With some ten thousand years between the first cultivation of grain and the 1834 invention of the combine, mankind has, as you might expect, come up with a number of ways to accomplish this. Pliny the Elder, writing around 77 AD, described three methods in favor at the time: beating with a flail; using a crushing stone or board; and spreading the wheat out on a floor to be trampled by a train of oxen.

I had lent out my oxen for the weekend and didn't own a flail — two heavy sticks connected by a short chain — which looks like something you'd find smacking the buttocks of a member of Parliament in a London S and M den, so I had to improvise, pulling out an old straw broom I'd been saving for the occasion. Anne and I laid a handful of wheat out on a new canvas tarp, and I threshed away.

The result of all my frenetic flailing was a bushel of dented wheat. Not a single berry emerged.

"Hit harder!" Anne urged, like a high school cheerleader rooting for her favorite (I hoped) linebacker. Cheered on by Pom-Pom Girl, I hit harder. A few strands of the broom flew off. The wheat bounced up and down on the tarp. I hit harder and still harder until, winded, I sat back on the tarp to catch my breath. A few lonely kernels of grain lay scattered among the debris. It was going to take something firmer than a broom to coax this stuff out.

"How about the back of a shovel?" Anne suggested.

That seemed a bit rough, but I didn't have a better idea, so I flailed away at the wheat with a shovel for a few minutes. Sure enough, the canvas soon became littered with popcorn-size kernels of wheat. But an examination of the seed heads revealed that only about half the kernels were being released. We found that rubbing the battered seed heads in the palm of a hand or drawing them between thumb and forefinger released the remaining grains, but in a few minutes, our hands were raw from the coarse chaff, and we had to put on gardening gloves.

After a bit of this, with progress pitifully slow, I concluded, "This doesn't make sense. What's the point of all this flailing if we have to strip each seed head by hand anyway?" I went down to the workshop and returned with the wooden mallet I use on my woodworking chisels. Then, a handful of wheat held to the tarp with my left hand, I beat it with the mallet in my right. That was the ticket! Some wheat remained behind, but not nearly as much, and many heads were totally clean.

But after a half hour of beating the tarp-covered lawn with a mallet, the ground beneath had become soft and yielded to the blows, which in turn became less effective. I kept moving around to new, firmer spots, but even with a large tarp, they were becoming more and more difficult to find, and I was getting tired.

"You beat for a while," I said to Anne, handing her the mallet while I went over to the woodpile, returning a few minutes later with my chopping block, a small tree stump that I use for splitting firewood.

Pounding on a firm surface caused the tough hull to release its grip on the berry with only a few blows — no additional stripping required. Now we were cooking. The job went much more efficiently if the seed heads were bundled together (guess there *was* a reason beyond art to gather the wheat into sheaves), so one of us bunched while the other pounded, and the tarp gradually filled with grain and chaff, along with broken pieces of straw.

Occasionally we stopped to shovel the wheat and chaff into a large bucket over which I'd placed a homemade sieve originally made for screening compost. Running our hands in the wheat and chaff along the screen, we were rewarded by the musical sound of grain tickling into the bucket. Most of the chaff fell in, too, but the sieve screened out the large pieces of straw and revealed seed heads that hadn't been fully threshed.

After six hours, weary, sore, and sunburned, we had threshed our little crop of wheat, and I understood why the Latin word for the threshing board is *tribulum,* which has the same origin as *tribulation.* This was tribulation if I'd ever seen it. Thank goodness for the combine, which cuts, threshes, and cleans the wheat all at once, right in the field.

Our bucket of wheat and chaff was mainly (by volume, at least) chaff, and we still faced the job of winnowing, that often-cited act of "separating the wheat from the chaff." But that would have to wait for another day. It was evening, and I needed a hot shower and a cold drink. Anne had one request as she peeled off her gloves and fell back onto the grass, exhausted.

"Promise me you won't grow cotton next summer."

WEEK
33

Miller's Crossing

"You are dealing with forces, young man, when you
speak of Wheat and the Railroads, not with men . . .
Men have only little to do in the whole business."
— Frank Norris, *The Octopus,* 1901

What a bizarre and comical sight. This was a commercial, state-of-the-art roller mill? It looked like something straight out of an old Disney cartoon. Mike Dooley and I were the only human presence on this large factory floor among the rows of large square machines, a couple of dozen in all, each a little smaller than a Volkswagen Beetle. These awkward steel contraptions were all shimmying — and I do mean *shimmying* — as if to a sound track only they could hear.

Standing on four robotic-looking legs that literally flexed at rubberized knees, they were swaying their metallic hips suggestively, bouncing up and down exuberantly, and just generally looking silly and weirdly animalistic. I could picture them late at night, when the mill was dark and empty,* switching on the lights and holding a surreptitious hoedown, then scurrying back into place the instant before the night watchman (with droopy mustache, of course) flipped on the light.

"What are they doing?" I yelled to Mike over the din.

"Look inside." Bits of bran, flour, and grain were vibrating atop a wire screen, the smaller particles falling through. These were sifters, and their gyrations seemed to do quite an effective job.

I'd found my way to this Clifton, New Jersey, mill, one of several owned by the Bay State Milling Company, by once again looking for the silos (shades of my trip to Bobolink Dairy). "They're the only ones in Clifton," Mike had told me. This old industrial city seemed an unlikely place to see twin silos rising above the factories and office buildings.

Which goes to show how little I know about mills. The other landmark Mike had mentioned were railroad tracks, and as I pulled into the parking lot, it occurred to me that "near the silos and the railroad tracks" could probably suffice as directions to pretty much every wheat mill in the nation. Wheat, as it has for a century or more, still comes from the Midwest in railroad cars, is stored in silos until milled, and goes out in trucks as sacks of flour. The story of wheat is largely the story of transportation, whether the grain is floating down the Nile or riding the rails of the Southern Pacific.

On the verge of milling my backyard wheat, I thought an understanding of the process might be useful. This is partly how I'd ended up at this Bay State mill, which also happens to be one of the plants that produces the King Arthur flour I'd been baking

---

*The mill is actually never dark and empty.

with every week. I had another reason for being here as well. During the past nine months, I'd learned that every bag of flour sold in the United States since World War II was enriched, replacing the vitamins and minerals that milling removed. I'd found out why niacin was among those vitamins, and I'd learned the saga of the heroic New York doctor who risked his life and reputation to find the cause of pellagra. One thing continued to bother me, however. I still wasn't swallowing the conventional wisdom that corn was responsible for the pellagra epidemic. Certain facts didn't add up, particularly the evidence that the American diet was moving from corn to wheat at the epidemic's peak. What better place to understand what might have happened to wheat than at a roller mill?

The steel-roller mill represented a radical departure from the way wheat had been milled into flour for millennia. Even before there was bread, wheat had been crushed with stone, first by hand, then, from about Roman times, with rotating stone wheels. In the mid-nineteenth century, a Hungarian inventor devised a milling process that ground the wheat between pairs of chilled-steel rollers, producing the whitest flour the world had ever seen. Much of this flour went to the royal court in Vienna, where it was prized for use in the delicate pastries we still call Viennoiserie, as well as in another Viennese invention, croissants. Americans who were treated to their first taste of these delicacies at the 1873 Vienna International Exhibition brought home a sweet tooth and a demand for European-style white flour.

As it so happened, the American gristmill was reaching its limits at about the same time. Softer southern wheat was being replaced by hardier, high-yielding varieties of hard spring wheat grown in the northern plains, a wheat so hard that it resisted grinding, often becoming scorched from the heat of the millstone before it yielded to the pressure. And unlike winter wheat, whose bran tended to flake off in chunks through grinding and could easily be sifted out, this hard spring wheat had a more brittle bran husk, which shattered into fine particles that inevitably ended up in the flour, which was white in name only. Thus in 1878, when a large gristmill in Minneapolis, the milling center of the nation, was destroyed by a "flour bomb" — highly explosive flour dust suspended in air — killing eighteen people and leveling not only the mill but two adjacent mills and the surrounding business district as well, rather than rebuild the stone mill, the owner brought over some Hungarian engineers and built America's first steel-roller mill.

Within a few decades, the roller mill was well on its way to displacing the stone mill. Standing on the milling floor at Bay State, I could easily see why. Grain was flying through these machines at an incredible rate. These rollers ran virtually unattended, twenty-four hours a day, seven days a week, and, unlike a stone mill, a roller mill didn't need to be shut down every couple of weeks for dressing of the millstones.

Given their reputation, the size of the rollers surprised me. I'd fully expected to see massive rollers on the order of a steamroller, but these were only about a foot in diameter and four feet long, individually enclosed in metal and glass boxes. There were dozens of them, but they weren't all doing exactly the same thing.

Mike had brought me to the first set of rollers the tempered grain passes through, the grooved break rollers. These gleaming steel rollers were rolling inward toward each other, but at different speeds, allowing the slower roller to grip the kernel while the teeth on the other one broke it open. The rollers were not crushing the grain at all but opening it up.

"Think about the problem," Mike explained. "You have to

shave off the inside of a spherical object. How do you do that?" I was stumped. "Well, how do you get cantaloupe off the rind?"

Suddenly it was clear. You start by breaking the kernel open so that subsequent steps can shave off the endosperm — the starchy part of the kernel that becomes white flour — from the bran. There would be eighteen passes through rollers in all, with further separation of bran and endosperm occurring at each stage. So, I asked, do rollers simply do this faster than stone wheels?

Not just faster, but better, Mike explained. Stone mills *crush* the grain, so tiny bits of bran and germ, too small to be sifted out, end up in the white flour, while roller mills *scrape* as they peel the endosperm from the bran. In fact, they scrape so efficiently that if you wanted to build a devitaminization machine, you couldn't do much better than a roller mill. Only 20 to 30 percent of the wheat's original vitamins remain in the resulting white flour. The bulk of the nutrients are found in the pieces that are sieved out: the germ, the bran, and, most significantly, the aleurone layer, a thin coat under the bran where most of the B vitamins (including niacin) are stored. Why do we strip all the healthy stuff out of our flour? Because Katie isn't the only one who loves croissants (and white bread and hamburger rolls). The goal is to get the bran out, and the vitamins are collateral damage. If millers had their way, they'd prefer to stop refining a little sooner, because the finer you mill the wheat, the more flour dust you create, and flour dust suspended in air is highly explosive, whether in a stone mill or a roller mill.

Mike wasn't eager to engage me on the subject, but I knew that mills are still blowing up all the time. In the decade preceding 1997 — that's *1997*, not 1897 — there were 129 explosions in flour mills and grain elevators, so imagine the risks a hundred years ago, before sophisticated filtration systems were developed.

This mill certainly felt safe, if not antiseptic, but I was ready to move on. I had one last question for Mike. "When did the roller mill become popular in America?"

He thought for a minute. "After the turn of the century. Many of the steel-roller mills running today were built in the teens and early twenties."

Bingo! The dates coincided precisely with the pellagra epidemic. For me, this was the last piece of the puzzle. I was more convinced than ever that bread, not corn, was responsible for the American pellagra epidemic, and I'd seen firsthand how it might have happened. However, I'd soon feel a little bit like Goldberger fighting the skeptical establishment myself. When I returned home, I e-mailed the author of a recent biography of Goldberger with my theory about the connection between white bread and pellagra.

"I, too, have heard the roller-milled white flour theory of pellagra," he answered.

So I wasn't crazy. This was a legitimate (if obscure) theory.

He continued, "I have not seen evidence to substantiate the claim."

Well, I had.

Blown Away (by an Unusual Destiny in the Blue Sea of August)

His reasons are as two grains of wheat hid in two bushels of chaff; you shall seek all day ere you find them, and when you have them, they are not worth the search.
—William Shakespeare

The threshed wheat and chaff half-filled an eighteen-gallon plastic bucket. But how much of that was wheat? When I ran my hands through it, it seemed to be nearly all light, fluffy chaff. A couple of weeks went by before I had a chance to find out, when I awoke one morning, not to the call of my conscientious wheat-eater bird, but to the welcome sound of wind rustling in the leaves. A cold front had moved in, bringing dry air and a stiff breeze. It was a perfect day to winnow.

Anne (lucky for her) was working, but Katie was free until the afternoon.

"I have a deal for you," I said as she stumbled downstairs midmorning. "I'm going to give you a chance to do something that I guarantee no other kids in this town — maybe the county, even the state! — have ever done."

Katie knew a rat when she smelled it.

"Does this involve wheat?" She had seen how tired Anne and I were after threshing.

"It'll be fun. Trust me." For once, I was right.

Winnowing wheat — another chore taken care of by the combine right in the field as it cuts and threshes — is traditionally done by tossing the wheat and chaff into the air with a pitchfork. In even a light breeze, the chaff drifts off with the wind, while the denser kernels fall to the ground.

With the stiff breeze at hand, this looked to be a snap. Katie and I spread out the tarp, stood near the center with our backs to the wind, dipped our cupped hands into the bucket, and tossed the grain into the air like a couple of referees throwing a jump ball.

At that precise moment, the wind reversed 180 degrees and blew the chaff back into our faces. The wind was both erratic and shifting. When it did strike, though, we quickly tossed handfuls of wheat into the air, marveling as the chaff drifted away. Soon we had gone through the bucket. What fell back onto the tarp was cleaner, but still half-chaff. We broke for lunch.

"This isn't looking good," I said over a sandwich.

"We'll get there eventually, Dad," Katie chirped, always the optimist.

"That's not what I mean. I think that bucket is all chaff. We'll be lucky to get a loaf of bread out of this."

Katie plucked a few grains of wheat out of her hair and handed them to me, a touching gesture. Truly we had nothing to spare.

After lunch, we continued winnowing, and gradually, almost imperceptibly, as we continued to go through the shrinking pile again and again, each time decreasing the proportion of chaff in the wheat, a small hill of golden grain started to rise on the tarp, covering Katie's bare feet and reaching to her ankle bracelet.

She giggled. "Dad, we're making wheat! I'll bet we've got enough for a dozen croissants right here!"

By the time Katie hopped on her bike and headed to her lifeguard job at the town pool, the bucket was mostly clean wheat.

Winnowing the last 10 percent, however, threatened to be 90 percent of the work, given the erratic winds. The remaining work was lonely and frustrating without Katie. If I tossed modestly, too much chaff returned to the ground. If I tossed higher, a sudden gust often carried some of the precious grain away with the chaff. Then I had a brainstorm. If chaff is that light, it should float in water, no? Wheat kernels, on the other hand, would sink. Couldn't I take advantage of this to quickly do the final cleaning? All I had to do was run some water into the bucket of wheat, skim off the chaff, and spread the remaining grain out on the tarp to dry.

Just to be sure, I did an Internet search with the terms "wheat winnow water" and found myself reading the abstract of an article from a scholarly journal. It seemed I wasn't the first to hit upon the idea. Gorillas in the wild have long been observed separating wheat from chaff by crushing it in their hands, then blowing the chaff away — exactly the same method of threshing and winnowing that the farmer Erle Zuill had demonstrated. What was exciting in this article, however, was that the author had found a family of gorillas who'd learned a new, more efficient method: dipping a handful of wheat and chaff in a stream and letting the chaff float away.

Wow — my idea *had been validated by apes*! Still, I couldn't find any mention on the Internet of humans actually cleaning wheat this way, so before proceeding, I sent off an e-mail to Mike Dooley at the mill. A beep on my laptop signaled his reply a few minutes later.

Bill,
    I would certainly try to avoid using the water. You take a risk of causing the wheat to germinate. Once germination starts, enzymatic reactions commence which convert starches into usable

energy in the form of sugars, a process called malting. This will destroy your bread-baking abilities . . . (but might be a nice addition
to a milk shake). Very impressive approach by the gorillas . . .
but my experience has taught me that very few made it past the
first semester of Milling Science and Management in the '70s
while I was in school!

Point taken. Mike suggested I use an electric fan instead to
free me from the vagaries of the temperamental wind. I figured
that another few hours on the tarp in front of the fan would get
the job done.

Except that when I finally got around to doing the last of the
winnowing, I discovered that many of what looked like clean
wheat berries were, on closer examination, still encased in a thin
membrane of husk. It took another full day of rubbing the wheat
on an old window screen, a handful at a time, to remove these
stubborn husks, leaving my hands raw for days afterward. In the
end, though, I had wheat.

From my small planting, I'd harvested twenty pounds of
beautiful golden wheat! Yet it wasn't the amount I'd grown that
moved me; it was something less tangible. Nothing I had ever
grown in the garden — not corn, tomatoes, leeks, or roses — had
given me as much of a sense of accomplishment as growing wheat.
I suspected I had tapped into some genomic key, connecting with
my agricultural ancestors on the Russian steppe some two, five,
even ten thousand years ago.

I'd reestablished a connection I hadn't known I'd missed.
Misty-eyed, I felt as if I'd just done something very important,
but I couldn't quite say what or why. I suddenly wanted to know
more about my ancestors — that is, my father's ancestors, those
Russian peasants and coal miners and priests — who had survived centuries of harsh nature and harsher rulers. I thought

about how locally grown, milled, and baked bread was almost certainly the only thing standing between life and death for my great-great-grandfather. That wasn't so long ago, just four generations.

Yielding to a sudden urge, I went out to the garden and, using a hoe, started turning the stubby remains of the wheat back into the soil, giving it a proper burial. As I settled into my to-and-fro rhythm, replicating the survival strategies of my ancestors, I found myself again thinking about why I'd been drawn to bread, to wheat. Was I satisfying some biological or emotional imperative, witnessing the resurfacing of a suppressed primitive urge?

Drifting off to sleep that night, in a state between wakefulness and unconsciousness, I had a kind of *2001: A Space Odyssey* experience, feeling myself racing backward through the centuries, seeing my ancestors living in cities, then, moving back in time, in villages, huts, and caves, all the while growing rye and wheat, planting and harvesting, threshing and winnowing. Growing and harvesting wheat had connected me to the ages, triggering an unexpected awakening. And I hadn't even ground it into flour yet.

Lecture to Young Men on Chastity

Languor, lassitude, muscular relaxation, general debility and
heaviness, depression of spirits, loss of appetite, indigestion,
faintness and sinking at the pit of the stomach, increased
susceptibilities of the skin and lungs to all the atmospheric
changes, feebleness of circulation, chilliness, headache, melancholy,
hypochondria, hysterics, feebleness of all the senses, impaired
vision, loss of sight, weakness of the lungs, nervous cough,
pulmonary consumption, disorders of the liver and kidneys,
urinary difficulties, disorders of the genital organs, spinal diseases,
weakness of the brain, loss of memory, epilepsy, insanity, apoplexy.
— Sylvester Graham,* on the perils of frequent
(more than monthly) copulation between married couples,
A Lecture to Young Men on Chastity, 1834

*Graham, a nineteenth-century Presbyterian minister and advocate of
vegetarianism, temperance, and abstinence, also advised that ketchup and
mustard cause friskiness, leading to insanity; self-gratification results in
blindness, paralysis, and senility; chicken pie causes cholera; and white bread
promotes promiscuity. He developed graham flour, a whole wheat flour in
which the bran is ground more finely than the endosperm, to promote health
and abstinence. Your correspondent, in severe need of libido reduction this
week, can report, having baked a loaf of graham bread, some success. Modesty (that is, my wife) prohibits me from elaborating, but before you rush off
to buy libido-depressing graham crackers for your spouse (or teenager), note
that Nabisco "original" graham crackers are made today with white flour,
high-fructose corn syrup, partially hydrogenated cottonseed oil, and soy leci-
thin. The thought of that alone is enough to depress one's libido.

Terror Firma

I've built . . . full-sized ovens in half a day.
— Kiko Denzer, *Build Your Own Earth Oven,* 2007

How to Build an Earth Oven in a Weekend;
or, A Recipe for Disaster

1. Set aside a *month* of weekends, because regardless of what Kiko Denzer writes (and preaches in Maine), that's closer to what you're going to need.
2. Drag your son out of bed at the crack of dawn and, using pickax and shovel, dig a footing deep enough to reach the frost line (allegedly forty inches in my neighborhood, but you may have to settle for less) and wide enough for a grave, because before the project is over, you're going to want to kill yourself, I guarantee it. With any luck, you will strike clay, which you should set aside for the oven itself, which you will get around to building later. Much later.
3. Instead of simply ordering a load of stone from your local building-supply company, who would dump it in a convenient location adjacent to the hole, follow Denzer's posthippie admonition to fill your footing/grave with "urbanite," his word*

---

*Some potentially dangerous confusion here: I was ready to fill my hole with Upper West Siders I'd recruited from a New York City Starbucks before I realized Kiko had totally redefined an established word.

for the debris you scavenge in your yard and neighborhood.
As much work as this is, it does have the advantage of cleaning your yard of old bird feeders, hardened sacks of mortar
mix, lawn mowers, and other junk your town won't take.

4. After a day of lugging all this debris to the foundation, make
half a dozen trips to your local home center to buy bags of
stone, because all that damned urbanite you scavenged filled
only a third of your enormous hole, and the small stones you
pour in just vanish at an impossible rate.

5. Crawl out of bed the next day and start to build a base for
the oven so you won't have to bake lying on your stomach.

6. Instead of buying those easy-to-assemble interlocking
bricks used for building retaining walls, insist (for aesthetic
reasons) on using old-fashioned red brick for the base.
Construct a four-foot cylinder of said brick, three feet high,
taking pains to keep the structure level on your sloping site.
Don't bother using mortar, for mortar is messy and time-
consuming, and besides, it seems to me that there will be no
place for the brick to go once the cylinder is filled with yet
more fill (see steps 3–4) and the thing is topped with a heavy
oven (see steps . . . uh, well, we won't be getting that far this
weekend. Or next).

7. As the brick wall rises, continue filling with more debris.
And more. After several hours of stripping your yard of
anything that isn't moving, you may be tempted to loosen
your definition of "debris" somewhat, but resist the urge
to go after low-hanging fruit, such as loose stones from
an existing wall, the foundation of your home, or the
neighbor's cat. Trust me on this, especially if your wife
has a sharp eye.

8. When the last layer of brick is in place, top off with small
stones to fill in the gaps between the larger pieces of fill.
Smooth with hands, then step back to watch, with horror,

as the entire structure collapses, the fill pouring out like flour from a broken sack.

9. Open a beer. Rebuild next weekend, using mortar.

Indian Giver

Illegal aliens have always been a problem
in the United States. Ask any Indian.
— Robert Orben, humorist and head speechwriter
to President Gerald Ford

"You're in an unusually good mood today," Anne noted as, whistling, I prepared to load a *pain au levain* into the oven.

"Parchment paper," I explained. "I can't understand why no one ever told me about this. It's like finding religion."

No more worries about the dough sticking to the peel, no more cornmeal or flour burning on the oven floor. Just cover the peel with a piece of parchment paper, and slide the whole thing, paper and all, into the oven. What a relief! Bread, however, was taking a backseat to another project I had going today. I was making flour. With an Indian artifact grindstone that Mike Dooley had lent me as I left his mill.

"How do you know this is a grindstone?" I'd asked, skeptical. To me, it looked like a rock.

"Notice how symmetrical it is." Mike traced a path along its perimeter with his hand. "See how it's smooth on the flat side, and rough on the rounded side. And these little pockmarks are from the tools used to shape the stone. Nature doesn't do that."

But Native Americans do. Or, once upon a time, did. I asked how old it was.

"No way to tell. Could be a hundred and fifty, could be five thousand. I know for a fact that some of the arrowheads in the settlement where I found this in eastern Kansas were thousands of years old. You can date them from the style. Why don't you grind some of your wheat with this," he said, placing the stone in my hands.

Grind my wheat with a rock? Who did I look like, Pocahontas? But I hadn't yet come up with an alternate way to grind it, having somehow neglected to address that tiny detail, and the notion of using the artifact was intriguing, so I accepted the rock.

The grindstone, 3½ inches wide by 6½ inches long and 3 inches high, weighed just over four pounds — a little less than a bag of flour — and felt good to hold. I marveled that it had been shaped by stone tools. But this was just half of the mill. If I was going to use it, I needed a companion piece on which to rub this one, with the grain in between. A slightly concave stone lifted from a freestanding wall on our property fit the bill. Hmm. I *did* say ("A Recipe for Disaster," step 7) I'd resist low-hanging fruit when scavenging, but the rock was too perfect. I resolved to replace it when I was done.*

Out on the picnic table, I poured a handful of wheat into the hollow of the stone and, with both hands, ran the Indian artifact grindstone over it. The stone simply rolled over the kernels of wheat as if they were marbles. I applied some more pressure. Same result. Then I really put my back into it, rubbing

---

*Last time I saw it, it was still in the corner of the porch.

vigorously back and forth, squeezing my eyes shut for an extra "umph!"

I opened them to a miracle. The stone was covered in white dust. I had made flour! The suddenness of it took me off guard, for I'd expected that the first grinding would crush the wheat into smaller pieces, and I would grind those further, and so on — after all, I was doing this by hand — and eventually I would get something resembling coarse flour, but the rock was already covered in fine flour, looking not much different from what comes out of the five-pound bag from the supermarket.

I was a miller.

Atop the flour sat a rubble of broken kernels and flakes of bran. Encouraged, I rubbed some more, and some more, as grain flew all over the place. Occasionally brushing the flour and bran into a bowl, then tossing another handful of wheat on the stone, I continued grinding, playing with the motion, moving from a back-and-forth action to a tight circular one, humming a mock Indian song — that is, I'm sorry to say, the Atlanta Braves war chant.

Two hours later, a small mound of flour forming in the bottom of my bowl, Anne came outside to check on the progress of her white man and was impressed. "Flour! But how are you going to grind the bran flakes?"

"I'm not. You're going to sieve them out, Minnehaha. We're making white flour."

This was the greatest surprise of the entire endeavor. I'd expected that I could only get whole wheat flour from hand grinding, but I'd learned more about wheat in the past two hours than in eight months of reading and research. It was one thing having Mike explain what was happening inside Bay State's steel-roller mills; I had discovered firsthand what makes wheat so uniquely suitable for milling. The three parts of wheat — endosperm, bran, and germ — react very differently to the pressure of the stone. The starchy endosperm, the white part of the kernel, literally shatters into powder (aka flour), while the tough bran breaks off fairly cleanly into large flakes that can be sieved. The tiny wheat germ, the embryo of the seed, is malleable owing to its high oil content and thus gets flattened. The different mechanical properties of each part of the seed are what make milling and separation possible, and I realized we could take advantage of them ourselves to make white (or whitish) flour from our garden-grown, Indian-stone-ground wheat.

Traditionally, stone millers silk-screened the ground wheat — like printing a T-shirt, but forcing wheat instead of ink through the fabric — in a process called bolting, but Anne and I used an old window screen in an aluminum frame. While I continued to grind, Anne rubbed the flour back and forth with our metal bench scraper. What fell through was unmistakably white flour, with small flecks of bran and germ.

"Can I put this on yogurt?" Anne asked, looking at the bran that remained on the screen. I expressed some doubts about the culinary properties of raw wheat bran, but we saved it, anyway. Plus, I wanted to use it to decorate the tops of the loaves I was going to make with my flour.

The net result of our long day was a mere eight ounces of flour and a quart container of bran. On the one hand, it was heady and exciting to be milling with this ancient grindstone that had passed through the hands of countless Indians (I no longer had to be convinced of its authenticity), and the prospect of baking with my own stone-ground wheat was almost thrilling. On the other hand, we'd hardly made a dent in the bucket of grain. I'd have to find another way to grind the rest.

Shortly after, an e-mail from Mike threatened to make that issue moot. I'd given him a sample of my wheat berries for analysis, and he was surprised by the results. "This wheat appears to be soft red winter. Would that be right? If so, it may not want to bake a good loaf of bread."

It may not want to bake — what?! I called him. "Are you sure?" The protein level had come in at barely 9 percent, far below the 11 to 12 percent level of even all-purpose flour, let alone bread flour, which is nearly 13 percent. My flour was apparently more suitable for making, say, croissants than *pain de campagne.*

The protein level, of course, is a measure of the gluten critical to bread making. Soft wheat, whether winter or spring, is far lower in protein and is used in pastries, piecrusts, and cookies, where bread or even all-purpose flour would be too tough. What is sold as "cake flour" is from the softest wheat, with a protein level of only 5 to 8 percent.*

"We overnighted some to our Minneapolis lab to double-check our own laboratory findings. It sure looks like soft red," Mike said.

No wonder it'd been so easy to grind.

Anne saw me scowling and asked what was wrong.

"White man tell me I grow wheat for many moons," I said, "to make flour only good for cupcakes."

---

*These listed percentages are of the milled white flour; the protein levels of the whole wheat berry are a fraction to a full percentage point higher, as the bran is high in protein.

WEEK
38

Terror Firma Redux

I have hope because what's the alternative to hope? Despair?
If you have despair, you might as well put your head in the oven.
— Studs Terkel

"I'm going to have to build the oven base over again, with mortar," I moaned to Anne.

"What's so wrong with that?"

"The project is escalating. Now we're into a permanent structure."

"Not necessarily."

I had that coming. Having waited way too long to start this thing (thinking I needed only a weekend — gee, where'd I get that silly idea?), I'd have to finish it up myself. Zach, who'd shared much of the hard labor on our first attempt, was preparing to return to college and unable to do more than periodically stop by and check on my painfully slow progress with the brick and mortar. I despise masonry work — the mixing, the dust, the mess, the cleanup, and the weight, my God, the weight! Mortar must be among the densest stuff on earth. The base rose slowly because I was building not just a wall but a circle of nineteen bricks. This meant that the nineteenth brick (or part thereof, since I also had to split bricks) needed to meet back at the first brick, at the same height. There was no room for sloppiness or eyeballing.

Every brick had to be set with a bubble level, and carefully. Not to mention the fact that I was building this circle with rectangular bricks, angling them to form a circle. Getting mortar into the pie-slice-shaped wedges between the bricks was a real chore.

The only thing I did do well was mix mortar. It was just like making dough. As with dough, I found it easier to start a little wet and add dry mortar to get the right consistency, rather than to start dry and add water. As I replaced my fragile wall with sturdy brick and mortar, I couldn't help feeling like one of the Three Little Pigs, especially when I looked at the building materials that were scattered around: straw, sticks, clay, and brick. Surely this was one oven that the Big Bad Wolf wouldn't blow down (though the Big Bad Building Inspector might, now that I had a "permanent structure"). By six o'clock, ten hours after starting, the base was finished (and so was I). Kiko's "build an oven in a weekend" was proving a tad optimistic, to put it mildly. Two weekends of work, and I hadn't even started on the actual oven yet.

After cleaning up my tools, I staggered inside, feeling an old hernia for the first time in years, swigged down a prescription painkiller/anti-inflammatory with a cold beer (because the label warned "take with food"), and was looking forward to slipping into a hot-enough-to-peel-your-skin-off bath when I heard Katie talking to Anne in the next room.

"Dad doesn't look so good."

I couldn't make out Anne's response except for the word "bread."

Bread? What day was this? Sunday, and I hadn't made bread this week! I'd promised myself I'd bake every week for a year without fail, and this wasn't how I wanted my streak to end: in a hot bathtub with a cold beer. I considered my options. Time was short; energy shorter. There was only one thing to do. I hadn't used it in years, but it was still in the pantry, taking up lots of space while collecting dust, like, I suspect, three-quarters of the

other ones in America. Really, when was the last time you used
your bread machine?

———————————————

The oddest thing about the bread machine is that it was invented
in Japan, where rice, not wheat, is the primary dietary starch.
But that's the Japanese for you, automating the production of a
food they hardly eat. The machine arrived in the United States
in 1987, and within ten years bread-machine sales had grown to
$400 million annually. Anne and I contributed about $175 to
that total when, like many Americans, we found the temptation
of daily, warm, home-baked bread too seductive to resist. Also
like many Americans, we hadn't used our machine in years.

Certainly, baking bread in the machine was easy. I measured
out and added all the ingredients, after which it was basically
(apologies to Ron Popeil) set it and forget it. Tonight's loaf would
be ready in a couple of hours, versus the eight that my usual peasant bread took. The dough, aided by gentle heat and a heavy dose
of yeast, rose more, but the crust, because it was not exposed to
intense oven heat and dryness, was soft and flavorless, as with
commercial bread. Cooked in an enclosed plastic box, the loaf was
more steamed than baked. And without a *poolish* or a *levain,* its
taste was bland and uninteresting. The bread machine seemed to
have been designed to reproduce not artisan bread but commercial bread, the cellophane-wrapped kind. With one big difference:
commercial loaves don't have a whopping hole in the center of
the loaf, left by the kneading paddle. My model produced a huge
gap that protruded into half the slices, making it difficult to get
enough bread for even a few grilled cheese sandwiches.

Well, I said I wanted holes in my bread; I got them.

The machine did have one thing going for it. I was free to soak
in the bathtub for an hour while it made the bread, all by itself. As
I lay submerged, with the lights out and shades drawn, reflecting

on the day, the week, and the months, my reptilian brain, as Clotaire Rapaille calls it, took over. And it said, Billy, what on earth are you doing? Killing yourself spending hours scavenging for "urbanite," mining clay, threshing wheat, grinding flour like it's 1491. By the way, how's the bread coming, fella? What's that? It's downstairs steaming in a machine?

I ran some more hot water into the tub as the last light of summer faded from the sky. I had to get back on track and seize control of my life — and my bread. My mind drifted back to a thought I'd had the week I'd taken a Zen approach to bread: The perfect loaf was already there, waiting to be discovered. I had to elevate myself to reach it. I had to get myself out of the ditch I was digging, figuratively and literally, and focus on the baker, not the bread.

I decided right then and there where to start. The next day, Zach went back to college, and I moved into his bedroom.

WEEK

39

A Lot of 'Splainin' to Do

> The ingredients for bread were always the same:
> flour, yeast, water, and salt. But the difficulty was that there were
> ten thousand ways of combining these simple elements.
> —Julia Child, *My Life in France,* 2006

"I think I'm sleeping in Zach's room tonight," I said with feigned nonchalance, carrying my bathrobe and pillows out of our bedroom.

I waited till I was just out of sight before adding, "And maybe tomorrow night as well. Maybe for a while."

There. It was out.

Anne wordlessly followed me into Zach's room, then shadowed me back into what used to be *our* room as I returned to get some things. I decided it'd be best if I didn't transfer too many of my possessions just yet. Anne's shadowboxing, meanwhile, required a response.

"It was Julia's idea," I said clumsily.

"Julia?"

As Ricky Ricardo used to say, "Lu-ceee, you got a lot of 'splainin' to do."

Let's start with Julia.

I'm referring, of course, to the late Julia Child.

I had been reading her memoir and had learned that Julia and her husband went through an astounding 284 pounds of flour in order to perfect the baguette recipe for volume 2 of *Mastering the Art of French Cooking.* Like me, she'd struggled with the crust. Like me, she'd tried all kinds of ways to create steam in the oven before finally finding a solution: dropping a hot metal ax head into a pan of cold water! (You can just picture Julia, wearing a welder's helmet and asbestos gloves, holding a pair of tongs with a red-hot, glowing ax head at the other end.) Also like me, she had eventually discovered slow, cool fermentations, *autolyse,* and even Raymond Calvel. In fact, she'd returned to France to meet the professor when she'd reached a dead end in her baking. After a single afternoon in which Calvel revolutionized her approach to bread, Julia returned home "euphoric" and redoubled her efforts to bake the perfect baguette.

Why? In her own words, because "I was simply fascinated by bread and determined to learn how to bake it for myself. You have to do it and do it, until you get it right." I'd found a soul mate. I've always adored Julia Child — at least her television persona, which is all I know — and now I felt as if I had a companion on my journey. With the benevolent spirits of Beard and Child smiling down on me, how could I fail? I resolved to soldier on.

Soldiers need sleep, however, which is why I had my pillows tucked under my arm. Julia had also given me the courage to do something I'd been thinking about for some time: moving into a room of my own. I'm a finicky and featherlight sleeper, and an early riser. Anne, meanwhile, was often writing up her patient charts late into the night and coming to bed after I was asleep, and no matter how quietly she tiptoed, I'd wake up. On the other hand, how Anne slept in the same room as me was a mystery, as age had brought a third companion into our bedroom, my increasingly heavy snoring.

With Zach back at college, we had a bedroom with a desk available for my home office. Why not move in? I'd broached the subject once before — we also had a tiny guest room — but Anne had vetoed it out of hand, using silly words like "intimacy" and "marriage." This time, though, I showed her Julia Child's passing reference to the house she and her husband had built in France, with "my bedroom on the left . . . and Paul's bedroom on the right. (He was a sometimes insomniac, and I was known to snore. We decided it was best to spend nights apart . . .)." Anne raised her eyebrows but didn't argue. Not only was she as much a fan of Julia's as I was, but apparently she was ready for a good night's sleep as well.

Sleeping arrangements out of the way, I faced the next problem: taking my bread — and its baker — to the next level.

Feeling Like Manure

"Wheat is life, boy. Don't let no silly bugger tell you different."
— Christopher Ketteridge and Spike Mays,
Five Miles from Bunkum, 1972

"I'm thinking I need to get some hands-on instruction," I confessed to Anne after another so-so loaf of peasant bread. "I need to make myself a better baker."

"Didn't you learn anything at the kneading conference?"

Oh, did I ever. I learned that if you want to learn to bake the best bread, you go to where the best bread is. Half the bakers I'd met in Maine, both amateur and professional, had been to France, to bake bread, taste bread, or both. Not to mention Julia Child, Steven "the Professor" Kaplan, Charlie van Over — everyone who was interested in bread went to France. And here I was, trying to bake breads with French names in New York. Well, if I was going to take a bread-making course, why not take it in Paris?

I broached my idea with Anne, who, after a millisecond of thought, agreed to a week of sightseeing in the City of Light while I studied baking. Thus before you could say "pain de campagne" I was enrolled in the week-long *boulangerie* class at the École Ritz Escoffier, the cooking school at the Hotel Ritz.

First, however, I had some unfinished business here in my own backyard. The clay "oven" at this point consisted of no more than a round brick base surrounded by mounds of clayey earth, rocks, bricks, plastic buckets, and a wheelbarrow filled with rainwater. I'd stepped out of last week's bath convinced I should give it up, but the allure of baking bread made from my own wheat in an oven raised like Adam from the dust of my garden was still powerful. Besides, I was so close, only a "Kiko weekend" away now.

The next step was to construct the oven floor, firebrick set into a mixture of clay and coarse sand. It so happened that I had some sand left over from an old project. I grabbed a bucket and shovel and headed down the hill to the compost heap, where I'd left it, thinking Kiko would be proud that I was scavenging it.

After clearing away the weeds that obscured the sand, I easily filled the bucket and brought it back up, then shoveled some clay through a homemade sieve — similar to the one I'd used to thresh the wheat — to remove the pebbles and rocks. It was enjoyable work on this perfect late-summer morning, the Catskills clearly visible in the distance, the work easy, the pace pleasant. In fact, I couldn't think of a better way to spend the day. As the sun warmed the morning air, I peeled off my layers down to a T-shirt. In two short weeks, I'd be baking at the Hotel Ritz.

Autumn in Paris, a city with more bakeries than New York has delis. France, a country that has twenty words for bread, the way that Eskimos have dozens of words for snow. Not only to study bread in one of the world's most famous kitchens but also to be surrounded by great bread? The prospect was breathtaking.

Not as breathtaking as what happened next, though. Afraid I might be a little short of sand — I didn't want to start mixing and have to run back for more — I went down for one last bucketful. Bending at the waist, I plunged the shovel into the soft mound of sand. Simultaneously, the tip of another shovel was plunged deep into my lower back.

At least that's what it felt like. I gasped in agony and stayed bent over, afraid to try to straighten up, as waves of pain radiated from my sacroiliac up my back. "This is nothing," I muttered out loud. "You just twisted funny." I figured that if I gave it a moment, it would pass.

It didn't. I thought it best to go back to the house. I should be able to walk, I reasoned. After all, I was still standing.

And then I wasn't. I didn't exactly lose consciousness, but I didn't exactly keep it, either, and I didn't so much fall as crumple backward onto the soft compost heap, joining the other discarded refuse of the yard: rotting peaches, decaying grass clippings, decomposing weeds, and composting manure. The heap was surprisingly soft and warm and comforting. I let my body relax, closed my eyes, and settled in.

WEEK
41

"Nous Acceptons Votre Proposition"

I know a bloke who knows a bloke who knows a bloke . . .
— Ben Kingsley in *Sexy Beast*

I studied the e-mail that had come in overnight.

"Nous acceptons votre proposition," it read. Oh, good, they accept my proposition.

What proposition? And who was "nous"? I didn't recognize the name or the e-mail address, and the sender hadn't included my original text in his reply. Or had this e-mail been in response to a fax?

I had no idea, because I'd sent out dozens of e-mails and faxes over the past few weeks, all with the same request in the same bad French. The seed planted by the cover photograph of *Baking with Brother Boniface* had grown as mightily within me as the ancient, twisted tree on the book's cover, and the more I'd thought about baking in an ancient abbey, the more the idea seized me. I wanted to bake bread in a place that was really old, a place that could put me in touch with a *real* tradition of baking (not the Johnny-come-lately, mere hundred-year-old Ritz).

I had zeroed in first on monasteries because they're old and steeped in tradition, then on European monasteries because Europe is older than America, and finally on French monasteries, once it turned out that I was going to be in France, anyway.

Anne laughed when she heard of my quest. "You? In a monastery?"

It did seem a bit incongruous, especially since you couldn't get me into a church these days, much less a monastery. Still, the mocking hurt a little, perhaps because of my own queasiness with the idea. "It's not a religious pilgrimage," I said a little too defensively. "I just think it would be neat. And all the monasteries accept guests for spiritual retreats."

My utterance of the word "spiritual" shocked her even more.

"I'm spiritual. In my own way." Although exactly what way that was, I couldn't say.

She dropped the subject, seeing how uncomfortable she was making me, but in fact I thought staying in a French abbey might be quite atmospheric and even a little — for lack of a better word — romantic. And if there was anything I needed after an increasingly frantic three-quarters of a year of baking, threshing, and oven building, it was a retreat, spiritual or otherwise.

Yet finding such a place had proved to be far more elusive than I'd expected in a country known for both bread and monasteries. Surely the two must intersect somewhere. Charlie van Over had been right, though: it seemed that these days, baking monks were rarer than singing nuns. The difficulty was compounded by my third requirement, which proved to be my undoing on several occasions — it had to be an abbey that would allow me into the kitchen as a participant, not just a paying guest in the dining room. I had contacted noted bread-book author and teacher Peter Reinhart, as Charlie had suggested (Peter was enthusiastic but unable to offer any leads); I had struck out with an equally enthusiastic Brother Garramone, a monk who'd had a bread-making show on PBS for a few seasons; and now I was down to my last lead, the author of a book called *Europe's Monastery and Convent Guesthouses*. Kevin Wright, despite having visited just about every monastery in France, didn't know of any that baked their own bread, but he did provide me the e-mail address of an American monk in France who might be able to help.

E-mail and *monk* in the same sentence? That didn't seem kosher, but when you think about it, e-mail (if you happen to be a monk) has got to be about the best thing since sliced bread. Although few monasteries impose a strict vow of silence these days, unnecessary talking is frowned upon. But no one said anything about e-mail. Or Web sites, which I found many monasteries have set up.

Wright's contact in France e-mailed me back, telling me that they certainly didn't bake bread at his abbey, but that he did know the name of a monk who was baking at a medieval abbey in Normandy. I contacted that abbey immediately. Alas, they reported, this baker had left two years earlier, and as a result they no longer baked bread, but there was a monk in Provence who baked. I contacted the abbey in Provence. Not true. But they knew of a monk . . .

At one point I found myself five deep in monks! I'd spent

weeks getting nowhere, going through Wright's book, e-mailing every ancient abbey that had an e-mail address and faxing the ones that didn't, spending entire days on this task as my departure date for France neared. With my prospects dimming and my trip fast approaching, I had apparently (for I had totally forgotten about it), out of desperation, tried a long shot with the Benedictine abbey in Normandy, the one whose guest master had lamented that they hadn't had fresh bread since their *boulanger* had left.

"I have a proposition," I'd written in French, spending hours digging through my French-English dictionary to write a ten-line e-mail. "You need some good bread. I need a spiritual retreat and would like to bake in an ancient abbey. I'll come for a few days to make bread for *les frères*."

Who could resist? For good measure I added that my bread had just won second place in a New York competition (note, I didn't say New York *City*), and I included a photograph of one of my better-looking *boules,* glowing warmly under the incandescent kitchen lights.

I didn't expect anything to come of this — after all, the notion of a seventh-century abbey inviting a lay American (non-Catholic at that) into their brotherhood to bake bread was absurd — so I didn't give any thought at all to the two misleading notions I'd recklessly advanced: one, that I was an actual baker (reading that I'd nearly won a "New York" competition must've had them thinking I'd defeated the likes of Sullivan Street Bakery and Amy's Bread, not a handful of Syracuse housewives); and two, that I could actually communicate with a live person in French.

The fact that the abbey's guest master didn't even respond to my ridiculous proposition didn't surprise me. I had now revealed myself as a crackpot. So when the following e-mail from Prior Jean-

Charles popped into my in-box several weeks later, I used two translation tools and read it three times to make sure I understood.

> Nous acceptons très volontiers votre proposition de venir passer quelques jours à l'Abbaye et de faire un peu de pain pour la communauté. Nous achèterons un peu de farine . . . Peut-être serait-il aussi envisageable que vous puissiez montrer à un frère comment on fait le pain . . .

They had accepted my offer to spend a few days at the abbey to "make a little bread for the community." The delay, the note explained, was due to the absence of the abbot himself, who had to approve such an unusual (if not unprecedented) arrangement. But wait, what was that "peut-être" part at the end? "Would it perhaps also be possible for you to show a brother how to make bread?"

My God! That's why they'd accepted my offer — I was to train a new baker! Train a baker? *I* was the trainee. The situation was absurd and terrifying. I would be taking a class, learning how to bake my first week in France, then teaching a novice the next. Anne, I should point out, wasn't the least bit fazed by this; in medical school they have a saying, "See one, do one, teach one," but I was freaking out. Apparently I was to be the head *boulanger* myself, baking for an entire monastery — in essence running a small bakery! The largest batch of bread I'd ever made in my entire life consisted of exactly two loaves. How could I have made such a reckless proposition? A follow-up e-mail mentioned that they hadn't used their bread oven in years and hoped it would still work. Bread oven? With, like, steam injectors? I had no idea how to work a commercial bread oven.

I could not perpetuate a major fraud on a one-thousand-three-hundred-year-old abbey that had stood for two-thirds of Christendom. Painfully I started to compose a reply, admitting my deceptions, confessing that I'd overstated my qualifications, spoke French on a first-grade level, and was sorry for the trouble. Left unsaid was the fact that if there was a hell, I sure as hell didn't want to spend eternity in it.

I wrote the note, but I never sent it.

I stared at the computer screen for a long time, reading the prior's note over and over, and started to see the request in a new light. I wasn't just being asked to train a monk or to bake some bread; I was being asked to repair a broken thirteen-hundred-year-old chain, to return fresh bread to this abbey, to reignite a tradition that had tragically been extinguished. It was an opportunity to repay a debt, to do for this abbey what the abbeys of Europe once did for the rest of us — keep knowledge alive during dark times.

In return, the abbey offered me something as well: a chance for repentance. For nine months I'd been imposing myself on others, barging into their bakeries and homes, asking favors and a million questions, and now I'd been suddenly and unexpectedly offered a chance to give something back.

L'Abbaye Saint-Wandrille, founded in 649, with a broken thirteen-hundred-year tradition of baking bread, had entrusted the reestablishment of that tradition to a New York nonbeliever.

Good Lord!

VI.

Vespers

Vespers, celebrated at day's end, takes on the character of evening. The day is almost over, our work is done. This is the hour of wise age, of resting in thanksgiving and humility after the struggles, successes and failures of the day of one's productive life.

God Bless the TSA

Tip on flying... Book an afternoon flight. The airport security
personnel has warmed their hands already on other passengers.
—Jay Leno

Weight: 201 pounds
Bread bookshelf weight: 60 pounds

I'd like to briefly interrupt the narrative to sing the praises of
an oft-maligned group, the TSA officials who guard our nation's airplanes. After all, they don't make the rules, and they,
even more than we griping passengers, constantly have to adapt
to the changing, often-silly regulations those geniuses in Washington keep dreaming up: Tweezers are out; cigarette lighters in.
This week, liquids are banned; the next, you can bring all the
liquids — in three-ounce bottles — that you can fit into a single
ziplock bag. Shoes are off; shoes are on; shoes are off.

And what do these underappreciated, beleaguered workers get
for their troubles? Passengers like me.

In my defense, I was on a mission from God.

As I approached the X-ray machine with my precious cargo, I
decided honesty was the best policy. Thus after I'd pulled out my
laptop and Baggie of toiletries, I displayed the half-gallon plastic
container with a locking lid and said, as casually as if I were de-
claring chewing gum, "Sourdough."

I might just as well have said, "Gun!"

Hedging my bets, I had also put a quart of my starter into a small gym bag and checked it along with my suitcase, but I figured there was a fifty-fifty chance it would get tossed when the bag was inspected, even though I'd written "SOURDOUGH" in large block letters on it. (I figured "LEVAIN" wouldn't help much.) Plus, if it did make it through, I wasn't sure what eight hours at forty thousand feet in the cargo hold would do to it. Thus my hopes were pinned on the *levain* I was carrying with me. Not only had it become indispensable to my bread, but I was hoping that this twelve-year-old starter — *my* starter, now — might become part of the tradition of the thirteen-hundred-year-old abbey.

Every TSA worker in the terminal chimed in on the discussion while the line built up behind me. Apparently there was no precedent on sourdough. Finally I was rather impatiently waved through the metal detector and asked to wait on the other side. Anne was relieved to see me.

"What's happening?"

"I don't know. Maybe you should go on without me. I may be here awhile. You have the address?" Bags continued exiting the X-ray machine on the conveyor belt, but none of them was mine. I couldn't figure out what was going on. We waited a few minutes more.

A loud male voice rang out from in front of the monitor at the X-ray machine. "What is this stuff, *dough*? Who's got the dough?" Jeez, where had this guy been?

"It's mine," I called, and I started to head back toward the machine, which, with passengers streaming toward me, created even more chaos.

"Stay right there!" he barked. I froze, then sheepishly headed back to Anne. All this commotion had apparently attracted the notice of a supervisor, who thankfully took charge. "What do we have here?" he asked politely but wearily.

"Sourdough. A medieval abbey in France is expecting it." I tried to read his reaction, but his trained poker face remained flat. He started to run a wand around the container of *levain,* which had stiffened into a plastique look-alike. I told him the abbey had kept the flame of civilization alive during the darkest of the Dark Ages but, after thirteen centuries, had forgotten how to make bread. This *levain* was the link to repair the chain.

Still no reaction. Trying to straddle the line between pressure and humor, I added, "The future of Western civilization is in your hands."

Just then, Anne, to my horror, opened her mouth to speak before I could stop her. The last time she'd done that in an airport, voluntarily reciting to U.S. Customs, *unsolicited,* every item we'd purchased and whom it was for, she sounded so forced and nervous that I expected to be strip-searched.

"Bill's bread won second prize at the New York State Fair!"

"Keep quiet and show some leg," I wanted to hiss. She was wearing jeans.

Still expressionless, he put down the container. Something else in my bag had caught his attention, something I hadn't even considered.

"What's this?"

He held up my small digital kitchen scale. Which, under the circumstances, did a more-than-passable impersonation of a timing and ignition mechanism for the plastique accompanying it. At least I wasn't carrying any wire. Or razor blades.

"It's a scale, for baking bread."

"You need a scale for bread? My mother never used a scale."

"More accurate than measuring by volume." I couldn't believe

I was having this conversation with a TSA official at Kennedy Airport.

"Hmm." He took the top off the scale — I'd never even known it came off — and wanded underneath before replacing it.

"Well, you get the prize," he said, breaking into a smile. "Strangest carry-on of the month. Have a nice trip."

I slumped into the first seat I saw in the terminal, drained and sweaty.

"That was close!" Anne exhaled.

"Not really." I pulled out my ziplock bag filled with small, colored plastic bottles labeled "Shampoo," "Conditioner," "Lotion," and so on.

"Did you wonder why I was bringing so much hair conditioner to France?" I asked. "In my carry-on?"

Her mouth fell open. I could see she was a little hurt at being kept in the dark.

"Some things it's better not to know," I explained.

Anne, aware of the limits of her own poker face, agreed. "Well, I'm glad that's over with, anyway."

"Not quite. We still have to get it past French customs. Come, let's find the gate. We're going to Paris!"

I felt a twinge in my back as I stood. Oh well, it was nothing that eight hours in a coach-class seat with my knees jammed into my chest couldn't cure.

Puttin' On the Ritz

If you're blue and you don't know
Where to go to, why don't you go
Where fashion sits,
Puttin' on the Ritz.
— Irving Berlin

I didn't expect the service entrance to the Hotel Ritz to be completely unmanned, but neither did I anticipate five hundred armed antiterrorist police, including two hundred members of the elite French CRS riot squad, dressed up the wazoo in body armor.

"Guess they heard I was coming," I quipped to Anne as I presented my confirmation documents for the bread class to the Ritz security guard at the rue Cambon entrance. "Wait here for a sec. Let me see what time I'll be done tonight." She looked around nervously at all the rifles. "Don't worry," I reassured her. "You're well protected."

When I returned five minutes later, Anne had vanished without a trace. My first instinct was to call her, but we'd left our cell phones, incompatible with Europe's cellular network, back at our hotel. I asked some Ritz staff on cigarette break if anyone had seen her, but she's hard enough to describe in English, let alone in my primitive French. It wasn't like her to just up and leave, but, hoping she had given up on me and wandered off, I went back inside to start the first day of my *cours de boulangerie,* feeling a touch unsettled. Why all the security? The hotel felt more like a military encampment than the famous Ritz, whose very name is synonymous with (after crackers) luxury, service, fine dining, and expense, the hotel that has for a hundred years been the Paris home to kings and princesses, writers, and actors.

Ernest Hemingway claimed to have personally liberated the Ritz in 1944, but the hotel's Hemingway Bar was more likely named in honor of his bar tab. Other luminaries whose celebrated stays helped fuel the legend include F. Scott Fitzgerald (who wrote "The Diamond as Big as the Ritz"), Marcel Proust, King Edward VII, Rudolph Valentino, Charlie Chaplin, Greta Garbo, and Coco Chanel, who made the Ritz her permanent home for thirty years. Some say the place has lost a bit of its luster, but thanks to continuing cameos in such movies as *The Devil Wears Prada,* the Ritz continues to loom slightly larger than life.

This week, however, it was mainly a reminder of death. In class, rumors about the heavy security were swirling: Bill Clinton was staying there; a prominent Arab head of state was visiting. The truth, however, turned out to be a shocking and unwelcome reminder of the last time the Ritz had been in the news.

That was August 31, 1997. Dodi Al Fayed and his girlfriend, Diana, Princess of Wales, were at the hotel because (a) she was a princess, and as I said, princesses stay at the Ritz; and (b) his father owns the joint. The half-royal couple, in an attempt to elude the ever-present paparazzi, had departed the Ritz via the rue Cambon service entrance, where I'd just left Anne. The paparazzi weren't fooled, however, and the high-speed car chase that ensued ended with a horrific fatal crash in a tunnel under the Seine. Now, ten years later, a British jury conducting an inquest had come across the channel to reconstruct the events leading up to Diana's death, and the French police, still smarting from the stigma of losing the princess on their watch, didn't want any more trouble. And that included trouble from my wife, who, she'd later explain, had been first interrogated, then shooed away while I was inside. Whether she protested that her husband had won second prize in a bread contest is not known.

With that somber backdrop, I began class in the subterranean bakery of the Ritz. After some formalities, a young Vietnamese woman, who held the dual (and largely incompatible) roles of chef's assistant and translator, took the eight of us down the elevator even deeper into the basement, to the laundry, where we received our uniforms: from top to bottom, a towering paper *toque* that turned me into a seven-footer; a *tour de cou* (a white cloth napkin worn knotted around the neck); a *veste de cuisine* (a sharp-looking white double-breasted jacket), over which I wore a *tablier,* or apron, into which I tucked my *torchon* (dish towel); and last but not least, striped, blue gray *pantalon*, or pants.

It was this last item of apparel that created what you might call a crisis of confidence among one of my classmates, a Canadian (thank goodness he wasn't American) I'll call Nebbish. You know Nebbish. Everyone knows Nebbish. If you're a guy, he's the kid you went to high school with who always forgot his gym clothes, who refused to wear a jockstrap, who was forever losing the combination to his locker, and who regularly broke his eyeglasses. To women, he's the kid about whom you whispered to friends, "He's so *annoying*!"

Now, some four decades later, Nebbish was back in my home-ec class, and naturally, he had a question: "Do we have to wear the pants?"

Stares all around: from a Californian veterinarian whose husband had been transferred to Paris, two giggly Japanese girls with video cameras permanently affixed to their hands, a young

Brazilian woman of Chinese ancestry, a very cool Australian chef at the Ritz who was taking this as an in-service course, and Nebbish's eighty-year-old father.

Yes, Nebbish had brought his father to class.

"Whaddya mean, do you have to wear the pants?" Pop growled. "What's the matter with you?"

"Of course, you have to wear the pants," the Vietnamese assistant said.

"I can't."

"But you have to. It is part of the uniform."

"I can't."

"You can't."

"No, I can't."

"Why?"

A pregnant pause.

"I don't have any underwear on. I didn't know we'd be taking off our pants."

French chefs, as anyone who grew up on Looney Tunes knows, come in only two sizes: short and fat, and tall and skinny. Chef Didier, our instructor and a baker at the Ritz, was in the latter group. He was a pleasant enough fellow who sported a broad grin and didn't at all fit the stereotype of the ill-tempered chef. He even told us to call him just plain "Didier," but, trained by watching reality chef shows on TV, I found myself involuntarily answering him with a snappy and militaristic, "Oui, chef!" every time. He didn't seem to mind.

Becoming a professional baker in France is only slightly less difficult and time-consuming than becoming, say, a nuclear physicist in the United States. In the States, if you want to become a baker, you have a couple of options. You can find a bakery that will hire and train you. Or if you prefer formal training, you can attend a professional school like the San Francisco Baking Institute, where they turn you into a baker in eighteen weeks.

In France, to become a *boulanger,* you enter into the government-supervised apprenticeship system that has been in place since the Middle Ages. Didier's route to the *boulangerie* of the Ritz included a four-year apprenticeship after high school, where he was required to master not only bread, but also patisserie, chocolate, and ice cream.

Didier had to wait to finish high school before starting his apprenticeship, but tomorrow's bakers won't have to waste all that time learning algebra. Reacting to the shortage of bakers in the country, the French government in 2007 lowered the minimum age of apprenticeship to a medieval fourteen.

The *boulangerie* course taught at the Ritz was, in a bizarre way, a miniature version of the apprenticeship program. The emphasis was not, as would have made sense, on crafting artisan loaves for the home kitchen, but rather on learning how to make bread for restaurant service. This meant learning the standard formulas and recipes of the classical repertory and baking lots of bread. Lots. The seven of us (Nebbish père had dropped out after the first day) baked several hundred loaves over the course of the week. We baked baguettes, olive bread, bacon and sun-dried tomato bread, sourdough bread, rye bread, whole wheat bread, whole wheat bread with currants and spices, raisin bread, apricot bread, rye bread with whole garlic cloves, white sandwich bread, *pain au levain, pain de campagne,* and more baguettes. When we'd exhausted those variations, we learned decorative bread (I can now make a rose out of dough, a skill that I've yet to find an opportunity to showcase) and rolls.

Each batch started out the same way — loading up the commercial kneader with about twenty pounds of flour, then kneading, fermenting, and dividing into loaves. Because the Japanese girls, who were my partners, were too busy videotaping to actually make any bread, I did much of the dividing and weighing and had become quite good at it by the end of the week.

Only briefly, and in mockery at that, did Didier demonstrate hand kneading, when he was making a whole wheat loaf.

"You can knead it like this for forty minutes," he said, exaggerating the effort with huffs and puffs, looking like Ed Norton in *The Honeymooners* demonstrating how to "core a apple" the old-fashioned way, "or like this for eight minutes." He threw it into the huge, rotating mixer and smiled. And *autolyse*? As we say in New York, fuhgetaboutit.

Much of the dough we made went, after shaping, into a huge refrigerated unit called a retarder proofer cabinet, more commonly known as the marriage saver. The origin of the nickname is easy to understand. When I make bread at home, it takes anywhere from seven to ten hours from start to finish. My loaves usually come out of the oven around four in the afternoon. If I were running a commercial bakery, and my bread had to be out on the counter at 7:00 a.m. — well, do the math (if, that is, you haven't left junior high school to become a baker's apprentice). In fact, not all that long ago, a baker's workday started about midnight and ended in the morning. The sight of the baker's assistant sleeping atop the warm oven at noon was not an uncommon one.

What the marriage saver does is control temperature and humidity, keeping the dough chilled (35 degrees Fahrenheit at the Ritz) and moist overnight, and then, using a timer, bringing it back to room temperature (75 degrees) the last few hours so that the bread can rise and get ready for the oven, all while the baker is at home in bed. With his wife.

The biggest challenge of the class (other than rolling baguettes and *bâtards,* which I proved to be spectacularly bad at) was simply staying out of the way of the Ritz's *boulangers*. This wasn't a classroom kitchen but a working bakery, and bakers were constantly rushing through with trays of breads, crying "Attention!" and "Excusez-moi!" Nebbish took the opportunity to seek the attentions of a young female baker, using the novel approach of criticizing the baked goods he'd been eating daily in the restaurants of the Ritz. This seemed to me a self-defeating, hopeless way of flirting, but damned if she didn't go from biting-her-lip tolerance to jocular familiarity with him by the end of the week, making the rest of us (okay, me) gag.

I hate to admit it, but Nebbish had a point. The bread at the Ritz wasn't very good, the course wasn't very good, and none of the breads we'd baked all week were particularly good, including the much-anticipated *pain de campagne,* the Ritz's version of the loaf I was trying to perfect. To that end, when not in the bakery of the Ritz, I was running around Paris, visiting the best bakeries in the city in hopes of finding the perfect peasant loaf, if for no other reason than to assure myself that I wasn't chasing an apparition, that the crumb, crust, texture, and taste I was seeking, still so vivid in my memory, in fact existed.

Class ran from early afternoon to early evening, leaving my mornings free. Anne and I started at the temple, Boulangerie Poilâne, home of the famous wood-fired-oven-baked, four-pound artisan *miche.* I talked my way downstairs to the working bakery, or *fournil* ("Je suis un boulanger américain"), and warmed myself before the roaring wood fire of the famous, ancient brick oven while a baker removed the large loaves. Having spent a fair amount of effort trying to get steam into my own oven, I was a bit chastened to see that the method used for steaming what many consider the best loaf of rustic bread in the world (Americans shell out fifty-three bucks to have a single *miche* shipped to their home) is nothing more than a badly battered metal bowl of boiling water sitting over the fire.

Lionel Poilâne, arguably the most famous baker in the world, had died in a helicopter accident in 1992, leaving the family's million-euro bread business in the hands of his daughter, Apollonia. I'd say this recent Harvard grad was up to the task, judging by the ruckus (and free publicity) she'd recently raised by suggesting that the baguette, the very symbol of French bread (if not of the French themselves), wasn't French at all. Debunking the legend (repeated in class by Didier) that the baguette was invented by Napoleon so that his troops could strap the long, skinny loaves to their legs, Apollonia insisted that the baguette was actually a recent Austrian import (*quelle horreur!* — the last Austrian import of note was Marie Antoinette, and we know how the French dealt with her) and that all patriotic French people should give up their love affair with this foreign white bread and return to a traditional Gallic loaf.

And just what would that loaf look like? Why, Poilâne's four-pound rustic *miche,* made with *levain,* sea salt, and stone-ground flour. *Naturellement.*

Lionel Poilâne, along with a handful of other young bakers, had been an early leader in the movement to reverse the decline of French bread, a decline dating to shortly after the end of World War II. With pressure to keep prices down and quantity up, French bakers started taking shortcuts, using flour adulterated with extra gluten, ascorbic acid, enzymes, and even fava bean flour, in order to create a dough that could both rise quickly and stand up to rough mechanized kneading and shaping.* The resulting bread, which, unfortunately, you are still quite likely to encounter today in a typical neighborhood *boulangerie,* had the texture of cotton candy and the flavor of cotton.

---

*France was not alone; Italy suffered a similar decline and is undergoing a similar renaissance of its artisan bread.

Two of the young maverick bakers determined to return good bread to France, Eric Kayser and Dominique Saibron, set up artisan bakeries on either end of rue Monge, one of the oldest streets in Paris's Latin Quarter, so packed with *boulangeries* that one of the side streets is named rue des Boulangers. Other noted bakeries were located on the outskirts of the city. Anne and I visited them all, after each excursion racing home and eating the bread for lunch before I ran off to make another couple of dozen mediocre loaves at the Ritz. Anne, meanwhile, was having a blast wandering Paris, going up the Eiffel Tower, visiting museums, and strolling through the Tuileries. By the middle of the week, tired of watching Anne have all this fun, I was considering dropping out of the class and joining her, but the slim hope that I might just learn something kept me going right to the bitter end.

The bread Anne and I were gathering on our morning forays was anything but mediocre, and slicing into each loaf was an enjoyable little drama. Returning from Poilâne, Anne and I bent over the *miche* like a couple of archaeologists examining a rare artifact, bread knife in hand, while I sliced through the center, releasing a rich, yeasty aroma and revealing the brown crumb within — a crumb that was almost identical to my "unsatisfactory" loaves, moist and dense, devoid of holes and netting. We took a taste. The high-extraction stone-ground flour (meaning that most, but not all, of the original wheat berry makes it into the flour) provided a consistency and taste somewhere between whole wheat and white flour. Not bad. Nice sourdough flavor. But fifty bucks a loaf?

"I think I prefer yours," Anne said, bless her heart.

I took little solace in that, however, because it was starting to look as though the loaf I was trying to imitate didn't even exist. To be sure, we'd had some truly fine bread, both peasant loaves and baguettes, but not the loaf I was after. Until, near the end of the week, when I tasted Eric Kayser's *boule,* made with a liquid *levain* that he maintains in a machine he designed when he couldn't find anything that met his requirements.

"This is it!" I cried.

A peasant loaf with the rich taste of wheat and a dry, open, alveolar crumb. So it *was* possible! Then I ran off to class, wondering if Chef Didier and his colleagues were even aware of what was happening on rue Monge and elsewhere, where bakers were experimenting with liquid *levains* and preferments, while the Ritz was stuck in the classical repertory.

I shouldn't have been surprised; the more traditional an establishment, the slower it is to change. And this hotel — its kitchen was founded and once run by the legendary Auguste Escoffier, whose kitchen-staff hierarchy system is still in place today, whose hundred-year-old cookbook of five thousand standard recipes is still used in culinary curricula around the world — was nothing if not steeped in tradition.

Just when I was ruing the money and time I had wasted on this course, something happened that seemed to make the entire week worthwhile. It happened not, however, in the bakery but in the classroom, where we gathered each day for coffee, tea, and a brief lecture from Didier. Chef Didier was describing the flour system in France. Flour is difficult to translate from French to English because there is no direct equivalent of French flours in the United States. We have cake, all-purpose, and bread flour, which are differentiated solely by their protein levels. The French have many more flours (distinguished not only by protein level but by mineral content), none of which really corresponds to any of ours. French flours are designated by type. Type 55 is basically their all-purpose, although the Ritz uses type 65, which has a little more of the bran and a higher protein level.

I was only half paying attention, drowsy from a week of racing between Parisian bakeries and the Ritz, when Didier mentioned that you have to add malt to the flour in order to help the enzymes react with the yeast.

That caught my ear. I raised my hand. "There's no malt in the flour? In America, the malt is added at the mill."

Didier found this astounding. In France the baker has to add his own malt.

Uh-oh. My mind raced forward. In a week I'd be baking at the monastery. I'd asked them to buy some type 65, some whole wheat, and some rye flour. But not malt. All my loaves might be doorstops without malt! Where was I going to get malt flour?

My classmate the veterinarian, who was a vegetarian (I guess you don't eat what you heal), gave me the names of several health-food stores in Paris, suggesting that I might find some there. The next morning before class, instead of tracking down artisan bread, Anne and I went out on a hunt to procure malt. The clerks at these stores didn't even know what it was. We also tried to buy some rye and whole wheat flour as insurance in case the monastery couldn't locate any. Parisian supermarkets, we'd found, had six hundred varieties of cheese but hardly any flour.

"Avez-vous la farine complète?" I asked to blank stares. They didn't know what whole wheat flour was? In a health-food store? That was incredible. Had I said the right words? I asked Didier about it in class that afternoon.

He wasn't surprised. "You'll find whole wheat flour in the country," he said through the interpreter. "But in Paris, people are not so much concerned about their health. They want tasty food, not healthy food."

No argument there. I'd been living delightfully on a Parisian diet of pâté, cheese, duck, foie gras, and wine all week. Plus,

Poilâne notwithstanding, this was still white-bread country, where the baguette ruled. And with a *boulangerie* on every street corner, selling baking ingredients to Parisians was akin to selling snow to Eskimos.

I told Didier of my concern about baking at the monastery and my inability to find malt. Could he give me a bit? I figured since only a tiny amount was needed for a loaf, a small sandwich bag of malt flour should last me all week.

Didier hesitated but agreed, reappearing a few minutes later with a large jug from which he poured about a quarter cup of a black, viscous substance that looked and smelled like molasses.

"I was expecting flour," I said.

Didier shrugged.

The last of the two dozen or so different breads we made in our twenty hours in class was a *pain surprise,* a tall, round loaf that, when you lift off the top, is — *surprise!* — hollowed out and filled with tiny triangular smoked salmon and ham sandwiches, thickly buttered (the better to stick together). This is the type of banquet food that was last in fashion when Gertrude Stein dined at the Ritz, but it was still the climax of the baking curriculum.

Finally the class was over. After much shaking of hands and posing for pictures, we were told in no uncertain terms not to leave any loaves behind tonight. What was I going to do with this dreadful *pain surprise*? The veterinarian had the same dilemma. "Maybe I'll give it to the beggar who's at the Métro every day," she said. I wasn't sure if she was serious. But I left class first, and sure enough, right at the Métro entrance was a pathetic-looking woman sitting on the sidewalk, wrapped in filthy shawls, with a cardboard sign asking for money to buy food for her children. I'd passed her every day but hadn't noticed her, just another beggar in Paris.

But was she even (excuse the term) a "real" beggar or a con artist? Deciding it didn't matter, I bent down and handed her the loaf, pulling off the top, revealing the little triangular salmon and ham sandwiches inside.

"Pain surprise, madame. Du Ritz."

No con artist could fake the look of joy, mixed with a little shock, that washed across her face. She thanked and blessed me, and that night she and her children dined on food from the kitchen of the Ritz. Seeing her face was heartening, but I really would've liked to see the vet's face when *she* walked by.

The week at the Ritz had left a bit of a bad taste in my mouth (and I'm not just talking about the bread). The way it ended — giving my last loaf to a beggar — seemed not only appropriate but symbolic. My quest for perfect peasant bread had led me far from the peasants, and I needed to return. I had five days before I was due at Saint-Wandrille. I wanted to go someplace where bread was still vitally important, where it was a staple, not a plaything of the rich. I needed a place where the peasants last rioted over the price of bread, not two hundred years ago, but two weeks ago.

The next morning, Anne and I boarded different planes. Her afternoon flight followed the sun home to New York. I parked some clothes and my *levain* with a friend living in Paris and headed south to the continent where, six thousand years ago, the first loaf of leavened bread on earth was baked: Africa.

The Count of Asilah

> Full of hope, Edmond swallowed a few mouthfuls of
> bread and water, and, thanks to the vigor of his constitution,
> found himself well-nigh recovered.
> — Alexandre Dumas, *The Count of Monte Cristo,* 1844

"You have time? I take you to all the bakeries in town," the shop-keeper offered, already starting to close his shutters.

I had prepared for my visit to Asilah by reading Paul Bowles's novel *The Sheltering Sky,* a bleak, moody portrait of postwar Morocco in which the American expatriate narrator, savvy and experienced as he is, allows himself to be tailed by a stranger, rolled by a prostitute, and nearly killed — in just the first twenty pages.

This should've put me on my guard, especially as in my own first *seven* pages in Morocco, I'd already had my camera stolen, watched a prostitute leisurely and openly negotiate a deal with three teenage boys, observed my waiter sniffing cocaine (which may have explained his indifferent service — or improved it), been the beneficiary of a secondhand-smoke *kif* high during lunch, been fleeced by a "guide" working in concert with my taxi driver (to think that I trusted the taxi driver!), and nearly been assaulted by a rug merchant for committing the venal sin of leaving his store without buying a rug. And yet — and yet! — when this ceramics-shop owner in the medina (the ancient walled quarter of the city) offered to close his shop for *half a Saturday afternoon* to personally escort me to the best bakeries in town, I thought (if you can call this thinking), Why not?

After all, I was here for bread — here because once upon a time, in both Africa and Europe, bread was widely prepared at home but baked in communal ovens. This economy of scale made, and still makes, a lot of sense, particularly when fuel is scarce, but this dying tradition is found in so few places today that it is in very real danger of extinction. I wanted to experience it while there was still time, in the way that so-called doomsday tourists are rushing to see polar bears in the Arctic before they disappear. Which was the reason I had come to this small city in northern Morocco, one of the few that still had the traditional *ferrane,* or community oven, deep inside its medina.

There was another reason for being in this North African country: while I had been chasing the ghosts of the bread riots that fueled the French Revolution two hundred years earlier, the real thing — a small bread riot — had recently taken place in Morocco, practically under my nose! Owing to a multitude of factors — not the least of which were those sacks of yeast stacked to the ceiling at the Lallemand yeast factory I had visited, destined to be used to turn corn into fuel instead of food — the price of wheat had doubled worldwide during my year of baking. For most American families, this was merely an irritation, if it was noticed at all,* but in countries where bread is still a staple (including such flash points as Pakistan, Egypt, and Iraq), it threatened social and political stability.

Morocco was a country where bread was worth fighting for,

---

*The flour in a typical loaf of commercial bread accounts for less than twenty cents of the price; the remainder comes from manufacturing, packing, transportation, and marketing.

not some luxury item where a bad *grigne* (the slash on the top of loaves) might cause it to end up in the garbage. Yet I was still surprised at how omnipresent, how much a part of the daily routine, bread was. It seemed to be everywhere: sold from pushcarts around which Moroccans crowded the minute the carts stopped; stacked in every phone-booth-size pocket store (there must be one of these tiny stalls for every ten residents); sold from the half-dozen or more bakeries scattered throughout this modest town; and, not least, baked in the communal oven, the *ferrane*.

It was the *ferrane* that had led to my encounter with Ali, the ceramics merchant deep in the medina. Wandering aimlessly through the maze of alleys without seeing anything resembling an oven or even a bakery, I'd finally decided to do the unmanly thing and ask directions from the next shopkeeper I saw, who turned out to be Ali. He informed me in English that I had picked a bad time to come to bake at the *ferrane,* for Ramadan had ended yesterday, and with it the frenzy of baking in preparation for the six-day festival that was just beginning. The *ferrane* was closed for several days, and Ali couldn't say for sure when it might reopen — either Monday or Tuesday, he thought. Well, I was leaving on Tuesday. I'd come a long way to bake in a *ferrane* and didn't want to go home empty handed.

I considered Ali's offer to visit the town's bakeries. A short man (he told me he was known in the medina as Petit Ali), he looked to be in his sixties and had a weathered but warm face — not at all like the young, cocky rug merchant in the baseball cap. That particular transaction had begun with handshakes, introductions (he introduced himself as Eddie, making me think of the seventies sales icon Crazy Eddie), and assurances of friendship for life, and ended with my new best friend literally screaming at my back as I walked out. "You say we are friends, we shake hands, I treat you nice, then you do this!" he yelled, following me out of the shop.

"This," by the way, was wanting to discuss the purchase with my wife, who (I said) was napping. Whether she was really napping or not was hard to say, since she was in New York, but Eddie returned the lie by saying I had to decide now; he'd be closed tomorrow because of the festival. Right. I don't think Eddie would close for his mother's funeral. "Do not do this again in Morocco, my friend! I warn you!" he screamed as I scurried away.

I flinched at the word "warn," with its implicit threat, but at least I wouldn't have to see him again. Asilah was a big place.

A little rattled and, after a long day of travel, badly in need of a beer — not always an easy thing to find in a Muslim nation, I was learning — my heart leaped and my mouth watered when at last I saw an Amstel sign. I flopped into a seat on the sidewalk and ordered up a cold one.

"Sorry, no *bierre*," the waiter said.

I pointed to the sign directly above my head.

He shrugged.

I settled for a glass of mint tea, seemingly the drink of choice among Arab men. The tea was beautiful, served in a tall glass filled with mint leaves, kind of like the mojito I'd have greatly preferred, but without ice. Or rum. I looked around for sugar but didn't see any, so while waiting for the waiter to return, I took a sip — blech! There was more sugar than tea in this tea, which explained the rotting teeth on many of the old men.

As I was wondering if the water in the tea had been fully boiled, who should wander by but Crazy al-Eddie! He glared at me. I tried to pretend we didn't know each other, but let's face it, I can state with complete confidence that I was the only person in Asilah who was six foot four and blond.

Eddie moved on, so I lingered at the table, enjoying the parade before me. On this first night of the festival, everyone was out, the women in their showiest robes, the men in both Western suits and traditional Moroccan djellabas, those hooded brown, white, or (my favorite) creamy yellow robes. The djellabas gave the men a monkish look, particularly as many walked bent at the waist, hands clasped behind their backs in the way of holy men, reminding me, before I was ready to think about it, of my next destination, the monastery. Very few families walked together, the young people preferring to congregate with their friends. And young people there were! So many that it was striking. Sit in a sidewalk café in any American city, and you see couples in their thirties or forties or older walking by. Here in Asilah the average age of the passers-by seemed to be about seventeen.

Starting to feel festive myself, I joined the promenade down the main boulevard, which was closed to traffic. Every bad travel book ever written has a cliché along the lines of "So-and-so is a land of contrasts." Yet from what I was seeing, Morocco was precisely that. Young women in traditional robes strolled arm in arm with young women in jeans and T-shirts. Some bridged new and old by wearing a traditional silk blouse and head scarf over their Calvin Kleins. The biggest contrast was provided by the movie theater adjacent to the mosque. I wondered what the men on their way to prayer must have thought when they passed the theater's posters of scantily clad women with their come-hither looks.* When the call to prayer sounded over the loudspeaker at the mosque, I paused, expecting the procession to come to a momentary halt. Yet no one else seemed to notice. As the pro-

---

*It turns out I'm not alone: some Middle Eastern experts are predicting that Morocco may become the next battleground of Islamic fundamentalism.

cession continued, the call to prayer largely unheeded, I went to bed.

The next morning, as most of Asilah slept off the long evening, I tried to wake up with several cups of espresso at the outdoor café around the corner. To move things along, I went inside to pay the check, but I had only the two-hundred-dirham bills (the equivalent of about twenty-five dollars) dispensed by the ATM. The waiter, unequipped to handle such a large sum of money, headed outside to get change from a neighboring merchant, but he never made it through the doorway — Crazy al-Eddie was just outside, with a wad of bills acquired no doubt from less discriminating tourists than I. There was no getting away from this creep.

Wanting to put some desert between myself and Eddie, I hurriedly left the restaurant, realizing half a block away that I'd carelessly left my camera on the table. Idiot! I raced back, but of course it was gone. This wasn't Norway, where I'd once left my backpack, passport and all, on a bench, only to find it still sitting there, untouched, a good forty-five minutes later. I couldn't help wondering if Crazy al-Eddie had made his rug sale after all. Only I didn't have the rug to show for it.

Despite this rude introduction to Morocco, when Ali — you remember Ali, the shopkeeper in the medina — offered, illogically, to close his shop to bring me to bakeries, I inexplicably had only one question: "Do we need to drive?" I may be naive, but I'm not reckless enough to get into a car in Morocco with a stranger — I think.

"No, no, everything close by. We walk."

We headed out of the safety of the touristy medina into a weirdly postapocalyptic scene, a tangle of deserted streets populated by stray dogs and illuminated by numerous smoky trash fires that burned unattended, explaining the perpetual foul-smelling haze that permeated the town and everything in it, masking the salt air. As we got farther from the medina, I started taking snapshots at each intersection with the replacement camera I'd bought that morning, hoping it would provide a digital trail later if I needed it.

The streets became less populous, then even less populous, and before I realized it, Ali and I were alone. Not another human being was in sight. Even the dogs had vanished. Yet I didn't want to show fear or weakness, and I wasn't sure I could find my way back alone, so I recklessly continued on, becoming aware that I was weirdly paralleling the opening of *The Sheltering Sky*. Whose protagonist dies at the end, by the way. I also became aware of even more bizarrely paralleling another story, that of Hansel and Gretel, who lose their way in the woods and are lured into — yes — a house of bread!* With a large oven inside. I was even mimicking their ill-fated bread-crumb trail with the digital one I was creating with my camera.

As I was mulling all this over, Ali stopped in front of a shuttered storefront. "Very good bakery," he said. I looked at the Arabic sign above it. For all I knew, it could've said GLUE FACTORY.

"Closed for Ramadan. But now you can find later."

I couldn't have found this place again if my life depended on it. But if my life depended on anything, it was on finding my way *back* from it.

"Come. We check another."

I obediently followed him deeper into the neighborhood to another bakery. Also closed. In fact, every bakery in town was closed for Ramadan. Okay, enough games. What was this guy up to? I suggested we return to the medina. I was mainly inter-

---

*In later versions the house is sometimes built of candy.

ested in the *ferrane,* anyway. I expected Ali to lead me back to
his shop, where, rug-merchant-style, I'd be pressured to buy some
overpriced piece of pottery as his guide fee, but surprisingly, we
parted at the medina gates with a handshake. I knew I would
pay for it in the end, though. The longer the setup, the higher
the payoff.

I thanked Ali, and he went back to his shop while I went in
search of lunch. As I sipped my beer (I had found the restaurants
that cater to tourists and sell alcohol) and ate some fried fish, I
pushed a tomato, tempting as it was, to the side. I'd been careful
with my diet, avoiding all fresh fruit and vegetables, and had gone
so far as to brush my teeth with bottled water, so at least I wasn't
suffering *la turista,* more properly called *la diarrhée du voyageur*
in these formerly French parts. Yes, I'd had some misfortune, and
I was still ticked about the camera, but things could be worse.

Soon, things were worse. My intestines were in full revolt. I
raced back to the hotel, where I spent most of the next four hours
in the bathroom, a bathroom whose drain emitted a stench of
sewage gas so intense I feared a spark might set the place ablaze.
I doubly dreaded every trip there, as just breathing in that room
was enough to make you retch.

I needed some medicine, and quick, but where? I hadn't been
able to follow the hotel clerk's directions (in Spanish) to the drug-
store, so immediately after another bathroom visit, I hurried back
into the medina, where Ali was at his shop. I started to explain,
but before I could finish, he'd already blocked the door of his
shop with a ladder and was quickly leading me out of the medina,
back in the direction of my hotel. The pharmacy was just around
the corner. Armed with Imodium and the closest thing to Pepto-
Bismol I could find, I thanked Ali profusely and ran upstairs to
my room. The medicine calmed my intestines down a bit, allowing me to sleep through the night.

At about five in the morning, I was slowly awakened by a drone that at first sounded like a distant fire siren. It was soon joined by another closer drone, which I could make out as monotone singing. The first time one hears the Islamic morning call to prayer, it is rather startling and intimidating, particularly before dawn. There is nothing joyous or celebratory in the chant; rather, it is delivered with an intonation of foreboding, starting soft and becoming louder in an ominous, threatening tone that sounds like a warning to come to prayer *or else*.

On this morning, I welcomed being awakened by the call, because for me it was the call, not to prayer, but to bread. Ali had thought that the *ferrane* might be open today, so I switched on the light, took more Imodium, and prepared a *poolish* with the French flour I'd brought along. If the *ferrane* was indeed open, I wanted to bring my bread in as soon as possible, in case the owner decided to close up shop early because of the fete. If he didn't open, well, then, I guess I'd have a bit of a sourdough for tomorrow. Having come this far, I was prepared to improvise.

After making my *poolish*, I went back to sleep, not waking till nearly nine. I hustled down to the *ferrane* and saw open doors, but the entrance was blocked by a small table. The baker was inside. He'd be opening at ten, he said in French. I hurried back to the room to make bread. The *poolish* was now four hours old. Ahh . . . it smelled like home. Clearing off a shelf that was set into the wall at just about the right height, I spread out a piece of parchment paper and set about kneading. Slapping the dough onto the shelf, I pressed hard. Really hard. All the way to the floor.

Shelf, dough, and paper all came crashing to the ground. Good start. Fortunately the dough had landed on the paper, so all was not lost. Since the maid was right outside, making her rounds, I quickly closed the door and drew the curtains, moving my operation over to a low table, which is where I should've been kneading in the first place. But this was Morocco and my brain was under the Arabian Nights spell. I continued kneading at the table, finding my good cheer returning despite my aching back, stolen camera, and angry bowels. There is truly something restorative about making bread. After two hours of fermentation and a ninety-minute rise, I grabbed my container of dough and a single-edged razor and headed into the medina. Where I once again became lost, an easy thing to do. Fortunately I spotted a woman with a large board covered by a floured cloth on her head. I fell in behind and followed her to the *ferrane.*

When I explained to the baker that I had traveled from America to bake in his *ferrane,* he welcomed me warmly and brought me upstairs, where two women were preparing bread, one taking dough from an enormous mixer that kneaded eighty kilograms (about two hundred pounds!) at a time, measuring and dividing with an old-fashioned balance scale, the other quickly and skillfully forming small *boules* from the lumps of dough as fast as the first woman could weigh. The ceiling was so low that I couldn't stand up straight, but otherwise the scene felt unexpectedly familiar and comfortable.

The sight of *boules* surprised me because I hadn't seen any in town. The mystery was cleared up downstairs at the oven, where just before loading the loaves, the baker pressed down on each *boule,* flattening it out, poked three holes in it, and dusted the top with a little cornmeal before sliding it into the largest oven I had ever seen.

I made four razor cuts in my dough, and the baker carried it downstairs on a plate. He asked me in sign language if I wanted it patted down, Moroccan-style.

"No," I told him. I was making a *boule,* not a flat Moroccan *smida.*

"Comme ci?"

Yes, just the way it was.

He handed the loaf to a one-eyed assistant baker, who transferred it to the longest and most splendid peel I'd ever seen, made from the slightly crooked branch of a tree. But to my alarm, with a flip of the peel he sent the dough sailing toward the ceiling, where it turned onto its back before landing on the peel with a thud. He flipped it again, returning the dough, now devoid of any gas whatsoever, right side up, sprinkled on some cornmeal, and motioned for me to take the peel, a gracious gesture.

The oven door was almost at ground level, requiring me to get onto one knee (and for the baker to work from a crouch all day long). Seen from eye level, the oven seemed to stretch on forever, making the bread oven at the Ritz look like the Hasbro Easy-Bake by comparison. I took the tree-branch peel and gave my loaf a ride.

While the loaf baked, I spoke with the head baker. Ali, who'd closed his shop once again to help me, translated.

Did the baker know about the bread riots in the south?

He did.

Did he know about the larger nationwide riots in the early 1980s, which some say took the lives of over five hundred people?

He was a child then, Ali translated.

Was he concerned about the growing price of flour?

He was unfazed by the price increases. Last month it was high, but then, after the protests, the price came down. Bread is too expensive! No, it's not that high. It's outrageous!

Was my baker schizophrenic? "Wait a second!" I said to Ali. "Did he say all of that?"

"No, *I* said it's too high. Last month it was only one and a half dirhams" — eighteen cents — "and now it's two and a half dirhams!" Or about thirty cents.

This increase of twelve cents doesn't sound like the stuff of riots, until you realize that the per capita annual income in Morocco is only $1,570, and the price of bread, which is eaten at every meal, had just jumped a full 67 percent.

The *ferrane* charged the equivalent of six cents to bake a loaf. I daresay it costs me considerably more just to preheat my oven at home. With the increasing price of fuel worldwide, the community *ferrane* seemed like an idea whose time had come. Sadly, though, it was an idea whose time was passing. Moroccans were becoming more Western, too busy to make their own bread.

My peasant loaf finished, Ali picked it up. "Heavy," he said, signaling for one of the baker's loaves. He held one in each hand, playfully turning his body into a balance scale to show how much heavier my loaf was. Indeed, the *smida,* although only an inch or so high, was light and airy, made with whiter-than-white flour. It was also tasteless.

My intestines started growling again, so I grabbed my loaf and retreated to my room. I hadn't touched a morsel of food since the sickness had started over twenty-four hours ago, and I knew I had to eat — but what? What could I eat that wouldn't make me sick? I remembered what Clotaire Rapaille had said about *The Count of Monte Cristo:* "If you have the right water, and the right bread — the old-time bread — you have total survival."

I looked at my peasant loaf sitting on the table. I had made it with bottled water and French flour. It was the only food in this town whose ingredients I could be sure of, and it even had some nutritious whole wheat and rye in it. Thus I became the Count of Monte Cristo, living literally on bread and water for the next two days, nursing myself back to health with bread made by my own hand.

———————————

My last night in Asilah, I headed into the medina one last time to look for Ali. He still hadn't tried to sell me anything. I wanted to say good-bye, thank him for his help, and buy something from his shop.

He pulled up a stool and insisted I sit. "Would you like a drink?" he asked.

"No, thank you."

"Why not?" He was hurt.

Why not, indeed? This man had been very kind and helpful to me. The least I could do was not insult him and accept his offer of hospitality.

Ali brought me a Coke ("in the bottle, please," I requested) and poured himself a coffee. I asked him if he or his wife made bread at home.

"Oh, I'm not married," he said. Then he explained why.

"Many years ago, when I was a boy, I was in love with a girl, but my parents had chosen someone else. But I was so, so in love with her. And she with me." He clutched his heart, looking at me through his warm brown eyes. Ali's hair flopped carelessly across his forehead, making it easy to see the lovesick teenager within. "But my parents would not approve the marriage. I didn't know what to do. I didn't want to marry the girl they had chosen for me, but I couldn't dishonor my parents and marry the girl I loved without their approval. I couldn't bear seeing her every day. It was so painful."

He grew quiet, lost in time and memory and sadness.

"What did you do?"

"I left home."

For the next twenty minutes, Ali described how he bounced around Morocco, working odd jobs here and there, estranged from his family, brokenhearted, burdened by a love that, decades later, he was still trying to forget. My Coke grew flat, Ali's coffee cold, as his life achingly drifted by, the bottled-up memories pouring from a long-corked bottle like a sad genie. Eventually his story reached here, the seaside town of Asilah.

"My heart was broken. I couldn't sleep, I couldn't eat. My weight was down to forty kilos."

I gulped. Ninety pounds.

"And everyone said to me, 'Ali, why are you so angry? You are the bitterest man in the medina.' They were right. And one day I realized this is crazy, to go through life so angry at the world. So I stopped being angry." He smiled. I smiled back. His face fell. "But I don't think I will ever be married."

A long silence followed, during which I realized what Ali's true motives were in closing his shop and taking me to the bakeries, to the pharmacy, to the *ferrane*. Loneliness. I'd kept him at arm's length throughout the week because I thought he was after my dollars, when what he wanted was my companionship and friendship. I felt ashamed.

"You shouldn't give up," I said finally. "You would be a good husband."

"Have you seen the girl in the jewelry shop over there?" He motioned toward a shop adjacent to his. In fact I had. She was beautiful and young. "Last year, I asked her to marry me. She told me she wanted to think about it, and the next day she came to me, and said, 'You know that thing that you talked about? I cannot. And please, do not ever speak of it again.' She thinks I am too old. I was born in March of 1953."

I almost choked. "March *what*?" I demanded, more curtly than I'd intended.

He was a little taken aback by my tone. "March eleventh."

This "old man," whom I'd pegged to be in his sixties, broken by life, his remaining years trickling away in the medina while he sold cheap ceramics to tourists, was born exactly two weeks before I was! I could feel my heartbeat speeding up. I needed to leave.

I had earlier spotted a bowl I wanted to buy, but as I rose, and before I could say anything, Ali said, "I want to give you a gift. Please, pick out anything in the shop."

I insisted on paying, to no avail. So I picked out a second piece, which I paid for. I asked if there was something I could send him from the United States, something he couldn't get here.

"I would like to speak better English," he said. "My English is so bad now because no Americans or English come here anymore. Perhaps you could send me a book that would help?" He reconsidered. "But it will be very expensive for you to send. You shouldn't."

I wrote down his address and promised to send a book. Of course, what I really wanted to send him, what he really needed, doesn't travel by post.

WEEK

45

The Trials of Job: Travel Edition

Gird up now thy loins like a man; For I will demand of thee,
and declare thou unto me.
—Job 38:3

The scene at the train station reminded me of stories of the eve of the Occupation, when panicked Parisians packed rail stations and streets, desperate to escape ahead of the approaching Nazis. On this night, however, those of us who jammed the Gare Saint-Lazare were merely trying to get out of town before the transit workers went on strike.

When I think about that night, coming after a long day of travel from Morocco, I see a scene, in black and white, of women in long skirts, heels, and nylons, carrying chic suitcases, scurrying toward their huge, steam-belching locomotives as the clock ticks down to the strike deadline. I see men in fedoras and pin-striped suits kissing their wives good-bye, not sure when or if they'll ever see them again. And I see — and this is the only even remotely accurate part — I see an exhausted, sick American, sitting on the platform, slumped against a wall, nibbling on a piece of crust, quietly taking in the scene, waiting for his *levain,* the rest of his clothes, and his train.

I hadn't even planned to be at the station until the following morning, but just before leaving Morocco, I'd finally been able to check my e-mail and couldn't believe what I read: Karen, the friend to whom I'd entrusted my *levain,* was warning me that the French transit workers had announced a strike beginning Thursday — the day I was to take the train from Paris to Normandy. Karen suggested I try to get a train Wednesday evening instead of spending the night in Paris as planned. She would meet me at the station with my starter and the rest of my clothes.

Sounded like a good plan, if — and this was a big if — the trains were still running, which we wouldn't know until we met at the station. In keeping with true Gallic tradition, the Thursday strike was in fact rumored to be starting on Wednesday night, as early as 7:00 p.m. As my flight from Morocco wasn't scheduled to arrive in Paris until 6:30, and the train to Normandy didn't leave until 9:20, I could very well be stranded, not just in Paris, but at the airport, fighting hundreds of other stranded passengers for a taxi! I could not believe my bad luck. I felt like Humphrey Bogart, lamenting from the soundstage that passed for Morocco, "Of all the days and all the trains . . ."

Even if I were able to catch a train to Normandy late Wednesday, I couldn't very well come knocking on the abbey's doors at midnight. So just before leaving Morocco, I had frantically and luckily secured, at an outrageous price, what must have been the last available hotel room in Yvetot, the train stop closest to the abbey. Because of the late hour of my arrival, however, I'd first have to walk from the station to their sister hotel in town, pick up the key, and then find my hotel. *Mon dieu!* Couldn't someone from the hotel meet me at the station?

"Non, monsieur," the Frenchwoman chirped cheerfully.

Well, then, could they arrange for a taxi to meet me?

"Non, monsieur," she said again in that same incongruously chipper, singsong voice, the tone that said yes while the words said no.* The hotel, Madame insisted, was an easy walk from the train station. And the second hotel was an easy walk from that one. I gave her my credit card number and hoped for the best.

The flight from Tangier to Paris arrived, thank goodness, on time. As I left the baggage claim, I looked at my watch: 6:45. Fifteen minutes before the earlier of the rumored strike times. I raced to the commuter train, relieved to find that it was still running. Eventually I made my way to the Gare Saint-Lazare, where I sat on the cold floor, facing thirty train tracks, the station fad-

---

*This is a common phenomenon in France, and I later witnessed in person this technique that the French use to sound accommodating and helpful on the phone when in fact they are being obstinate and very *un*helpful. What they do is smile from the moment they pick up the phone until they put it down, which makes the voice cheerful and friendly, regardless of the actual content of the conversation.

ing from frenetic to eerily quiet as the last trains pulled out — or not. Up and down the platform, the departure times on each gate changed to CANCELED . . . CANCELED . . . CANCELED . . . I stared at the sign at gate 29, willing it to remain at 9:20.

I couldn't help wondering if I was being tested. It did in fact seem as if I had to prove my worth, my dedication to this mission, before being allowed into the sacred abbey. Injury, sickness, theft, strikes — I was experiencing the Trials of Job: Travel Edition.

This was a little tricky because, well, I didn't believe in God, probably not in any kind of God, but certainly not the kind who'd want to become involved in the daily petty struggles of us mere mortals down here on earth. Yet I felt comfortable with my assertion that I was indeed being tested, comfortable with being able to hold the simultaneous beliefs that (a) God didn't exist, and (b) He was testing me. After all, the theory fit the facts so well.

Whether my ordeal was due to divine intervention or a bad run with the dice, I couldn't help laughing out loud as I realized that what I would normally view as a nightmare to be avoided at all costs — wandering around a strange foreign city at midnight with my luggage, searching for not one but *two* hotels — was the circumstance that I now fervently, desperately hoped for. This was, remarkably, my best-case scenario.

To realize it, however, I would need to be on virtually the last train out of Paris. The station grew nearly deserted. Another sign switched to CANCELED, and another. Clutching my *levain,* I went back to staring willfully at the sign above gate 29, a beacon of hope, still improbably glowing 9:20.

A Time to Keep Silence

With curiosity and misgiving I walked up the hill...
toward the Abbey of St. Wandrille... I wondered if my
project had not better be abandoned.
— Patrick Leigh Fermor, *A Time to Keep Silence,* 1957

Day 1: *Monastic Idol*

A full three hours before sunrise, as the monks of l'Abbaye Saint-Wandrille de Fontenelle were in Vigils, the first of the day's seven services, I was headed to my own chapel of sorts — the abbey *four-nil,* or bakehouse — crossing the enormous courtyard under the chilly and starry Norman sky with my bucket of *levain,* acutely aware of the crunching of the gravel under my feet. Something above caught my eye, and I stopped and looked heavenward.

The world stopped with me.

Total, utter stillness. Not a sound to be heard anywhere, no voices, no traffic from the town outside the abbey walls. No early-morning birds, no distant barking dogs, not even the sound of my own breathing, which must have ceased for the moment as I absorbed the wondrous sight before me. To the east, directly above the abbey church, a star shone brightly, more brightly than any star I'd ever seen in any sky, a star that burned, I thought, surely as bright as the star of Bethlehem. Venus? Maybe, but I'd never seen the second planet from the sun shine so brilliantly. I looked for another explanation — perhaps there was an astronomical event, say, a supernova, that I was unaware of. It was possible; I hadn't seen a newspaper for weeks. Or was it the air over Normandy?

I wanted to stay in that spot, just staring at the sky endlessly, but instead I set the world's machinery in motion again, continuing across the courtyard to the dark, chilly bakery. It was time to feed the *levain*.

I had arrived by taxi the previous morning after taking a long, luxurious, and badly needed bath at the little hotel in Yvetot, which I'd found at midnight almost by accident, when I feared I was lost. As I lay soaking in the tub, washing off Morocco, sending deep heat into my tired back, I wondered if my project had not better be abandoned. I would've been quite content to stay put in the hotel for a few days, taking baths, sampling Norman cuisine, and lying in the soft king-size bed while watching French television coverage of the rail strike that had paralyzed the nation. I had indeed been on the last train out of Paris.

With my destination at last so close, this entire ridiculous enterprise — posing as an expert baker, baking in an unfamiliar oven, with unfamiliar flour, in an unfamiliar and intimidating place, communicating in a foreign language that I barely spoke — was starting to feel like just about the worst idea ever. I remembered a conversation I'd had with Katie shortly before leaving.

"Dad, what are you going to be doing in France?"

"Training a new baker in a monastery built in 649."

"You?" she blurted out, her eyes wide. "Why are they trusting you?"

"They think I'm a master baker."

"How'd they get that idea?"

"I told them I'd won second place in a New York bread contest."

The last time I saw Katie, she was doubled over in laughter, and justifiably so, but a deal is a deal, a promise is a promise, and having persevered to make it this far, I knew I had to see it through.

My stomach kneaded into a nervous nausea, I stepped out of the cab and through the gates of l'Abbaye Saint-Wandrille de Fontenelle. Before I'd gone ten paces, the tension started to drain out of me. The grounds were calming and soothing. Sunlight streamed through the mist, emerging in the kind of rays you see in religious or romantic art but almost never in nature. Before me soared the stone ruins of the ancient church, stark and beautiful under a crisp blue sky. There wasn't another soul in sight.

Entering a doorway marked RECEPTION, I found an elderly layperson at the desk. I tried to explain in French who I was, but nothing registered. Perhaps I wasn't expected after all. He tried calling someone, to no avail, so he directed me to the guesthouse outside the abbey walls, directly across the street. I dropped my bags at the door and rang the bell.

No answer. This was some welcoming committee. I was thinking about that king-size bed I'd just left in Yvetot, when a balding, slightly rotund monk in round glasses came scurrying by, his black habit rustling.

"Ah, you must be the baker," he said rapidly, in a distinctly British accent.

Relieved, I said I was. He looked at the luggage I'd dropped in the doorway.

"Are those your bags?"

They were.

"No, no, no, no, no," he said rapidly. "He never gets anything right. You are not here. You are *inside* the abbey, with us." It was the first time, but not the last, that I'd hear myself included in "us" during the next few days. "Come, come, come, come,

come," said this Dickensian character in a French monastery as he whisked me away.

I struggled to keep up as we crossed the street, dragging my bags back through the abbey gate and into the interior guesthouse, where the *père hôtelier,* or guest keeper — a discouragingly severe-looking fellow whose tightly clipped hair doubled the size of his already generous ears — greeted me with the barest of nods.

"I take you to your cell," the *père hôtelier* said in English, the word "cell" reverberating with me as I followed him to a fifth-floor room in a five-story walk-up in what in New York City would be called a prewar building. Except the war that this building was "pre" was the French Revolution.

As we climbed the narrow, ancient spiral staircase, around and around, up and up, motion detectors switched on lights as we reached each landing, an improvement for sure over the dim candlelight that would've been the only source of illumination in this dark stairwell for most of its existence. The *père hôtelier* informed me that lunch followed the 12:45 service (or "office") called Sext, during which I was to sit in the front row of the church. I was to follow the monks into the refectory immediately after the service. In other words, if I wanted to eat, I was going to church today. I was eager to hear the Gregorian chant for which the abbey is known, but still, the assumption that I would be attending the service was a stark, perhaps intentional reminder that I was a guest at an abbey, not a hotel.

He handed me the key. "You are the only guest at the abbey," were the guest master's Bates Motel–esque parting words, making my remote location all the more mysterious.

I certainly hadn't been assigned the room for the view. The tiny cell was windowless save for one round window so small you'd complain if it was in your berth on a Caribbean budget cruise, and so high up that the only view it provided was of the sky. Otherwise, the room wasn't bad, with a single bed (nice, firm mattress on a board), a desk, and a sink, but the room's sharply angled ceiling, following the roofline, reminded me of the kind of attic apartment that rental agents had always shown me in my young, nearly broke days, except that I'd never been in an attic apartment whose ceiling was punctuated by massive hand-hewn beams. Their presence, while undeniably adding a certain ambience, closed the room in even further, literally forcing me to my knees to retrieve clothes from the bureau.

I had been expecting a room with a nice window. Just before leaving home, I'd stumbled upon an out-of-print book by a British writer, Patrick Leigh Fermor, who'd come to Saint-Wandrille after World War II, looking for a quiet, contemplative place to do some writing. Later he described his time at Saint-Wandrille and two other monasteries in *A Time to Keep Silence*. Of course, his visit had occurred over half a century ago, so I didn't know how relevant it would be to mine. The answer soon became apparent. Hardly anything had changed, except that he had a room with a garden view. A bathroom with two shower stalls and a toilet stood directly across the hall, in effect giving me a private bath. All in all, it was a fine cell.

Ten minutes before Sext (so named because it is, by the old Roman clock, which begins at sunrise, the sixth hour of the twelve-hour day), I pushed open the heavy door of the church and was immediately blinded by the darkness. I stopped for a minute to let my eyes adjust, afraid to take another step for fear of stumbling over a precious relic or a monk. But there were no monks and fewer relics, precious or otherwise, in the austere, bare church, with one notable exception: a medieval-looking black and gold box, with a glass front, mounted on the wall. I peered through, and as my eyes adjusted to the darkness, I was startled to find someone peering back. It was the thirteen-hundred-year-old skull of the founder of the abbey, Saint Wandrille himself!

In 649, when the owner of this skull, a monk named Wandrille, came to this pastoral valley to found the abbey that carries his name, Christianity was still in its formative years; Muhammad, the founder of Islam, had been dead just seventeen years; and nearly a millennium would pass before Columbus would land in America.

Wandrille's abbey, which is said to have boasted a three-hundred-foot-long basilica, flourished until 852, when Viking invaders sacked and burned the buildings. The monks escaped with their lives (and, more importantly, their relics, including the skull of their founder), spending years wandering northern France before finding refuge in Belgium.

In 960 the community returned and rebuilt the abbey, initiating a period of prosperity that saw the abbey's population grow to three hundred monks and spawned, over the next thousand years, some thirty saints. During the darkest of the Dark Ages, when centuries of knowledge were being destroyed or lost throughout Europe, the monks of Saint-Wandrille and other monasteries throughout Europe kept knowledge alive. Saint-Wandrille was renowned for its school, where not just religion but the arts and sciences were taught. Just as important were its library and scriptorium, where texts sacred and secular were preserved, painstakingly copied and illuminated, protected from the barbarians, and preserved for future generations.

The abbey's trials were far from over, however. The coming centuries would bring more fires (both accidental and intentional), sackings, governmental interference, and persecutions. Napoleon allowed the magnificent fourteenth-century Gothic cathedral to be used as a convenient "superterranean" stone quarry around 1800, leaving only the ruins standing today. The current church was a fifteenth-century Norman barn that had been disassembled and relocated stone by stone to the abbey, then built into the present church largely with the monks' own hands from 1967 to 1969.

Unlike the great churches of Europe, with their richly carved furniture, paintings, marble statues, and enormous stained-glass windows, which flood the faithful with colorful filtered light, Saint-Wandrille's interior was almost barren, its small windows set so deeply in the thick stone walls that whatever light made it into the church was gobbled up by those walls, darkened from years of burning incense. This church was, in fact, as bare, as dark, and as gloomy as the Middle Ages themselves.

I wondered if the very austerity was the point. This was a church built not to attract the community at large or to seduce or intimidate the heathen, but for the use of the monks, who were not here to be entertained. There was nothing in this church to distract them. I would float this theory several days later to Brother Christophe, the Dickensian monk who'd brought me into the abbey that first day. He agreed, but added, "Still, it could be lighter. It's so bloody dark!" There was, however, one notable source of ever-present radiance: a spotlighted, nearly life-size gold crucifix almost magically levitating over the altar, suspended on thin chains that were all but invisible at certain times of the day. The position of Christ, his back arching out from the cross, added to the feeling of levitation, giving the impression that he might simply free his bonds and soar from the cross, down the length of the church, at any moment.

My eyes having adjusted to the darkness, I took a seat in the second pew, ignoring the guest keeper's instructions to sit in the first because it was roped off from the rows behind (did he mean the first pew, or the first pew behind the rope?). Services are open to the public, but there were only two other people in the church, both elderly. Waiting for Sext to start, I became dimly aware of an uncomfortable sensation. My feet were freezing. In fact, my entire body was becoming chilled, even though it was shirtsleeve weather outside. I made a mental note to "dress for church" — meaning, in this case, to wear every piece of clothing I'd brought with me.

The huge church bells rang out, and the monks filed into the church in their black robes from a passageway behind the altar. Actually they didn't so much file in as amble in over a period of several minutes, during which we three laypeople stood in respect. The monks, about thirty in all, arrived in ones and twos, taking their places in the choir, two rows of choir stalls on each side of the altar, facing one another. As would be the case with every service I attended, a few stragglers came in late, after the service had started.

The abbot, who looked to be about eighty, entered last. Then the service began, fifteen minutes of nearly unbroken Gregorian chanting of the psalms, the two sides of the choir alternating verses, answering each other in stirring antiphony. The voices, particularly from several of the young soloists, were so beautiful that I later jokingly asked if you had to audition to become a monk. What a great idea for a reality show, I thought: *Monastic Idol.*

The psalms were sung in Latin as our little congregation followed the monks through a baffling sequence of standing, bowing, and sitting. Or almost sitting. The monks in the choir never got to sit for this brief service. Instead they reclined back into their choir stalls at about a twenty-degree angle, looking a bit funny and informal in their identical black robes, as if they might be leaning on the rail on an ocean liner's ecclesiastical cruise, except with a psalm book, not a drink, in hand. The strange bow they did was equally fascinating, a deep, stiff, ninety-degree bow from the waist, making them look like picnickers who'd lost something in the grass. Fearing for my back, I never tried to imitate it.

At exactly one o'clock the short service ended, and the monks filed out toward the refectory for lunch, while the *père hôtelier* with a little wiggle of the hand nervously signaled for me to follow. What a jittery fellow! On the way he whispered that I should have been on the other side of the rope, in the front row. Damn! I had screwed up already! Yet it wasn't so much an admonishment as it was an explanation of the privilege being afforded me.

"You have a *right* to be there," he said, indicating that I should use the door from the courtyard, an area closed off to visitors, and this door opened to the inside of the rope. Which raised a question.

"Where am I allowed to go?" I asked, assuming that parts of the abbey were off-limits to the overnight guests.

He seemed surprised. "Anywhere. You are one of us."

We entered the refectory, a breathtaking medieval hall over a hundred feet long, built in the tenth century. Both long walls were lined with beautiful windows that flooded the room with light, a welcome change from the dreary church. One of the walls was decorated with Romanesque arches, and the open, vaulted ceiling gave the room an airy feel. A row of tables, pushed together to form a continuous table perhaps a hundred feet in length, lined each of the long walls. The monks sat with their backs to the wall, facing one another across the room, mimicking the arrangement of the choir. A third row of tables, reserved for guests, ran plumb down the center, just so everyone could keep an eye on us.

The *père hôtelier* and I were the last ones to enter the room, and I was startled to see that the monks and several guests were all standing at their places, almost at attention, while just before me, a young monk stood poised with a silver pitcher of water and a matching bowl. The hotelier signaled for me to put out my hands, and a moment later, the abbot of l'Abbaye Saint-Wandrille de Fontenelle did as abbots have been doing here for 1,358 years: he officially welcomed me by ritually, and with humility, washing my hands.

Then, following the hotelier's signal, I made the excruciatingly long walk to my assigned seat at the far end of the hall — my place was marked with a heavy silver napkin ring embossed with my room number, 13(!) — as the standing monks watched, getting their first look at the *boulanger américain*. (I'd soon learn that everyone had been anticipating with curiosity my pending arrival.) We all stood at our places while the abbot said a brief prayer; then the monks all shifted down one or two places toward the front of the room to fill in any empty seats, and lunch was served.

Fearing that monastic life would leave me hungry, I'd planned to stock my room with snacks beforehand, but with the last-minute rush to beat the strike, there hadn't been time. I needn't have worried. Lunch consisted of a robust and well-prepared meal of beef bourguignon, incredible french fries — real Belgian *frites,* cooked, I suspected, in duck or goose fat since that's the only way you get *frites* that good — lettuce picked that morning from the abbey's own garden, and, for dessert, flan and strong black coffee.

My heart sank, however, at the sight of the beautiful-looking baguette, with a golden crust and perfect *grignes,* that sat on a simple breadboard at the center of the table. Oh, no, how was I going to compete with this? I tentatively took a nibble, then relaxed. It was more pleasing to the eye than to the palate. I knew I could make better bread than this. At least, I knew I could at home.

Meals at the abbey are eaten in silence — among the monks and guests, that is. As food was brought to the table by waiter-monks, the abbot, standing a few feet above us in a little perch built into the wall, began reading aloud and continued until lunch was over. The tone of his voice — a strange monotone chant — said "prayer," but the words, as far as I could tell, said "history lesson." I couldn't make out exactly what the reading was about, but I recognized the words "États-Unis" and "américain," so it certainly wasn't ancient history. The other words I kept hearing were "histoire de Michelin."

I figured that Michelin, in addition to writing travel guides, must also have a French history book, or even a series, titled *Histoire de Michelin,* sort of like the *History of Herodotus* or something. Later I would have a chance to ask Brother Christophe about it.

"That history lesson at lunch, what period of time was it covering?" I asked. "The French and Indian Wars?"

"Oh, no, it's quite contemporary. It's about Michelin."

"The man?"

"No, the tire company."

"The abbot is reading the history of a *tire* company?"

"It's rather interesting, in fact."

Not as interesting as the discovery that the monks had daily "story time." And that monotone chant! If I did readings like that, I'd clear customers out of a bookstore faster than a bomb threat. But of course the abbot had a captive audience.

I thought about this style of narration later and decided that like many things about the abbey that at first seemed baffling or even ridiculous, a method to the madness did eventually emerge. Chanting the text in a monotone serves several purposes: It re-lieves the reader of having to study the text beforehand, to un-derstand what words to give emphasis to, and it sounds the same no matter who reads it. As with the drabness of the church, the monotone guarantees that the focus stays on the story, not the storyteller. And never, ever, is there any mumbling.

Just before the reading began, I caught a couple of the younger brothers playfully making faces at each other across the refectory, one pretending to clean his ears with his napkin. It heartened me greatly to see humor at the abbey, as I'd been a little intimidated by the nervous and severe-looking hotelier. Of course, the fact that I had disobeyed his very first instruction by sitting in the second row in church didn't help. The sixth-century Benedictine Rule, which still governs daily monastery life today, dictates that all abbeys shall receive guests — in fact, receive them as (gulp) Christ — but it is the hotelier's job to make sure that they don't interfere in any way with the monks' lives of prayer and contemplation. He had a lot of responsibility, and if I screwed up, say, by sitting down at the abbot's table or interrupting the history lesson with a loud burp, it was his head.

I didn't become familiar with the Rule until I'd returned home, but the level of specificity in this document is remarkable. Even the procedure for the mealtime reading is spelled out. "Not just anyone who happens to pick up the book shall read," the Rule instructs. "The one who should read should begin on Sunday and do so for the whole week." Such detail was necessary. Saint Benedict, writing a hundred years before the founding of Saint-Wandrille, was trying to restore order and discipline to the monasteries, which even in those early years of Christendom had become loose and corrupt.

I mostly welcomed the mandatory silence at meals for the freedom it provided from having to make obligatory small talk with strangers ("Do you come here often?"), but at times it became something of a farce. There were six of us at the guest table at lunch this first day (a mixture of day guests and some new overnight guests who'd arrived), and we used sign language — as specified in the Rule — for offering to pour cider and the like. Some mouthed, "Merci." An occasional whisper ("Say, could I have some more of those terrific fries?") while the abbot was droning on about radial steel belt tires would've gone a long way. As a matter of fact, at one point I *wanted* more french fries, but other than poking the diner next to me — a gloomy, blond young man wearing rectangular eyeglasses, jeans, and a red nylon jacket tightly zipped to his chin, making him look as if he'd just descended from the French Alps — in the ribs, I had no way to communicate that critical piece of information.

As the monotone continued, everyone at the table, picking up on some signal that only I had missed, folded his cloth napkin and placed it back in its ring. I followed suit, wondering if this meant I'd see the same napkin at dinner. It did. And the next day. And the day after that. The monks took this frugality one step further, each using his napkin to clean out the inside of his drinking glass and wipe down the table before stowing the napkin, along with his silverware and glass, in a small wooden box, ready for the next meal.

With such a substantial midday meal, I suspected dinner would consist of lighter fare, but that night's menu started with a fabulous, thick green vegetable soup, followed by chicken cordon bleu and roast tomatoes (from the abbey garden), and for dessert, french toast — recognizably the dreary baguettes from lunch, transformed into a sweet dessert.

Practically every monk in the place, though, was trim and fit. The French paradox at work? Not exactly. The secret here is that meals are not a lingering affair. Food is plentiful but is whisked in and out at such a frantic pace that to get a full stomach, you have to eat quickly — two chews and down the hatch — or you'll leave hungry. During my stay, the typical dinner, a three-course affair consisting of soup, entrée, and dessert, was concluded in a

Maalox-inducing nineteen minutes! I hadn't had to eat that fast since junior high school lunch period.

Near the end of dinner one night, I followed as the guests again put their napkins back into their rings. The man across from me, however, laid his ring on top of his folded napkin. A moment later, the *père hôtelier* rose and, looking particularly stern, strode quickly over, picked up the napkin ring (silently, it goes without saying), and walked quickly down to the far end of the hall, where he dropped it into a drawer, while the poor fellow sat with downcast eyes. Had something happened? Was he being thrown out on his ear? Maybe for sitting in the wrong pew?

No, it was just another ritual, one that I would eventually experience myself (thank goodness I'd be prepared for it). When you arrive, the abbot washes your hands; when you leave, the hotelier returns your napkin ring to the sideboard. That way, everyone knows it is your last supper.

After lunch that first day, a short middle-aged monk, a tall young monk, and a medium monk, all wearing glasses, were outside waiting for me.

"Are you the baker?" the medium monk, who was apparently there to be a translator, asked in fluent English. He introduced me to the tall monk, Bruno, who was to be my apprentice, and to the short monk, Philippe, the abbey's accountant, who looked every bit the part. Philippe, whose English actually wasn't bad, had been placed in charge of me for the visit because he'd been the assistant to the last baker and knew his way around the *fournil*.*

---

*My 500-word French vocabulary increased to 501 during this trip when I learned that a *fournil* is where the bread is baked; a *boulangerie* is a shop where bread is sold (and possibly baked as well).

The four of us went over to take a look at the mothballed bakery, but the monks didn't have much time. It was already two, and the next service — None (or "ninth") — was at 2:15. I had expected to be working in a corner of the kitchen, but the abbey had a dedicated *fournil* opposite the large courtyard, the last in a row of shops, housed in a long fourteenth- to seventeenth-century building, that included the laundry, the woodshop, and the commercial business that supported the abbey, a document-digitization service. I was tickled by the fact that, given its renowned history of copying medieval texts, Saint-Wandrille was still in the document-preservation business, but none of the monks seemed to appreciate the irony. Instead they viewed the business as an annoyance that they'd just as soon unload if they could find a replacement source of income.

The bakery itself seemed to date from not long after the Middle Ages. The first thing I saw as we entered was an old, belt-driven commercial kneader, which, I was told, was purchased in the 1930s. "We won't be needing that. We'll knead bread by hand," I said breezily.

Philippe and Bruno exchanged nervous looks. Had I said something wrong? Philippe then introduced me to the enormous oven, which was comparatively new — only a half century old, with a panel of dials and toggle switches bearing mysterious labels like "Petit Chauffage" and "Grand Chauffage." About ten feet deep and six feet across, it took up most of the bakery, although the baking area inside was less than a foot high. I'd have to watch the rise of my *boules* in that thing. I peered inside. The top of the interior looked like the business end of a toaster, covered with rippled wires that would glow red when this behemoth was powered up. I was thrilled to see that the oven had a heavy firebrick floor and a steam injector. Philippe opened a manila envelope and pulled out a stack of worn papers, the original instructions for the oven. If there's one thing monks excel at, it's record keeping.

I looked around. There was a very small workbench and a crude proofing cabinet made from plywood, which held ten shelves of greasy black bread trays, each molded to hold a half-dozen long loaves. We wouldn't be using those, either.

I showed Philippe and Bruno the *levain* I'd brought from home. They weren't quite sure what it was or how it was going to be used. I explained that we could either use instant dry yeast (which they'd never heard of — Philippe had only used fresh cake yeast in the past) or *levain,* or a combination of both, to leaven the bread. I pulled out my recipe for *pain au levain,* which required half a kilo of starter for a good-size *miche.*

"But to feed the abbey, we will need so much of it," Philippe said, peering into my half-gallon container. "Eighteen kilos a day."

Eighteen kilos? That was, like, forty pounds.

"How do you figure?" I asked. "You only need a half kilo for a loaf."

"We used to make thirty-six loaves of bread a day."

"Excusez-moi? Combien?" How many? Surely he hadn't said thirty-six.

"Thirty-six," Philippe repeated in English.

"Thirty-six *petite* loaves. This makes a big *miche.*"

"No, thirty-six one-kilo loaves." Eighty pounds of bread.

I gulped. That didn't make sense. There were only thirty-five monks at the abbey. Even adding in a few guests, I'd figured a good-sized *miche* feeds six, so we'd make six a day. I explained my math to Philippe.

"Yes," the accountant replied, "but we eat bread three times a day, and we bake only three times a week. At breakfast, it is all we eat. And on weekends, we sometimes have twenty or more guests."

No wonder they were worried about kneading by hand. That also explained the presence of the enormous industrial oven, purchased when the abbey had not thirty-five monks but sixty. I clearly wasn't prepared for this kind of volume. Or was I? Suddenly, what I had thought was a wasted week at the Ritz, mixing huge batches of dough, dividing, weighing, and working with a commercial oven, seemed to have served a purpose. Even, one might say, been part of a plan.

"We'll just use the *levain* for special occasions," I said, trying to appear cool and confident but realizing that, even to do a couple of loaves, I'd quickly have to build up the little bit I'd brought with me. In fact, it was time to feed it right now. "You have some flour?" I asked.

Philippe pointed to a large sack standing on the floor. "See?" he said. "We got exactly what you asked for."

I looked at the label. It was marked "Boulangère Spéciale" and had a long list of ingredients:

Farine de blé type 55
Farine de triticale
Gluten de blé
Farine de blé malté 80 g/ql
Amylases fongiques 15 g/ql
Acide ascorbique 4 g/ql

In other words, pretty much the type of flour that had ruined French bread, loaded with additives like ascorbic acid, extra gluten, and enzymes to ensure a rapid, tall rise, the flour that Poilâne, Kayser, and Saibron had been campaigning against.

The only additive missing was the bane of the postwar baguette, fava bean flour. And the *boulangère spéciale* was type 55, not the type 65 I had asked for. I bit my lip. Oh, well, at least I wouldn't have to worry about finding malt (my little bit of malt syrup had since dried up), but how could they have gotten this so wrong?

Still, I didn't want to hurt the feelings of my hosts. Philippe was so pleased he had obtained exactly the flour this *boulanger américain* had requested. But where was the whole wheat, the *farine complète*? I was willing to try to make bread with this flour, but I didn't want to make Wonder bread. We needed some whole wheat.

"Où est la farine complète?" I asked Philippe.

He seemed confused by my question. There were twenty-five kilos of it right in front of me.

"No," I said in French. "This is white flour, not *complète*."

He pointed to the writing near the bottom of the bag: "Boulangère Complet." The flour was complete, having everything the baker needed, including added malt and gluten. That explained the confusion, but I marveled again how some people in France didn't know what whole wheat flour was.

I decided to let it drop for now. Thank goodness they had obtained the bag of rye flour I'd requested. We discussed how to get started, and I suggested that we just bake two loaves tomorrow to acquire some experience with the oven and the flour. Philippe and Bruno had been thinking along the same lines, and we agreed to start at 8:15 a.m., after Lauds.

Before leaving the *fournil,* though, I needed to feed the *levain.* The twenty-five-kilogram bag of flour was sewn shut. I was struggling with it, when the monk who was acting as translator reached under his habit and whipped out a large pocket knife with a locking blade that wouldn't have been out of place in South Central Los Angeles.

"What the he . . ."— I caught myself just in time — "heck are you doing with *that* thing?"

"All the monks are required to carry them," he deadpanned. "Except when we sleep, for fear we'll cut ourselves."

I cut open the bag and returned the knife. Clearly I had to revisit some of my notions about monks. As my companions scurried off to None, I settled into the old bakery — for the next few days, *my* bakery! — blowing the dust off peels, finding some *couches* for forming the loaves, trying in vain to coax some heat out of the radiator (the place was freezing), and planning out the next day. I realized that if I was making a *pain de campagne* at eight, I'd have to feed the *levain* by 5:30 a.m. or so.

Before I knew it, evening had come and the bells were ringing for Vespers. I entered the church from the door in the courtyard, following two new guests, who, before sitting, knelt and said a silent prayer. For the first time in many, many years, I did the same. This is what I said, this Prayer for Nonbelievers Who Nonetheless Could Use a Little Help:

> Dear God, if you exist and you are the kind of God that these good men at this abbey are sure you are, a God who is aware of each and every one of us and listens to and even sometimes answers our prayers, I don't often ask anything of you, but I have endured sickness, theft, strikes, scam artists, and wandering a strange city at midnight to get here, only to find a 1930s mixer and the wrong flour. I ask you just one favor: Please, dear God, don't let me screw up tomorrow. Let the bread be good.

Day 2: *D-Day*

High on the list of Things I Never Thought I'd Hear Myself Say: "If we start the *poolish* after Vespers, we can refrigerate it overnight, take it out to warm up before Vigils, knead the dough after Lauds, let it ferment during Terce, form the loaves just before Sext, and bake after None."

Which would bring us back to Vespers. I triumphantly tapped the point of the pencil down on my notebook. "Bon!" I said out loud, letting out a huge sigh of relief.

Our first day of baking had not gone well. The oven thermostat was off by 50 degrees Celsius (a full 90 degrees Fahrenheit), so our test loaves were scorched in the oven. (I should've known something was wrong when the parchment paper I'd brought along instantly turned to ash.) The *miche* I'd made with the *boulangère spéciale* flour had risen so much, I was afraid it would hit the heating coils on the oven ceiling. Most troubling of all, though, was another, more vexing problem to be solved: fitting the bread making into the busy (and inflexible) schedule of the monks.

I had come to Normandy with my artisan sensibilities, slow, cool fermentations, five-hour *poolishs,* and six-hour *levain* risings — all unwelcome alms to a monk-baker who had to run off to church seven times a day, not to mention his assorted study groups and other commitments (including playing the organ on Sundays). I was amazed by how tied to the clock abbey life was. A monk doesn't technically need a watch, for the bells still toll, as they have for thirteen centuries, fifteen and five minutes before each service, but every monk I saw wore one. Bruno's was a sharp-looking digital model.

The liturgy of the hours, starting with the predawn Vigils at 5:25 (which lasts up to an hour and ten minutes) and ending with the close of Compline at 9:00 in the evening, with five other offices and two fixed meal hours in between, left little time for much else. Here is the schedule we were faced with:

Service	Time	Average Duration (hours: minutes)
Vigils	5:25 a.m.	1:10
Lauds	7:30 a.m.	0:40
Terce/Mass	9:45 a.m.	1:00
Sext	12:45 p.m.	0:15
Lunch	1:00 p.m.	0:45
None	2:15 p.m.	0:15
Vespers	5:30 p.m.	0:30
Dinner	7:30 p.m.	0:30
Compline	8:35 p.m.	0:20

Plus another afternoon gathering for the monks in the chapter house, various study groups, and time devoted to private prayer. Not to mention that all of the brothers also had jobs. They were doing the laundry, cutting the grass, cleaning the kitchen, practicing the organ, being guest masters, doing bookkeeping, managing the gift shop, sweeping the great halls, lighting the church, and being the homeowners of a thousand-year-old house (and being the homeowner of a mere baby of a hundred-year-old house, I have more than an inkling of what that involves). "When is there time for contemplation?" I asked Philippe, who seemed confused by the question.

"We only work for an hour and a half in the morning, and an hour and a half in the evening," Philippe answered. "There is time after Mass and in the afternoon, after None."

Perhaps, but not nearly enough time to make the somewhat

fussy and time-consuming bread I'd brought to Saint-Wandrille. I had thought monks took long, leisurely walks and had hours each day to do nothing but think and pray. These monks, though, always seemed to be rushing around, often late for services, always pressed for time. The rigorous timetable seemed to impose an almost military discipline on the monks, but after all, I guess discipline is the name of the game when one chooses the monastic life.

"We have to wait five hours?" Philippe asked with alarm, peering down at my bubbly *poolish*. "Then another three hours after that? We won't be baking until Vespers!"

He had a point. Even the mere baking of the *miche* had been a problem, since it took nearly an hour — an hour that had to be jammed in between services. In fact, Bruno and Philippe had had to run off to church, although the *miche* was still in the oven. I needed to come up with something that fit into their schedule, that could be made in quantity (which left out my state fair *miche*, leavened with only the wild yeast *levain*), and, most importantly, that Bruno could handle after I left in only two days. I could almost see Philippe and Bruno shaking their heads as they left for None. Tomorrow, Saturday, we were to make our first batch of bread for the abbey. Sunday was a day of rest, and Monday morning I was leaving for the Normandy coast before returning home the following day. In other words, I had one shot at this, and one shot only, to have any chance of repairing the broken tradition of bread making at Saint-Wandrille.

Gathering up my sheaf of recipes and my notebook, I stepped outside. Bells tolled ominously as the huge barn of a church drew in the black-robed monks like a giant magnet attracting iron filings, leaving a sudden, still void in the courtyard. I looked around. A speck in the enormous courtyard, I felt infinitely small and insignificant. Cross-legged on the ground outside the bakery, leaning back against its south-facing wall, I closed my eyes, feeling the energy of the sunshine flow into my face, down into my limbs.

I started pondering the problem, and suddenly pieces of a puzzle, cut during the previous forty weeks of wandering in the baking wilderness, started falling from my subconscious into place, fitting together with a remarkable synergy. Spending the afternoon at Bobolink, experimenting with *poolish* and *levain,* learning to weigh ingredients, knowing how to use the baker's percentage, loading the Ritz's commercial oven, and most of all, fiddling endlessly and single-mindedly with my peasant loaf recipe — I suddenly realized that all of it, whether I'd been staring at my navel or at microscopic yeast, was not only relevant but critical.

I laid out the schedule of services and the recipes. The first to go was the *pain au levain.* There was no way we were ever going to have enough *levain* to make that bread in sufficient quantity. Still, I had become so used to baking with my *levain* that the thought of not using it seemed heretical. Besides, I hadn't given up the fantasy that my starter would still be in use at the abbey a dozen, a hundred, or — why not? — a thousand years hence. I thought maybe we could use just a little in each loaf, not for leavening, but for flavor. I'd never tried this before, but I didn't see why not.

The next problem was the long wait for the *poolish* to develop, a process that was setting the baking back too far in the day. We could do just a straight dough in a couple of hours, but I had come to the monastery as an apostle of artisan bread, which to me meant using some kind of preferment. Otherwise the brothers might as well continue buying that dreary bakery bread. At home on a few occasions, I had done an overnight refrigerated *poolish* with success. I looked at the monks' schedule. If Bruno could manage to take the *poolish* out of the fridge on his way to Vigils at 5:25 a.m., it'd be warmed up and ready to use by the end of Lauds, around 8:15. That allowed sufficient time to mix, *autolyse*, and knead the bread before Mass. Then we could give it a good two-hour fermentation and return at 11:30 to divide, weigh, and form the loaves before Sext and lunch. After None ended at 2:30, we'd return for the actual baking.

I thought this timetable would work; now I just needed to come up with a recipe that combined an overnight *poolish* and some *levain*. I worked out a formula that made a half-dozen one-kilo loaves, using nice round numbers, a formula that we could easily double or triple or even quadruple as needed. I started with three kilos of flour spiked with five hundred grams of *levain*, then figured out how much whole wheat, rye, water, and salt I would need for that amount of flour.

Six months earlier, this would've been a tedious exercise of ratios and guesswork. But knowing how to use the baker's percentage — the very same method I had once derided — saved the day. I knew I wanted about 12 percent whole wheat (assuming I could find some) and 6 percent rye. Figuring how much salt to use was easy — salt is always 2 percent of the total flour weight. Where the percentage really came in handy, though, was with the water. I generally used a 68 percent hydration level, but, concerned that working with such a wet dough would be difficult for a novice, I settled on a 65 percent hydration formula. This would give us a moist but still workable dough for shaping. So all I had to do was add up the weight of all the flours and multiply by 0.65.

Not so fast! Fortunately I had screwed this up at home more than once, or I'm certain, given the fatigue and the pressure, I would've made the same mistake here. When calculating the hydration, you have to remember to account for both the flour and the water *in the levain*. That is, one hundred grams of my *levain* adds fifty grams of flour and fifty grams of water to the total. Doing all the math by hand, I came up with a recipe and checked it three times.

Bon. The only thing left was the yeast. I had brought with me a small box of instant yeast in foil packets just to get started, figuring I'd buy a one-kilo bag of SAF instant yeast (still made in Louis Pasteur's old town, Lille) along the way, but nowhere in France had I seen yeast in quantity. I marveled at the fact that I can walk into any number of stores in the States and buy a jar of French SAF yeast, yet it didn't seem to exist in France, another reminder that home baking seemed almost unknown here.*

The unavailability of instant yeast was immaterial, anyway. I could see that Philippe didn't trust the stuff. As he'd reminded me a few times now, when he was the assistant baker, they'd used fresh cake yeast. He'd questioned my dry yeast enough that I decided we'd go with fresh. Fortunately I had held some of it in my hand at Lallemand, or I might not even have known what it was. Never having used it, though, I didn't know the correct baker's percentage — that is, how much to use in my dough.

What was I going to do? Tomorrow was Judgment Day. We'd be making our first batch of bread for the abbey, and I didn't want merely to guess at the amount of yeast. Yet I was stuck without my reference books and without Internet access. Wait a second — I'd received e-mails from the prior. Surely there was Internet access somewhere. When Philippe returned from church, I asked if I could get on a computer to send an e-mail. This monk

---

*When writing *The Italian Baker* in 1985, Carol Field noted that there was not a single cookbook in Italy devoted to bread making at home — but thirty-five thousand commercial bakers supplying the bread.

with a degree in business took me to his Dell computer with a seventeen-inch monitor and an external security device that required a smart card. His computer setup was more sophisticated than mine at work, and I'm an IT director.

Logging on to my e-mail account, I sent e-mails with the attention-getting subject line "SOS from Normandy" to Charlie van Over (and his wife, Priscilla, because I knew that Charlie wasn't religious about monitoring his e-mail) and Peter Reinhart, hoping that one of them would respond before the next morning.

Afterward I met with Philippe and Bruno in the bakery. The two test loaves had cooled enough for a tasting. They had risen, yes, but had about as much personality as François Mitterrand. We needed some whole wheat flour. And I wondered again about that *boulangère spéciale* flour, with all the additives. I didn't think it was making very good bread. Furthermore I knew Philippe and Bruno were worried about the baking schedule, and I needed to address the issue. It was time for a little tête-à-tête.

"When I came here," I began, "I didn't understand how much bread you had to make, and how little time you had to make it. The recipes I've brought are no good for you. But I've worked out a new recipe that I think will be much easier and still make very good bread. I've never made it before, so tomorrow will be another day of experimentation." They seemed satisfied with that. "Also, I think you'd prefer to use fresh yeast. Perhaps we can get half a kilo from the bakery?" Philippe smiled. He seemed *very* satisfied with that.

"And we must have some *farine complète*." I explained the confusion, pointing out the word *complet* on the bag of flour, attributing the problem to my lack of French, which was partly true. But I could see that Philippe, who'd bought the flour, still felt bad. "And," I continued, building to the coup de grâce, "I don't like this flour. This is commercial flour, made to stand up to mechanical mixers and short rises. We are artisan bakers."

I paused to let the words sink in.

"We cannot make artisan bread with commercial flour. When you go to the bakery for the *farine complète* and the yeast, can you see if they have any type sixty-five without additives? And tomorrow we will make six loaves from my new recipe."

Bruno was intrigued. "You're making a new recipe up just for us? This bread has never been made anyplace in the world?"

"*Jamais,* Bruno." Never.

I showed him my scratch pad with the recipe. He grinned broadly as he read the title aloud: "Pain de l'Abbaye Saint-Wandrille."

Dough-caked bowls and tools littered the sink; flour coated every surface. For two loaves of bread, I'd made quite a mess, but I was too tired to clean up now, and besides, it was getting late. I went back to the room to change out of my flour-stained clothes.

After dinner — three courses served in a record fourteen minutes (geese on their way to becoming foie gras aren't fed that quickly) — I went back to my room to change into work clothes again. I still needed to clean the bakery and prepare the *poolish*.

Normandy cools off quickly after the autumn sun sets, but despite the chill, I didn't bother with a shirt or a jacket, but just changed into my jeans and pulled my apron on over my stained T-shirt. As I left the room, I happened to glance in the mirror over the sink and was startled by the image I saw looking back — the stereotype of a French baker, right down to the bloodshot eyes! The only thing missing was a Gauloise hanging out of my mouth.

I made the trek across the dark courtyard. It was eight thirty, although it felt like midnight. I'd spent fourteen of the past sixteen hours on my feet, preparing *poolish,* building *levain,* baking, formulating, and mopping. I thought I'd be living the life of a French monk in my four days here. How fatuous; I was living the life of a French *baker*. My spirits revived when I switched on the light in the bakery. Two bags of flour — a bag of whole wheat and a bag of unadulterated type 65 — sat on the table. Philippe had come through. Now the only question was, would the type 65, without malt, come through? Was malt really required to kickstart fermentation? I hoped not, for I had none. Perhaps the little bit of *levain* I was adding, less than a hundred grams for each one-kilogram loaf, would serve the same purpose.

I mixed the flours, made a *poolish* with a guesstimate for the fresh yeast I'd found in the kitchen refrigerator, and built up some more *levain* before returning to my cell. As it was after nine o'clock, the strict rule of silence was now in force. Not that you could generally tell the difference.

My head hit the pillow and I fell instantly into a deep sleep.

Day 3: *Pain de l'Abbaye*

Just after five thirty in the morning, I groped my way into the basement entrance of the dark kitchen, walking my hands along the cold stone walls until I found the stairs and some light at the top. Philippe had, as promised, taken the *poolish* out of the refrigerator on his way to Vigils, and it looked nice and bubbly, a good sign. Retrieving the *levain* from the walk-in refrigerator, I brought it across the courtyard to the bakery, once again pausing to admire — and wonder about — that brilliant star shining brightly in the east.

By the time Philippe and Bruno arrived after Lauds, at quarter past eight, I'd measured out the flours on the abbey's antique brass scale and wiped a couple of years of dirt out of the huge copper kettle of the commercial mixer, itself as much a relic as anything else at Saint-Wandrille. "Okay," I said, projecting as much optimism as I could muster. "Time to make the premier batch of *pain de l'Abbaye Saint-Wandrille*."

Bruno showed that infectious childlike grin. "First ever," he said.

"First ever."

Before we started, though, I needed to check my e-mail to see if my SOS to Charlie and Peter had been answered. I had responses from both. Predictably, their answers were different — Charlie's exactly double Peter's — but Charlie, whom Priscilla had paged out of a meeting, freely admitted he wasn't sure of his figures, as it had been a while since he'd used fresh yeast himself. I went with Peter's figures of 0.1 percent for the *poolish* (I'd used 0.075, a remarkably close guess), and 2 percent for the final dough. I'd learned that, when in doubt, less yeast is better than more.

We dumped the *poolish,* flours, and water — over fourteen pounds of dough — into the copper kettle, measured out eighty grams of fresh yeast, gave it a quick mix by hand, and let it sit for a twenty-minute *autolyse* while Philippe adjusted the heavy brass arms of the mixer. Every modern (or even not-so-modern) kneader I'd ever seen has a single dough hook, which, with some variation, spins while also moving around the bowl in an orbital motion, not unlike the action of my KitchenAid stand mixer at home. But this museum piece had two solid-brass arms, which resembled a giant salad fork and spoon. The bowl rotated slowly while the two mixing arms swung back and forth in opposite directions, just missing each other as the spoon passed through the two prongs of the fork. It was a mesmerizing and wondrous sight to behold.

After five minutes we switched the machine off, scraped the dough down into a mound, and threw a cloth over the bowl. I looked at my watch. Even with a lengthy *autolyse* and much fiddling with the machine, it was only quarter past nine — we'd finished with time to spare before Terce. So far, so good. I asked Philippe and Bruno to meet me back in the *fournil* to form the loaves at eleven thirty, giving them some free time, and the dough a good two-hour fermentation.

By half past eleven, the dough had risen nicely — a little too nicely, in fact. So much for needing malt. The *levain* in the *pool-ish* had packed more wallop than I'd expected, so next time we'd cut the yeast in half. As Bruno divided the dough into 1.1-kilogram pieces on the digital kitchen scale I'd brought from home, we discussed what shape to form the loaves into. I was, of course, partial to the *boule,* but Philippe saw a problem.

"The long loaf is a better shape, as every brother gets the same-size piece. With the round one, the middle slices are much bigger than the ends."

This eerily echoed Clotaire Rapaille's comments on bread de-mocracy, but with the opposite reasoning: Rapaille had thought the *boule* more egalitarian, for no one got stuck with the pointy end piece, the *croûton.* But Philippe, reflecting the austerity of abbey life, was more concerned about the size of the portion.* I showed Bruno how to form one *bâtard,* which is shaped like a skinny football, then had him do the rest. His first loaf was a blunt-end cylinder, so I started to demonstrate how to roll the ends into nice points (a technique I'd just learned at the Ritz), when Philippe interrupted.

"But it is better not to have the points!" he insisted. "So every-one gets the same-size piece."

I thought Philippe was carrying this a bit too far. "But then it

---

*The fact that either of these men even considered this issue is in itself illustrative of the differences between France and the United States, where such a thing would, unfortunately, never be given a nanosecond of thought.

is not a *bâtard,*" I said, smiling. "It is a cylinder. The bread must please the eyes as well as the stomach." I could hardly believe what was coming out of my mouth, yet I couldn't help myself. It was as if Chef Didier had stowed away in a portion of my brain and come with me from the Ritz.

Leaving it up to Bruno, I changed the subject, showing him how to flour and fold the heavy linen *couche* to hold the shape of the loaves. Bruno was a bright, eager student and a quick study. We assembled six loaves and fired up the ancient oven. Seeing me covered in flour, and nervously looking at his watch, Philippe offered, "You don't have to go to Sext, you know. It is not required of the guests."

"But it leads right into lunch." As far as I knew, it was the only way to get fed.

"Yes, but you can also meet in the *salle d'hôte.* The *père hôtelier* always checks in there first, to see if any new guests have arrived."

Odd — the *père hôtelier* had neglected to mention that option. Even odder, I turned down Philippe's offer. Surprising myself, I found I *wanted* to go to Sext, to sit in that cold, dark church for fifteen minutes, to hear the voices of the monks, soothing, calming, and uplifting. I was being drawn, whether I wanted to be or not, into the rhythm of monastery life. I had wondered beforehand if attending church services might reindoctrinate me into Christianity, but the chanting in Latin, while beautiful, was to my ears unintelligible. For all I knew, they could have been singing about the internal combustion engine. Yet I enjoyed the services and found that my time in the dark, austere church, listening to Gregorian chant, had the effect of sharpening my senses. I'd started to notice, for example, the repetition of significant numbers, the bells always tolling at the end of a service in repeating sets of three rings (representing the Holy Trinity), and how the lighting of the church varied throughout the day, starting fairly dark for the predawn Vigils, then growing lighter for Lauds and Mass, and dimming again as the day wound down. Always lit, of course, was the ever-present crucifix, hanging from the ceiling, Christ poised to loose his bounds and fly down the length of the church.

Before hurrying to Sext and then following the monks to lunch, I had thrown on a sport jacket but hadn't had time to change out of my floury jeans, and as I walked down the long refectory, past the rows of monks standing at their places, Bruno eyed me head to toe and grinned broadly. I winked and shook the leg of my pants as I passed, leaving a little puff of flour behind, and almost caused him to burst into laughter, which no doubt would have been a major breach of protocol.

You are one of us. Indeed, it was beginning to feel that way. Which made what I did after lunch easier. I approached the guest master, who was turning out not to be such a stern fellow after all, but rather likable, about staying another day. "Bruno's going to be a terrific baker," I explained. "But he's not quite ready."

Which was precisely half the truth.

Philippe was pleased but felt guilty about my decision when I told him later. "But I thought you wanted to go to Honfleur," he said in that gentle voice of his. It's true, I had wanted to spend my last night in France in a comfortable bed in a *chambre,* not a cell, spending more than sixteen minutes at dinner, lingering over Normandy oysters and getting drunk on Calvados. Yet suddenly the thought of spending a day in a touristy village, which sounded a bit like a Norman version of East Hampton, the streets filled with British day-trippers from across the channel, was only slightly more appealing than landing on nearby Omaha Beach in the face of Nazi machine gunners. I preferred where I was.

Bruno was visibly relieved that I was staying, and he had a

request: he liked the country loaves we were making just fine, but he had really been intrigued by the *levain* and wanted to make a true *pain au levain,* with no commercial yeast at all, on our last day of baking.

"Bruno," I said, starting to feel some real affection for this brother, "you are truly a baker. Monday, we'll make a loaf like Poilâne's."

It being a Saturday, a handful of weekend guests had arrived. The glum Alpine hiker was still there in his red jacket. (Would he *ever* take that damned thing off?) I found myself, now a veritable veteran of abbey meals, showing the newcomers — three young men who'd arrived together and a Dutch priest — the ropes, pouring cider for everyone, putting my napkin in the ring at just the right moment. The father abbot read us some more about the Michelin Man, and then it was almost time for church again.

After a fine None service, Bruno, Philippe, and I assembled in the bakery. With the schedule imposed on us, the loaves were proofing longer than I would've liked, but the bakery was chilly — in the midsixties — and I figured they could survive and still have enough left for a good oven spring. I had no choice, really, but I thought about all the times I had raced back to the kitchen — from the store, from the garden, even, memorably, from bed — a slave to a strict schedule, sure that if I was ten minutes late the bread would be ruined, yet here I found myself liberated from worrying about such precise timing. The only timing I was concerned with was that of the seven Divine Offices.

Bruno scored the loaves with a *lame* and slid them into the oven with a good spritz of steam. The loaves swelled instantly in this marvelous oven with its massive brick deck. A mere half hour later, the *bâtards* were done, shiny from the steam and looking quite professional, if a bit puffy. Now there was nothing to do but wait for the verdict in the morning. And clean the bakery, which was coated with flour. As I reached for the broom, Bruno shooed me out. I protested, but he wouldn't hear of it. "You've been living in here," he said. "Go for a walk."

Hanging up my apron, I threw on my jacket and headed out to really see the abbey grounds for the first time. We were in the third of what would be five unbroken days of warm sunshine in Normandy in October, a time of year, I'd been told by one of the monks, when cold rain is far more likely. I sat on a bench for a moment and contemplated how this weather seemed providential, a reward for my earlier travails. But that would require a belief in a divine Providence, one, no less, who would alter the weather for millions of other people — possibly to their detriment (maybe farmers needed rain or fishermen cloud cover) — to reward me alone for a loaf of bread! "Not possible," I muttered, "and why am I even having this insane conversation with myself?"

As I ambled on, an amazing thing happened, a small, welcome miracle in its own right, one that I could freely accept: I stopped worrying about the bread. In fact, I stopped *thinking* about the bread for the first time since my arrival, so overwhelming was the beauty and peacefulness of this ancient place. My mind free, I drank in the solemn magnificence of the grounds, walking past neatly trimmed formal shrubbery, along the Fontenelle River, through apple orchards, discovering espaliered pear trees on a south-facing wall, and hiking to the remote seventh-century chapel that had been built by Saint Wandrille himself.

I was hungry, and as I passed an orchard near the chapel, a bright red apple beckoned. I looked around. There was no one in sight. Surely they wouldn't begrudge me a single apple. The temptation to pluck this low-hanging fruit was irresistible. As I reached out for it, I wondered if the picking of fruit was explicitly forbidden, and at the flash of that word, *forbidden,* my arm recoiled as I realized with horror the symbolism of the act I was about to commit.

I had come *that* close to inviting disaster. It was time to return. On my way back I walked through a small cemetery with two rows of markers, the graves of deceased monks, on either side of the path. One stopped me dead in my tracks: a headstone marked BILLY with the year of my birth! This was getting weird. Forbidden fruit, unexplained celestial events, now my name and the year of my birth on a tombstone! Was this all a dream? I dropped to a knee both for stability and a closer look. The stone wasn't reserved for me. It was the grave of one Jean-Baptiste, better known, apparently, as Billy, who died the year I was born. I took out my camera and snapped a picture, the act reconnecting me with reality.

A few minutes later I was back in the courtyard. I had been out for two hours, and not once had I encountered another living soul. The thought occurred to me that I was more likely to encounter God. Not that I really expected to, but it did, for the first and only time in my life, seem possible in this ancient, otherworldly place to realize some kind of divine *experience:* a vision, a voice, an epiphany. I stayed on my toes, alert to His presence, but all I could see were the timeless ruins, the sparkling stream, flowers and herbs, fruit trees heavy with ripe apples and pears, birds chirping in the trees, church bells ringing in the distance, all of it drenched in that incredible Norman sunshine, and, above all, perfect, transcendental solitude.

Day 4: *Le Verdict*

Normandy is still dark at seven thirty in the morning, so imagine what it's like at five when the bells signal the monks and, on this occasion, one amateur baker to rise for Vigils. I wound my way down to the guesthouse kitchen (where guests serve themselves breakfast, the only meal of the day not taken with the monks), only to find that the hot water dispenser for instant coffee hadn't yet been switched on. With a few minutes to kill before Vigils, I crossed the courtyard to feed the *levain,* stopping midway to look at that extraordinary star. If anything, it had grown brighter, looked closer. Then, wrapped in a wool sweater and my lined, hooded leather jacket, I entered the dimly lit church. Only a handful of monks entered behind me. Even the abbot didn't show up. "It's very difficult," Bruno said later when I expressed surprise at the poor attendance. A couple of *frères* sleepily wandered in late, as always, and a few yawned repeatedly throughout the service. A quarter of the dozen assembled blew their noses or coughed.

Like all the services at the abbey, Vigils is sung, but this one is sung with a difference: Vigils is a one-note song. For a full hour and ten minutes, the monks chanted psalms in monotone, while I questioned my decision to attend. I thought I'd dressed sufficiently, but I was freezing. And badly in need of coffee. I could see myself coming down with one beaut of a cold when this was all over.

The only saving grace was that most of the service was conducted seated, relieving my empty predawn stomach from the jack-in-the-box routine — Up! Down! Stand! Kneel! Stand! Sit! — of the other services. Even the monks were allowed to sit, rather than lean, for this one. Still it was brutal, and *so* cold. Afterward I hurried back to my room to take a long, hot shower, which was a challenge because the faucet was on a monastery-appropriate twenty-second timer, like the faucets on public washroom sinks. With some experimentation, I found that by leaning against the knob with the top of my buttocks, I could keep the water on while remaining in an acceptably comfortable position. After I'd thawed, I barely had time to wolf down a couple of slices of very stale baguette and a cup of instant coffee in the guest-house kitchen (while the monks were at this very moment judging my *pain de l'abbaye* in the refectory!) before the five-minute warning tolled for Lauds.

Adding a corduroy shirt under my sweater and jacket, I scooted back to the church. I didn't regret it. Lauds is perhaps the most beautiful of the services, almost uninterrupted antiphonal chanting, although since it came on the heels of the hour-long Vigils, I'd expected it to be brief, fifteen minutes or so. It turned out to be closer to forty. It wasn't yet quarter past eight in the morning, and I'd already spent nearly two hours in church. How did these monks get anything done? I wondered. Then I remembered: this *was* what they did.

After spending a few minutes in the *fournil,* it was off to Mass at quarter to ten. The monks entered in a procession, some dressed in muted green frocks. These were the *pères,* whose extra study had elevated them to the rank of father. I was surprised to see Bruno, such a young man, in green. Brother Bruno was in actuality Father Bruno. Later I would ask him about it. "You're young to be a *père,* no?" Bruno, I knew, was thirty-six.

"No. I've been a monk for eighteen years." He thought for a moment. "Half of my life," he said, sounding surprised, as if he'd never stopped to think about it before. But that's quite possible. Bruno was doing something that he didn't ordinarily have an opportunity to do: chat with a visitor, as guests are normally not allowed to speak with the monks. I had extraordinary access to the community, a fact that I knew and appreciated, and I'd like to think some of the monks appreciated it every bit as much. They, after all, were the cloistered ones.

I was appreciating some other advantages of my unusual status as well. As my breakfast of bread and water (flavored with instant coffee, but still bread and water) was leaving me famished well before lunch, I'd taken to visiting the kitchen midmorning with a breezy, "Bonjour, chef!" and grabbing an orange or a small container of yogurt, along with my *levain,* on the way out.

After lunch I was afforded a private tour of the abbey with Brother Christophe, the monk with the British accent whom I'd met at the guesthouse door the first day. We strolled the buildings for an hour as Christophe, who was remarkably versed in the abbey's history and architecture, played docent, revealing to me the symbols hidden in the bas-relief sculptures and filling in my century-size gaps in French history. I asked him if he'd heard of *A Time to Keep Silence.* I probably should've known this beforehand, but it was like asking a U.S. senator if he'd heard of the Gettysburg Address.

"Heard of it! That's why I'm here," Christophe answered, amused. He had come across the book in his native Canada some years earlier (he acquired his accent during his schooling at Oxford, where he earned a master of arts degree in history) and had been inspired not only to visit a monastery but to become a monk. "We have a signed copy in the library."

A decidedly modern beep sounded as we walked around the medieval cloister, its pavement covering tombs of the founding abbots. Oh, no, I hadn't absentmindedly taken my cell phone with me, had I? I patted down my pockets while pretending I hadn't heard anything. No, I was clean.

The beep sounded again. It was close; it must be me — what could it be? A low-battery warning or something?

"I'm so sorry," I said to Christophe while I frantically searched for my phone, my camera, or anything else that could be beeping.

"Oh, it's me," he said casually, and pulled a pager out from under his robes. My jaw almost dropped to the tomb of the fourteenth-century abbot directly beneath my feet. Christophe excused himself and made a phone call. As the tour wound down and we walked across the grounds, I gently edged the conversation from architecture to religion. I had come to the abbey protected with a healthy shell of skepticism and in a mood to discuss — maybe even challenge — the rationale of the cloistered life. These monks, as commendable as they were, weren't exactly Mother Teresa. That is, they weren't out feeding the hungry, or defending the poor, or running hospitals or schools, or even, as their predecessors had done, copying texts during the Dark Ages. What, then, *were* they doing? "How do you see your role in the modern world?" I asked.

Christophe thought for a moment as we looked down at the quickly moving Fontenelle. "To pray." He paused and was about to elaborate, then stopped. "To pray. I'll just leave it there."

"To pray," I said. "It's as simple as that."

"It's as simple as that."

To pray. For all of us. That was the end of my much-anticipated debate over the cloistered life, since it seemed like a perfectly sensible answer, and I could find absolutely nothing in it to challenge. Four days ago the skeptic in me might have, but on this afternoon I accepted Christophe's answer as he and the monks of Saint-Wandrille had accepted me — willingly, unquestioningly, and, most of all, without judgment. No one had asked about my religious convictions, about my commitment, about my motives for being here; it was utterly impossible to question theirs.

Up until the moment I asked Christophe that shamelessly loaded question, I would never have known I was speaking with a monk. The same was true of Bruno and Philippe. These men — all the men I'd met at Saint-Wandrille — wore their piety lightly. Perhaps that's why I took to them so easily. I suspect I'm not alone in generally feeling uncomfortable around priests, ministers, and the holy, some of whom wear their holiness as a badge.

Priests, like cops, move and speak in a certain way that is un-
mistakable. They don't even have to be overt about it. Trust me,
nothing is worse than running into your minister in town and
hearing, "I haven't seen you in church for a while."

By contrast, the monks at Saint-Wandrille spoke so strongly
with actions that they didn't need words. Christophe's simple
answer — to pray — had, I thought, a corollary: To be. Not to
preach. To be. As he might say, it's as simple as that.

Patrick Leigh Fermor wrote about the feelings of claustropho-
bia and oppression he had felt in his first days at Saint-Wandrille,
and I had made sure I'd packed some Valium, as I fully expected
I might feel trapped, if not experience a full-blown panic attack.
I never needed it. With each passing day, the rhythms and traditions of the abbey seeped deeper into my soul, aided and fueled
by the still-unbroken autumn sun, and the pure joy of being with
these stimulating, intelligent, gentle men in this mystical and
timeless place had overcome any feelings of isolation or foreign-
ness. In fact, never had I felt less foreign.

Of course, I had another reason to be happy, as well. I had my
own French bakery.

It had become my home away from home, and after a few
days of baking, the chilly room had started to warm up, to smell
comfortably of flour and yeast and bread. We had managed to
tame the oven and had mastered the antique mixer. I was hap-
pily spending fourteen hours a day in the *fournil*, becoming a
familiar sight in the courtyard (and in the church), and receiving
nods and smiles from the monks as I scurried across the quad in
my T-shirt and stained blue apron, on my way to the kitchen or
the guesthouse. If I looked strange, the tall, middle-aged, flour-
dusted American who had come to bake bread, no one let on.

The *fournil* was in fact where I was headed now, and moments
after entering the courtyard, I saw another familiar tall figure

enter directly across from me, carrying *levain*. I'd been avoiding Bruno and Philippe all day long, for I didn't want this wonderful feeling I was experiencing to be spoiled with bad news about the bread.

There was no avoiding the verdict now.

————————————

With my long strides and Bruno's even longer strides, the distance between us closed quickly, and I soon saw that Bruno's grin was as wide as the courtyard. He could hardly contain himself.

"They loved it! The brothers all loved the bread! Every one! They want to have it all the time, instead of the old bread! They were so happy to have good bread, and bread that's good for you!" As we walked toward the bakery together, this shy young man, who hadn't even offered a handshake on my first day at the abbey, instead keeping his hands clasped under the billowing folds of his scapular, patted me on the shoulder — not once but twice — as he said, "And all because of you!"

"You're the *boulanger* now, Bruno," I said, too startled by the gesture to return it. "If you hadn't volunteered to bake, I wouldn't be here right now."

Bruno had more exciting news. "One of the brothers told me it tasted like the bread he'd had in Paris."

Bruno had mastered the technique of speaking to me slowly, using a third-grade French vocabulary, so we were able to more or less converse in French, but had he just said what I thought he'd said?

"Notre pain?" I asked. Our bread?

"Oui, notre pain!"

Bruno wanted to confirm something. "And this bread has never been made before, correct? You made this recipe just for the abbey, yes?"

I answered in the affirmative, to his visible relief. Apparently he'd been repeating that tale and needed to confirm it, as the legend of the *pain de l'abbaye* was already spreading. Bruno had two reasons to be excited, of course. Not only had he formed the loaves that had garnered such rave reviews, but the unqualified success of the bread most likely meant that Bruno now had the new job he desired: the abbey *boulanger*.

Of course, I was also thrilled — or more accurately relieved — but still a touch skeptical. Bruno was too much of a fan to be objective. Soon, though, other reviews started drifting in as we weighed out the flour and made the *poolish* for the next day's loaves. A knock came at the door, and I waved in a monk I hadn't yet met.

"I want to congratulate you," he said in English. "The bread is magnificent."

Even Philippe, who hadn't been impressed with our test loaves, was won over. He was more excited than I'd ever seen him, telling me with great pride that a suggestion had already been floated that they start selling the bread in the abbey gift shop. Bruno quickly put the kibosh on that idea. He knew he had yet to even bake a single loaf on his own. Feeling in an expansive mood, I asked Philippe if he and Bruno could be my guests for a dinner in town to celebrate. I wanted to do something for these fine men, either of whom would give you the hair shirt off his back.

"Thank you so much," Philippe answered. "That's very kind. But we simply cannot." I had figured as much, but it was worth a try. Bruno, I noticed, looked disappointed.

Philippe left Bruno and me to finish up, and it was dark when we left the bakery, matching strides as we crossed the courtyard, bringing the *levain* and *poolish* to the kitchen.

"Look," Bruno said, gesturing with his head toward the living postcard in front of us. A full moon was hanging directly over the refectory, adding its circle of moonlight to the rectangles of light softly glowing through the translucent windows.

We both looked at it in silence. Finally Bruno said, "It's beautiful, isn't it?"

"It's perfect, Bruno. It's perfect."

Day 5: *The Monk, the Baker, and the Atheist*

My last full day at the abbey was a blur of yeast and chant. I attended all seven offices, from Vigils, at 5:30 a.m., to Compline, which ended just before 9:00 p.m., and in between baked seven loaves of bread with Bruno — another batch of a half-dozen *pain de l'Abbaye Saint-Wandrille*, plus the *pain au levain miche* that Bruno wanted to learn.

Bruno was surprised when he heard I was doing the sweet seven.

"I want to see what your life will be like as the baking monk," I explained, another of the half lies I was becoming distressingly comfortable with.

Alone in the bakery for much of that day, Bruno and I discussed the future. Bruno thought he could bake three times a week, and he already had an assistant baker lined up. In my wildest dreams I couldn't have anticipated such success. So perhaps I was feeling a little cocky and just a little too comfortable with my new best friend when I decided to have a little fun, and to let him in on a secret.

"That *levain* you love so much, I told you it's twelve years old, no?"

"Oui."

"That it's from Alaska?"

"Oui."

"That it was given to me by an atheist?"

Bruno froze and looked up, his face contorted in alarm.

Damn! I realized I had made a mistake, had misjudged, had forgotten where I was. What I thought was merely a little irony was a spiritual crisis for this young man. I could see the whole week going down the drain. How incredibly stupid of me! You don't joke about religion with a monk!

"But he's a very good man," I added quickly, frantic to save the situation. "Very generous, very kind, and dedicated to bread. I think he would be happy to know that his *levain* made it here and that the abbey is baking bread again."

Bruno relaxed a bit. "Make sure you tell him his *levain* is in an abbey," he said, with a wry smile.

"Oh, I will. I *will*."

Then Bruno let me in on a little secret of his own, one that, like mine, also threatened the resurrection of the abbey *fournil*. The acceptance of the bread had been almost universal, but not quite. Only one person in the abbey wasn't happy with the bread. Unfortunately it was the abbot. He had trouble with his digestion and didn't like this slightly darker, denser bread. He wanted a baguette.

"I'll leave you the recipe," I told Bruno, wishing I had another day to spend with him. "Baguettes are very easy and quick. In fact, you can make up a big batch once a week and freeze them in plastic bags. Your oven is still nice and warm at dinnertime if it's a baking day, and you just put the baguette from the freezer into the oven. The abbot gets a fresh, warm loaf of white bread. When he breaks it open . . ." I mimed inhaling a loaf of bread, closing my eyes, and smiling. It was easier than continuing in French, which was exhausting. Bruno nodded and laughed. He got the idea. We both knew, if the abbot ain't happy, ain't nobody happy.

My final meal at the abbey featured *moules frites,* a real treat. Steamed mussels and, best of all, more of those great french fries.

When the food was brought out, though, I immediately saw a problem. In the best of circumstances — say, quiche — it was a challenge to eat enough before the food was whisked away. How on earth would I ever eat enough labor-intensive baby mussels to fill my growling stomach? As I dug the little mollusks out with my dinner fork, growing more frustrated with each shell, I glanced at the long table across from me and realized I was doing it all wrong. The monks had solved this problem. Most used half a shell to scoop out the mussels, far more efficient than my attempts to pry them out with a fork, but a few dropped all niceties altogether and were eagerly slurping them right out of the shells. Now, that was *really* efficient.

I adopted the shell-scoop method, but what I really wanted was more of those *frites*. Alpine Hiker, the collar of his jacket almost covering his mouth, was still seated to my left, and the plate of *frites* was to his left, so near, yet so far. He failed to notice that my plate was empty (violating one of the unwritten rules of abbey dining — scratch that, it *is* written, in the Benedictine Rule, which clearly states that "the brothers shall serve the needs of one another, so no one needs ask for anything"). So, feeling rather at home now, and with little to lose, I swallowed hard, leaned over, and broke the rule of silence while the abbot burned rubber, whispering, "Frites, s'il vous plaît." Lightning did not strike, no one hustled over to escort me out, and I got to enjoy more *frites* before it came time to lay the napkin ring on top of my by now well-soiled napkin. Right on cue the *père hôtelier* snatched it up, marched the length of the hall, and dropped it into the drawer with a clink.

After dinner, back in my room and tired from a day of baking and bowing, I was half-undressed when I happened to glance at the abbey schedule under the clear desk protector. I still had one more office to attend. I quickly bundled up and headed to the church for Compline, the only office I hadn't been to yet. Operating in true monk fashion now, I was late, and the service had already started. Even for this church, it was dark, so dark I could hardly see where I was walking as I groped my way to the front pew. The only light glowed dimly from behind the altar. As my eyes adjusted, I could make out the monks in the choir, faces hidden deep inside their hoods — Compline being the only service during which they wore their cowls. It was a thoroughly spooky, medieval scene. And about to become spookier. As usual, my eyes drifted up to the life-size, gold crucifix hanging above the altar.

It was swaying.

I looked around but didn't see a source of moving air. All the church doors were closed, and there were no electric fans in sight.

Yet, dear Mother of God, it was swaying! Almost imperceptibly, but back and forth ever so slightly, as if Christ were on a playground swing, not a cross. Or was it? Was I hallucinating? My eyes fixed on the cross, I tried to find a reference point behind it, a mark on the wall, so that I could determine whether the cross was swaying or I was, but the church was too dark. Disturbed, I needed something familiar to look at. I lowered my eyes to the choir and sought out Bruno, towering above the others. I could only make out his shadowy silhouette. His face hidden deep in the recesses of his hood, he was no longer my new best friend, his ear-to-ear grin lighting up the *fournil*. He was a stranger — unfamiliar, unfathomable, unapproachable. I shivered. I was back in the cold darkness of an earlier century.

It was time to go home.

Day 6: *Pain Surprise*

I woke to unexpected good news. My airline seat had been miraculously upgraded to business class. It looked to be a relaxing, easy trip home today. Before packing, though, I wanted to have breakfast and attend Lauds because, mindful of the selfish prayer I had uttered on my first day here, I had some unfinished business in church. A surprise treat awaited in the guest kitchen, where someone — presumably Bruno — had left half of the *pain au levain miche* we'd made the previous day, turned on its cut end, just as I had instructed on my first day. I smiled. When I turned the bread over, I was stunned at the beautiful, open crumb and the distinctly alveolar structure. This was my bread? I had never baked a loaf that looked like this.

I cut a slice, the knife leaving a yeasty fresh-bread aroma in its wake, and took a bite. The bread bit back, announcing its presence, filling my mouth, my mind, my soul, with a medley of flavors and textures. The crumb was firm but yielding, with suggestions of rye and whole wheat, and just enough *levain*. I let the bread play on my tongue, which delighted in finding and poking through the generous holes, the vacuum of life left from the wild yeast's frenetic anaerobic activity as, fueled by the intense heat of the abbey oven, it furiously metabolized, leaving little contrails of gas until, at about 125 degrees Fahrenheit, it exhaled its last breath.

I bit into the dark brown crust, crackly but not overly hard, remarkably and naturally sweet and complex, the product of those Maillard reactions I'd been seeking. I took another bite. And another. And one more, just to be sure. This was the best bread I'd ever tasted.

I had baked the perfect loaf.

The quest was over. Yet I felt cheated — there was no one to celebrate with. In fact, I was four thousand miles away from anyone who could even appreciate what this meant. Then I remembered where I was and realized that this was an occasion for contemplation and reflection, not hugs, noisy shouts, and champagne. I did at least get the pealing of bells, although they were intended for Lauds, not me. I took a photograph of the bread and scurried to the church one last time.

Afterward I'd expected to meet only Bruno in the bakery, but a small farewell committee awaited me: Bruno and Philippe, of course, but also the prior, Jean-Charles, and the monk whose pocket knife had opened our first sack of flour what seemed like ages ago. I returned Bruno's computer flash drive with all of the recipes on it, including one I'd written up the previous night for baguettes. Jean-Charles then made a short, gracious speech, thanking me, and presented me with a wrapped gift, "something for the eyes and something for the ears," which turned out to be a gorgeous book of photographs of the abbey and a CD, recorded at Saint-Wandrille, of Gregorian chant.

In turn, I thanked Jean-Charles for this unforgettable experience, for allowing an American amateur baker to bake in their *fournil* and stay at this *abbaye magnifique*. Jean-Charles, embarrassed at my effusiveness (or perhaps my French — who knows what I really said), laughed. The festivities were cut short by some bad news: *la grève* had returned, with scattered strikes wreaking havoc with rail traffic into Paris, and trains running intermittently and off-schedule. They wanted to rush me to the station and an earlier train. I had ten minutes to pack.

Saying my good-byes quickly, I almost missed Bruno, my dear apprentice, shyly standing back. "Oh, Bruno!" I laughed, returning. He put out his hand. I shook it, then spontaneously embraced and kissed him, French-style, on each cheek. "Bonne chance, mon ami," I whispered in his ear.

I may have arrived by taxi, but I was leaving by chauffeur. Philippe drove me to the station in the abbey's little car, winding past pastures and farms as I nervously glanced at my watch. Along the way, we reflected a bit on the week.

"Bread is important to the church as a symbol, no?" I said.

"Bread *is* the church," Philippe said as we pulled into the train station nearly simultaneously with what would turn out to be the last train into Paris until evening, delivering me from the abbey in the same dramatic fashion in which I'd arrived.

With one last wave to Philippe, I ran aboard with my bags. As the train pulled out of the station, out of Normandy, out of the Middle Ages, I collapsed into a seat.

And wept.

VII.
Compline

Compline (from the Latin which means
"to complete") marks the completion of our day
and leads back into the darkness of the night,
but a darkness different from that of vigils.
This is the darkness of God's
mysterious presence.

What Would Bruno Do?

If my first days in the Abbey had been a period of depression, the
unwinding process, after I had left, was ten times worse.
— Patrick Leigh Fermor, *A Time to Keep Silence*

Weight: 196 pounds
Bread bookshelf weight: 64 pounds

To say I experienced a rough reentry back to earth is putting it mildly. I returned with the grace of astronaut Gus Grissom, whose *Mercury* capsule sank in the Atlantic when he allegedly panicked and prematurely blew off the door of his spacecraft while bobbing in the waves. No one was hurt, but no one was happy, either.

I had read of Patrick Leigh Fermor's difficulties in readjusting to outside life, but he had spent weeks at the abbey, and I a mere five days, so the moodiness and depression that followed caught me off-guard.

Arriving home on a Tuesday night, I went to work on Wednesday. That was a mistake. I called in sick Thursday and Friday, giving myself a four-day weekend. I needed time to think, to find my center of gravity, to understand what had happened in those five extraordinary days.

I hardly talked. I slept a great deal and, when in the kitchen, listened to the CD of Gregorian chant the abbey had recorded. I thought I recognized some voices. I could tell Anne was worried.

Finally I felt I had to broach the subject. I cleared my throat as we sat alone at the kitchen table. "I'm having some readjustment problems," I finally said.

She laughed nervously. "No kidding."

That was the end of the conversation. I had nothing to add.

The next day, Anne leafed through the book of photographs of Saint-Wandrille that I'd been given, looking for clues, and asked, "If you're ready to talk about it — what is it about the abbey that you miss? It looks like such a peaceful place in the photographs."

"I'm not ready to talk about it."

We sat in silence. It wasn't that I didn't want to talk about it. I just didn't know what to say. I considered trying to describe an image I'd had while sitting on a wall my last afternoon at Saint-Wandrille, an image I'd not been able to shake, but one so odd I hesitate to mention it even now.

It was of a dessert plate, of all things, covered with white chocolate sauce, over which lay a perfect circle of dark chocolate drawn from a chef's squeeze bottle. If you watch cooking shows, you already know what happened next: a disembodied hand bearing a knife descended and, with a quick stroke, pulled the circle outward at one point, disrupting the perfect arc, before withdrawing. Silently recalling that image, I held back tears. Finally I got up and left. I wanted to be alone.

Over the next few days, I became aware that the sharpening of senses I'd experienced while at Saint-Wandrille had remained. For the first time, I heard the drone of the overhead ventilation as I received physical therapy on my back (which had been pain free at the abbey but was now aching again). I noticed how a radio host signed off, not with the usual "Have a good day," but with "Make it a good day," which I must've heard a thousand times before, yet had never before *heard*. I found it very appealing. The voice of a yardman, a Haitian immigrant, in the lumberyard who acknowledged a two-dollar tip with "God bless you," instead of "Thank you," reverberated with me for days.

My mind wandered down previously unvisited corridors. Still in my first week back, while waiting with Anne in the eye doctor's office, I saw a poster with a diagram of the human eye. "Did you ever wonder," I asked when she returned from being dilated, "what kind of species might have evolved if there were no eyes? Vision is just an illusion, the result of light bouncing off an object and our eyes and brains making sense of it. But strictly speaking, it's not necessary for intelligent life."

"Well, there's slugs," she said, to satisfy me.

"Yes, and deep-sea fish and lower forms of life, like microscopic organisms, but that's because any animals that evolved with sight crowded out those without. But if no one had the advantage of sight, would there still have been higher forms of life that create music and poetry? And what form would that life have taken?"

Anne opened up the newspaper, no doubt wondering how long this business was going to last and when the old me was going to return. Problem was, I was becoming kind of comfortable with the new me.

"Vision," I repeated, "is an illusion."

The first crack in the thin crust that separated me from my old life came as I lay in bed early one morning, half-asleep, listening to the radio, undecided if I was going to the office or not. I'd dreamed about the abbey again, as I would every single night for the first six days I was home. (The dreams stopped, weirdly but appropriately enough, on the seventh night.) The topic of this morning's radio stargazing feature was a noteworthy but regular phenomenon in the heavens. Venus, the host explained, was rising in the east four hours before the sun, a particularly advantageous circumstance that made it glow particularly bright.

My eyes flew open, suddenly wide and alert. Of course, I'd known that my morning star — that brilliant star I had seen from the abbey — had an astronomical explanation, but I'd been clinging to the slim hope that it had been something, however improbably, cooked up for me. The fact that it was a regularly occurring phenomenon diminished its impact, making me wonder if the entire week had been, not a spiritual experience, but an illusion that my subconscious, sensing the need for a good show, had created.

The next crack in the crust shattered it to crumbs, when I received an e-mail from Brother Philippe, thanking me and inquiring about my trip home.

"The Father Abbot will ask the community on Monday evening if we want to continue making our own bread or not," he added. What? I thought it was a done deal, that the bread was a smash, Prior Jean-Charles was onboard, and if Bruno could throw together a decent baguette once in a while, the abbot would be happy. This sudden uncertainty made me jittery and shocked me back to my old self.

"Can you believe this?" I fumed to Anne. "They're putting it up to a vote? I travel eight thousand miles for them, and these overgrown choirboys are going to have a meeting and take a vote? Isn't anyone in charge there?"

I immediately regretted "overgrown choirboys," especially since Philippe, one of those choirboys, had added, "I will pray for you." I had wanted to hold on to that abbey feeling and was finding out just how difficult that was going to be. Less than a week after I'd left, it seemed that what happened in the abbey did in fact stay in the abbey. Saddened and ashamed by my outburst, I resolved at least to try to adopt the temperament of the monks, to ask myself before gritting my teeth over traffic or swearing over a burnt loaf of bread, "How would Bruno react?"

The next day, a handful of teenage French exchange students, including one who coincidentally was staying with us for two weeks, ended up at our house with their American hosts. I'd noticed that our student wasn't too crazy about American food, although she was too polite to say anything. I figured the others might also be missing French food — not to mention home — so I did something totally uncharacteristic for me, something I couldn't have imagined myself doing a month ago: I invited the whole crew to stay for dinner.

After digging up the remaining leeks in the garden for leek-potato soup, I made six baguettes and an apple tart with apples picked from our orchard. The aroma of baking bread, the flour in my hair, the dough under my fingernails, the challenge of baking without my scale, which I'd left with Bruno, brought me back to this life.

The girls, seven in all, eagerly wolfed down the soup, so busy eating that they hardly spoke. The bread on the table disappeared. Anne sliced some more, which also disappeared. One of the French girls, her eyes wide, looked up at Anne. "You are a good bak-eer," she said in a lovely accent.

Anne pointed to me.

"You?" She was stunned.

I smiled.

She ate another slice. "You are a *very* good bak-eer. This eez very good bread."

I bowed slightly. "Merci beaucoup, mademoiselle."

I saved the remaining two loaves for our student's breakfast each morning. She greatly preferred it to the English muffins we'd been feeding her.

Anne later said, "That was really nice of you to do that. I could tell the girls really appreciated it."

In reality, though, it was an act as selfish as it was thoughtful. For a few minutes, I'd recaptured the spirit of the abbey, where "guests are received as Christ," and, most importantly, found a way to get my crumbling psyche through the weekend.

That evening, Anne and I made love for the first time since my return. It felt good and warm and safe.

WEEK
48

Half-Baked

Fix, sell, or close.

— Former CEO of a major multinational conglomerate

Beep-beep-beep-beep.

"What's that?" Anne asked, coming into the kitchen. "Are you baking?"

"Not anymore."

The oven had shut down, leaving a half-baked two-pound *miche* inside to steam and a two-hundred-pound baker outside to smolder.

A cryptic "F2" flashed on the control panel. I pressed the Off button, which stopped the infernal beeping while I looked up the code in the owner's manual.

"It's a high-temperature warning," I reported.

"How high did you have it?"

"I think Katie needs help with her homework."

"How high did you have it?"

Since returning from the abbey, I'd been preheating the oven to its maximum setting of 550 degrees before steaming the hell out of it, hoping to reproduce that great Saint-Wandrille oven spring, with pretty good results. I hadn't reproduced the perfect *boule* of my last day at the abbey, but the bread had never been better, even though I was using essentially the same recipe I'd used before going to France. There was another mystery as well: I hadn't used parchment paper since watching it vaporize in the abbey's oven, yet the dough never, ever stuck to my rice-flour-dusted peel,* as if (I like to think) it had acquired a certain respect for me.

The oven, however, afforded me no such respect.

Beep-beep-beep-beep, it protested.

"Turn it off," Anne pleaded.

"It *is* off! Shut up!" I screamed.

"Hey!"

"Not you, the oven!" I hit the Off button again. It quieted down, like a baby with a pacifier, but soon started up again.

Beep-beep-beep-beep.

"Oh, for God's sake!" I muttered. "I'll fix you!"

I headed outside.

"What are you going to do?"

"Pull the plug on HAL." I went down to the basement and threw the circuit breaker. HAL went dark. And quiet. For good.

Two days later, our appliance doctor arrived, replaced the probe, collected two hundred dollars, and *then* pronounced the patient dead. The instrument panel was fried, he said (I didn't

---

*I'd switched from cornmeal, as rice flour makes less of a mess in the oven.

dare ask if 550-degree steam could be a factor), and the manu-
facturer no longer made the part. This was, mind you, not some
obscure Scandinavian company, but an American megacorpora-
tion (let's call it, in deference to HAL, "FD") whose celebrity
ex-CEO's motto ("Fix, sell, or close") should be modified, when
it comes to his ephemeral appliances, to simply "Throw away,"
because apparently fixing is not an option when they break.

"What do you mean, they don't make it anymore?" I said to
the repairman. "That oven's brand-new."

"Well, most people wouldn't consider twelve years old
brand —"

"My mother has an oven built in the fifties — the nineteen
fifties! — that she can still get parts for." Which is true. Of
course, on these older units, there are few parts to break. They
don't have timers, they don't have cycles, and most importantly,
they don't have circuit boards, yet they work great. If you stop to
think about it, an oven is probably the simplest appliance in your
home. All it needs is a heating element and the simplest of ther-
mostats, a strip of metal that curls when heated. An oven should
last a hundred years, and could, but that's no good for a company
like FD, so they top the thing off with a wholly unnecessary digital panel whose built-in obsolescence guarantees they can sell you
a replacement every decade or so. Determined to fight the system,
I told the repairman I'd find the part on eBay.

"Look," he said, trying to talk some sense into me, "even if
you can, with labor it's going to cost you as much to fix the oven
as to replace it. And the door needs a new spring. Half your heat
is leaking into the kitchen." As it was, I'd already dropped two
hundred dollars with nothing to show for it, so I gave in. Fortunately we had a second FD oven, a smaller convection unit, also
twelve years old, that I could use in the interim. I'd made bread
in it only once, using the convection mode, and wasn't pleased

with the results. Emotionally as well, it was going to be hard leaving the other oven, whose quirks and nuances I had mastered, this oven that had been my faithful companion these forty-eight weeks. Sometimes, though, you just have to move on.

A *Levain* of My Own

> If I could convince you of just one thing about making bread, it
> would be how little effort it takes to cultivate a sourdough.
> — Daniel Leader, *Local Breads*, 2007

Charlie van Over's *levain* was making great bread, but it was time to create my own personal, local *levain*. The wheat, after all, was local, the water was local, and if I could build a starter from local yeast, I'd literally be feeding on — becoming, in a sense — my environment.

And beginning a tradition. The notion was irresistible. But where to get local wild yeast? Actually yeast is everywhere — in the air we breathe, even in the flour we buy. I thought of just putting a batter of flour and water in the yard and seeing what local flora settled in, but images of spiders and fungi and pollen discouraged me. Then just before leaving for France I happened to read that the haze you see on grapes is actually wild yeast.

I didn't have any grapes, but I had seen something strikingly similar to that haze, more commonly referred to in our household as "that damned haze," since it had to be wiped off each and every backyard apple with a dish towel. For years I had wondered, What on earth *is* that stuff? Pollen? Pollution? A by-product of the apple? It reminded me of the haze that accumulates on the windshield inside a car (which is caused by outgassing from the plastics in the interior).

Thus I had my yeast source, but the problem was that every time I opened a book to learn how to make a *levain* from scratch, the directions were hopelessly confusing and intimidating: feed it every twelve hours, stir every six, discard half, put it in the refrigerator, take it out of the refrigerator, start with rye, switch to wheat, leave open, wrap tightly, watch for bubbles, mark the container so you know when the mixture doubles, and so on. Adding to the confusion was the vocabulary — words such as *chef, seed,* and *barm,* used to describe the various stages of *levain* development.

At the Ritz, however, Chef Didier had made a *levain* with no fuss at all, starting by letting a cut-up apple sit in a bottle of water for three days, then mixing in some flour. It seemed uncomplicated and foolproof. I cut up a nice, hazy apple from the harvest, added the peel of a second for good measure, and dropped it all into a bottle of our good Hudson Valley tap water (which I had first let sit out overnight to dechlorinate). Three days later, I measured out equal weights of apple water and my Indian-stone-ground organic wheat,* covered the bowl with plastic wrap, and waited.

Within twenty-four hours, small bubbles had appeared. I fed

---

*Of which I had only the precious small amount I'd ground in week 37. Having come to the conclusion that the Indians would take back Manhattan before I finished grinding all my wheat with their old grindstone, I'd had half the remaining wheat milled at Bay State and the other half stone-ground in a gas-powered portable stone mill at a farm festival.

the starter with more flour and water, and by the next morning, it was vigorously bubbling away. When I uncovered the plastic, I was greeted with the wonderfully tangy aroma of fermentation. I'd done it! It really was that easy. I fed it again and went off to work.

But what *had* I done? I felt as if I'd created life, which of course I hadn't. I had just encouraged the life that was there to reproduce at an accelerated rate. My starter was a rich mixture of wild yeast varieties (all wild yeast belongs to the species *Saccharomyces exiguous,* a different species from commercial yeast), flour, and the by-products of fermentation: alcohol, carbon dioxide, and an assortment of organic acids. I may not have started life, but I had started a tradition, one that might even outlive me (though I hoped not anytime soon).

Well, there are traditions, and there are traditions. This one appeared fated to be short lived, for upon my return home that evening, although my *levain de la maison Alexande*r had doubled in size, it contained no bubbles, a detail whose significance wouldn't become apparent until later. I unwrapped the plastic, stuck my nose in to inhale that yeasty aroma, and was almost knocked over by a foul, evil smell. I called Anne over to confirm.

"Eeww! Throw it out!" she pleaded, not aware of the emotional attachment I'd already formed to my two-day-old creation. Instead I discarded about two-thirds of it (Anne immediately removed the garbage bag from the house, apparently fearing that the thing might overwhelm us à la friendship bread) and fed it with fresh flour and water.

What happened? How had it gone from exquisite to foul in only eight hours? It wasn't until the next morning, in the shower (where I do some of my best thinking), that I realized something truly startling: I had M. Bigo's problem, the very same one that led Louis Pasteur down the road to the discovery of the chemistry of yeast! My *levain* wasn't just wild yeast; it was wild yeast and bacteria, and it is the bacteria that give sourdough breads their characteristic sourness. But over the past few hours, the bacteria had flourished, choking out the yeast, which explained the absence of bubbles, not to mention the foul smell.

My mind moved forward a hundred or so years from Pasteur to the Lallemand yeast factory in Montreal and the lessons I'd learned there. The trick in producing commercial yeast is in creating an environment that is more conducive to yeast than to bacteria. That means plenty of oxygen. I'd kept my starter tightly covered, partly because I'd seen fruit flies hovering in the vicinity, and after all, I'd figured, yeast thrives in an anaerobic environment.

I had forgotten the most important lesson to be learned from Lallemand: yeast undergoes fermentation, the kind desirable for bread, in the absence of oxygen, but to make it thrive — that is, reproduce, which is exactly what building your *levain* is all about — it needs plenty of oxygen. How could I have forgotten the deafening roar of the blowers in the yeast factory? My tightly wrapped, oxygen-starved bowl was not conducive to yeast reproduction but, like M. Bigo's, was quite receptive to bacteria.

Throwing on my bathrobe, I ran down to the kitchen, where I again discarded most of the sour-smelling starter, added fresh flour, and whipped vigorously, trying to introduce oxygen. Then, to allow some oxygen in, I covered it with a screen instead of plastic wrap. If a couple of fruit flies got in, well, that's life. I wasn't giving up yet. I owed it to Leeuwenhoek and Pasteur to see this thing through. After several more days of stirring, discarding, and refreshing, wondering if I was throwing good flour after bad, I opened the container and was greeted with the smell of ethyl alcohol. The patient had survived. And I had a *levain* of my own.

Cracked

Right now I'm having amnesia and déjà vu at the same time.
— Stephen Wright

Beep-beep-beep-beep.

Oh, no. I couldn't believe it. Was I having déjà vu?

Beep-beep-beep-beep.

The word "Probe" flashed on the oven's instrument panel, although I wasn't even using the meat probe. I turned off the oven. Still, the beeping continued.

Anne came into the kitchen and glared.

"Five hundred fifty," I volunteered sheepishly before she could ask.

At least this time, when oven number two cooled down, it stopped beeping and was still usable — as long as I stayed under 475 degrees — which was a good thing, because not only was I down to my last oven, but it turned out that this oven was making better bread than the oven I'd destroyed. I hoped to keep this one for a very long time.

Anne was baking a meat loaf a few days later, when she noticed something odd about the glass window set into the oven door. "How long has this glass been cracked?" A thick fissure ran the entire length of the window, most likely a result of cold water from my plant mister striking very hot glass. I would never use a mister again, switching to pouring a cup of water into a preheated cast iron frying pan set below the baking stone. As it turned out, this worked better, anyway. Still, the damage was done.

Anne asked if we could replace the window in this twelve-year-old oven.

"I doubt it." I pointed to the brand label: FD.*

It so happened that we had a tax meeting with Anne's accountant the next morning, during which I was ruing the fact that my bread baking had destroyed two ovens. His jaw dropped when I mentioned I'd been preheating to 550 degrees.

"But the thermostat goes up to five hundred fifty!" I protested. "Why would they let you set the oven to five hundred fifty if it destroys it?"

"The speedometer on my wife's Saab goes to a hundred fifty," he shot back. "That doesn't mean she should drive that fast!"

Good point.

All this oven carnage reminded me that, with winter fast approaching, I had a half-finished clay oven in the garden. With the gift of a rare late-autumn day in the upper sixties, it was now or never. I knew such work was risky, given my still-hurting back, but I would move carefully and take frequent rests. And schedule physical therapy for the next morning.

We had done this next part at the workshop in Maine, and it seemed fairly straightforward: Build a dome out of firmly packed wet sand, then mix up a batch of clay and sand and build up a four-inch layer — the oven wall — over the form. Let it dry overnight, cut out a door, scoop out the sand, and light a fire. According to Kiko Denzer's book, "This can easily be completed in half a day."

---

*In fairness to FD, I should point out that we were able to obtain a replacement window for a reasonable price.

Not in my book. I started at nine thirty with five hundred pounds of purchased (I'd wised up by now) sand — more, I thought, than I needed, but I didn't want to take the chance of running out in the middle of the project — and probably about four hundred pounds of the clayey soil that Zach and I had dug from the foundation. After completing the firebrick base, I dumped out the first seventy-pound bag of sand and started to form a dome. Soon I'd dumped out a second bag. And a third. And half the fourth, until ninety minutes and three hundred pounds of sand later, I'd finally reached the tip of the sixteen-inch stick I'd stuck in the center.

I stood back to admire my work. It was a mess, a badly lopsided hemisphere, bringing a flood of emotions and bad memories of elementary school art class. Taking a short piece of a two-by-four, I started whacking it around, pushing in the high spots, adding sand to the low, for about twenty minutes, until I finally had something that resembled a less imperfect hemisphere.

Time to mix clay. I had spurned getting my toes dirty at clay-oven boot camp, but now, on this warm November day, with an aching back, mixing by foot seemed an excellent alternative to using a backbreaking hoe. I changed into shorts, peeled off my shoes and socks, and jumped in. It was in fact quite effective — especially if you occasionally grabbed each side of the tarp and pulled it toward you, rolling over the mix of clay, sand, and water — and just a little bit fun, which I'd always suspected, as long as no one else was stepping on you. It was less fun to actually build the oven, going round and round the sand form, patting on successive inch-high globs of clay, four inches thick, working my way up the igloo, going through bucketfuls of the stuff at an astounding rate.

The sun was disappearing behind the mountains as I patted the last piece of mud into place. I lay back on the grass and closed my eyes, wondering how I ever got suckered into this lamebrain project. As much as I wanted to blame Kiko, I hadn't been seduced by him or even the brick oven at Bobolink. I was facing a force far more powerful, one that seemed at times as threatening as it was benevolent, stronger and more enduring than anything I had ever encountered.

I'm speaking, of course, of bread.

WEEK
51

Let Them Eat . . . Brioche?

Whenever weighty matters are to be transacted in the monastery,
let the Abbot call together the whole community, and make
known the matter which is to be considered.
— *The Rule of Saint Benedict,* ca. 530

Still no news from the abbey. I stayed in denial as long as I could, reminding myself that an ancient abbey moves slowly, but weeks after the supposed date of the vote, I had to face reality: the abbey would not be reopening the bakery. Most likely, after the initial excitement had worn off, cooler heads had prevailed, and they had realized how difficult it would be for a novice baker to supply three dozen monks with their daily bread. It was, after all, quite a commitment. I tried to be stoic about it. I'd given it my best shot, and that was all I could do.

Then I woke to this e-mail:

Dear William,

The news came yesterday evening in the chapter room after Vesper. The father Abbot announce that a great majority of the community prefer our own bread. So we will re-make our own bread but progressively that means for breakfast at the beginning and a bit more after. The Abbot want to take care of father Bruno who is nominate officially baker!

So you succeeded in your mission. Thank you very much!!! I think it would be a good day for you, isn't it!

I still keep you in my prayers with all your family.

—Fr. Philippe

It took a moment to sink in. The monks had taken a vote and preferred my bread to the bread of the French *boulangerie* in town.

I soon heard from Bruno as well.

"The father abbot has finally decided to permit the return of bread making. I am very happy," he wrote in French. I could hear his exasperation in the word *finally.*

"The abbey is a novel," he added, hinting at the intrigue behind the abbey walls, leaving me wanting to hear more. He closed by saying that I was in his prayers.

"I now have two monks praying for me daily," I joked to Anne. "I'm in clover!"

Bruno's note also included a request: Did I have recipes for brioche and croissants? Croissants again? What was with the damned croissants?

"Dad, I told you!" Katie cried when I showed her the note.

"Katie, do you have any idea how difficult croissants are to make? All those layers of butter and paper-thin dough? It takes years of practice. I've had, like, three good croissants in my entire life, and two of them were in Paris."

I wrote Bruno, telling him that croissants were quite challenging but that I would try some brioche recipes this weekend and
get back to him. You have to give the guy credit. He was nothing
if not ambitious.

His request for brioche, a rich (but not sweet) bread made
with butter and eggs, baffled me a bit, though. I've never understood the attraction of this egg bread. It is, however, a classic
French bread, immortalized in Marie Antoinette's alleged cal-
lous response to the starving masses' demand for bread, "Qu'ils
mangent de la brioche," or "Let them eat brioche."

Hang on a second — shouldn't that be "Let them eat *cake*"?
Only in this country, where brioche was long ago mistranslated
as "cake," an error that probably resulted from the fact that brioche was unknown in America two centuries ago. It's not exactly
commonplace even today. You can be quite certain that Marie
Antoinette knew her cake from her bread, and had she wanted
to say "cake," she'd have said "gâteau," not "brioche," if she ever
said any of this to begin with, which is doubtful, since similar
remarks ("Let them eat crust") had been ascribed to various unpopular royalty decades before the queen's birth.

In any event, with a host of other great breads available, I
wondered out loud why Bruno wanted to make brioche. Anne
pointed out that I didn't grow up with brioche, and who knew
what kind of hardwired memories it held for Bruno and the other
monks: Was it a special bread eaten only on Sundays? Would it
remind him of his mother or father? Bread, as I was learning, is
a powerful stimulus, capable of probing deep into the subconscious, if not into genetic memory.

I thought about Bruno's choosing to leave home at just
eighteen to live the sequestered life of a monk, making me
wonder what kind of home life he'd had up to then. Home . . .

Christmas . . . I suddenly realized Christmas was approaching. Bruno probably wanted to make brioche for Christmas!

Rather than delay any further, I located two brioche recipes, one that used equal parts flour and butter, and a more modest one with half the butter, mindful that butter was such a luxury at the abbey that it was only served with bread on Sundays. Both came out well, so I sat down with my online French-English dictionary and painstakingly translated as best I could. Then came the really hard part: composing an e-mail. Not only because, with an American keyboard, it takes forever to insert the accents that seem to appear in every other French word, but because I faced a real crisis: Do I use the *vous* form or the *tu* form in addressing Bruno — the formal or the familiar?

The entire time I was at the abbey, I'd been addressing him as "vous." This was partly out of respect for a monk and partly because this form was easier for me to conjugate, having had more practice. Traveling in a foreign country among strangers, you don't get many opportunities to use the familiar. On the other hand, I had kissed him. Surely there must be some rule that once you've kissed a person of the same sex, you can use the *tu* form. Bruno, however, in his note, had addressed me as "vous." Yet that might be because in a brief note I'd sent on returning home, I'd used the formal, and he was taking my lead. Argghhh! I pondered this *vous/tu* business for a good half hour, marveling (and frustrated) that the French never seem even to give it a thought; it just comes naturally.

Sticking with *vous* was the safer path, but it just felt wrong. I took a chance and went with the familiar, addressing this young monk as "tu." I'd find out whether I'd blundered or not when he replied.

Finally I did something I should've done earlier, when I sent my Moroccan friend Petit Ali a richly illustrated English dictionary, but I'd never thought of it. I ordered a French-language bread-making book for Bruno, one written by the great rue Monge baker Eric Kayser, with a card wishing Bruno a *joyeux Noël*.

WEEK
52

The Perfect Future in the Present

The perfect is the enemy of the good.
— *Voltaire*

It was twenty-three degrees and snowing when I went outside to light a fire. I pulled a lawn chair close to steal some warmth, but the clay oven was stingy, absorbing every kilocalorie that the fledgling fire inside generated. I really couldn't complain — this was the entire point, to transfer heat from burning wood to a large thermal mass of clay and brick, which would in turn transfer it to a mound of dough, transforming it into bread long after the fire itself had died out.

I hadn't planned on doing this in the middle of winter, and certainly not in snow, but my year of baking was remarkably, suddenly, and almost too soon down to its final weekend. What had started out as an experiment had become routine, then ephemeral. Before it ended, however, I had one last mission to accomplish.

As I sat outside in the snow, tending the fire, I heard a familiar birdcall, one I hadn't heard in months: "Wheat-eater, wheat-eater, wheat-eater, *wheat*!" He was back. In the middle of winter! Had my conscientious pal returned early for the event? I welcomed him, perched in the tree above me to see his wheat, finally, turned into bread.

I should've kept the sheet metal firing door in place, but I needed to see the fire, burning strongly now in its second hour. Watching the orange and yellow flames twist and dance their mesmerizing ballet, it seemed that what I was about to do was a miracle, as much a miracle as fire itself. Seeds of grass, wild microorganisms, and water were about to become bread. This is not anything that could happen in nature. A strike of lightning would turn a primeval swamp of amino acids into Jerry Lewis before wheat seeds left on their own would become bread. Bread happens only through the intervention of humans.

I'd planted seeds of grass, harvested and cleaned them, and crushed the resulting grain into flour. To leaven the bread, I'd nurtured a colony of wild microorganisms that had landed on my apple trees on their way to somewhere else. I'd vigorously worked the flour and water with my hands to coax the long, tangled gluten molecules to unwind. And finally, this oven, this oven that had been such a source of exasperation and pain, was about to perform the final step, providing the heat to transform the grass known as wheat into bread.

Fire, clay, grass. I felt primitive, and I felt good.

And not so good. Sitting in the freezing temperatures aggravated the pain in my back, still aching from building the oven, reminding me of the tribulations of the past year. In addition, I'd reawakened a hernia, broken not one but two ovens, moved out of my marital bed, and suffered food poisoning in Morocco, from which I had only recently fully recovered. In search of the perfect loaf, in search of understanding the miracle of bread, I'd driven hundreds of miles to visit yeast factories and flour mills, flown thousands of miles to study in Paris and bake in Africa. Yet my bread, although very good and vastly improved since the first week, never, except for the one mystical moment at the abbey, reached the mantle of perfection that I'd aimed for.

In Nathaniel Hawthorne's 1843 story "The Birthmark," one small imperfection — a birthmark in the shape of a hand — on the face of Aylmer's otherwise perfect wife starts to drive him crazy, to the point where he concocts a strong but dangerous potion that he believes will erase the blemish. His wife, Georgiana, to please her obsessed husband, agrees to drink the liquid, and in fact it works. Her birthmark starts to fade. And as the last trace of it vanishes, she reaches for one brief moment the pinnacle of perfection — and dies (though not before getting in a last rebuke at her unappreciative husband). Hawthorne ends the story this way: "He failed to look beyond the shadowy scope of time, and, living once for all in eternity, to find the perfect future in the present."

Novelists, by convention, aren't allowed to do this anymore — that is, speak directly to the reader and tell him what he's supposed to have learned.* Memoirists, I'm not so sure about. Anyway, what a superb phrase. I think that may be exactly what the monks at Saint-Wandrille are up to, focusing on the perfect future in the present of their shadowy scope of time.

Since returning from the abbey, I'd stopped tinkering with my recipe. Not only had I recognized the futility of trying to reproduce the sublime *boule* I'd made in Normandy, but I'd realized something far more important: it didn't matter. The goal had yielded to the process. Freed from the shackles of perfection,

---

*Which is a shame; it made writing term papers so much easier.

I'd spent the past few weeks actually having fun in the kitchen, maybe really for the first time. I made pizzas and baguettes. For breakfast one morning I made *ebelskiver,* a spherical, leavened, stuffed pancake from Denmark. I still baked peasant bread more often than not, to have in the house for breakfast or to bring to friends, or simply because fresh bread had become part of our diet and we missed it when it wasn't there. I'd also switched from a *boule* to a *bâtard* — yes, that was another prejudice I'd left behind in Saint-Wandrille, that peasant bread could only be a *boule.* The *bâtards* were even occasionally dotted with some gas pockets, and they seemed to have more flavor as well, possibly because the proximity of the crust to the interior allowed for greater exchange of those Maillard compounds between crust and crumb. I had also come to appreciate (apologies to Philippe, for he was right all along) the fact that in a *bâtard,* all the slices were the same size.

At high noon, the snow falling heavily now, both the dough and the oven seemed ready, and as my family gathered around the oven, I slipped the *bâtard* — made with my own hand-ground wheat, *levain* from yeast in my orchard, and Hudson Valley water — into an oven fueled by my apple branches.

I could legitimately say I was baking like an Egyptian.

Although Egyptians were no doubt more skilled at building fires. Concerned about generating enough heat on this snowy day, I'd overdone it. We could've melted steel ingots in that oven, which by now was more suited to glassblowing than baking. The dough cooked too quickly, charring on the outside. But no matter. I pulled it out, hearing the crust crackle and pop in the cold air, a sound I hadn't heard since the abbey.

"Listen, it's singing!" I cried, delighted, echoing Lindsay's words at Bobolink Dairy.

"Is that a good thing?" Katie asked.

"Oh, yes. That's a very good thing."

There was one other "very good thing," also a very big surprise. My backyard wheat, so low in gluten that it appeared to be soft wheat to the technicians at Bay State Milling who'd analyzed it, made fine bread, especially the half I'd stone-ground, whether in the clay oven or the electric. So much so that Anne, whose memory was apparently growing even shorter than mine, asked if I was going to grow wheat again this year!

"Only if you buy me a combine for Christmas," I answered.

After the bread had cooled, I opened a bottle of wine (French, of course) and proposed a toast, which came out sounding more like a benediction than I'd intended. "To our ancestors, and their ancestors, and their ancestors before them, who for six thousand years survived on this bread that we're about to eat."

As I sliced the loaf, I was acutely aware that across the Atlantic Ocean, the monks at Saint-Wandrille were also just sitting down to break bread for their evening meal — it was Sunday, so they'd have butter — and I added a silent toast to Bruno. While we ate bread and drank wine, a ritual nearly as old as civilization itself, Anne asked, "So, dear, what have you learned over the past year?"

Let's see . . .

Bread in a healthy diet doesn't make you fat.

Too much bread, washed down with wine, does.

The only thing more unsettling than having your faith shaken is having your lack of faith shaken.

Use a *levain*.

Do not undertake any project that promises it can be completed "in a weekend."

Do not drink the water in Morocco. Or the tea, or the coffee. In fact, you might think about skipping Morocco altogether. I hear Barbados is nice this time of year.

Trust strangers. Well, some. Only those that you can trust.

Choose one thing you care about and resolve to do it well. Whether you succeed or not, you will be the better for the effort.

Bread is life.

I should've added, "Monks use e-mail." Just before Christmas I'd received a note from Bruno:

> I do not know how to thank you for your kindness! I had not received a Christmas present since entering the monastery. I found a bit of the joy of my childhood! I do not know how to say thank you, I have nothing else to offer you except my friendship and my prayers.

His first Christmas present since entering the monastery . . . I'd read those words over and over again. Poor soul. Poor blessed, fortunate soul. He had, by the way, used the *tu* form.

I was even less prepared for Katie's question. "So, Dad, are you going to bake bread next week?"

What *was* I going to do next week? And the week after that, and the week after that? The year that had started so slowly had gone by so quickly. So much seemed unanswered, undone. I had only scratched the crust of bread, only begun to understand the possibilities in bread and in the baker. It didn't feel like the *end* of anything. It felt like a middle, or maybe even a beginning.

On the other hand, I was greatly looking forward to some freedom on weekends, to not having to plan a Saturday or Sunday around a five-hour fermentation and a two-hour rise, followed by a one-hour bake, to being able to work in the garden, or go to the market, or, yes, even have afternoon sex without scheduling it around the anaerobic respiration of a one-celled organism. I was ready to have my old aerobic life back.

"Dad?"

"Gee, I don't know, Katie," I finally answered. "I guess I'll see how I feel."

She and Anne both tried to hide their disappointment, but my answer had left the kitchen as deflated, dense, and cheerless as one of my early loaves.

"But I was wondering," I continued. "Do you think you might like some croissants?"

Recipes

A Note about the Recipes

The recipes that follow specify measurements in grams. If you have to ask why, you skipped week 14 ("Metric Madness"). Go ahead, read it now; I'll wait . . . I suppose I could buckle under to convention and provide (shudder) imperial volume equivalents, but trust me, you're far better off investing in a twenty-five-dollar digital kitchen scale. While you're at it, pick up a pizza stone, and you'll be ready to make the best bread you've ever tasted. *Bon appétit!*

Building a *Levain*

To paraphrase the baker and author Daniel Leader: if I could convince you of one thing, it's to bake with a *levain*. Furthermore, if you want to use any of the following recipes, you'll have no choice. Here's how I made mine. Other methods can be found in several of the bread cookbooks listed in the bibliography.

2 apples	350 grams all-purpose or bread flower
1 quart water	50 grams whole wheat flour

Prepare the apple water:

1. Let 1 quart of tap water sit out overnight to remove any chlorine.
2. Look for a hazy apple, preferably from a farm stand (the haze is wild yeast). Cut the apple into 1-inch chunks and

place, along with the peel of a second apple, into a container with 1 cup of the water. (Cover and reserve the remaining water for later.)

3. Let the apple and water sit covered, at room temperature, for 3 days, stirring daily. The mixture should be foaming a bit and should smell somewhat like cider by the third day.

Build the levain:

DAY 1

4. Combine 50 grams of whole wheat flour with 350 grams un-bleached all-purpose or bread flour (the additional protein in bread flour may be beneficial for the early starter).

5. Measure out 150 grams of the apple water through a fine strainer and add 150 grams of the flour mixture (you'll use the rest of the flour later). Whip vigorously with a whisk, scrape down the sides, and cover with a screen (a frying pan spatter screen is ideal) or cheesecloth.

6. Leave the *levain* at room temperature, whipping every few hours to incorporate air. It is important to keep the starter aerated during the first few days.

DAY 2

Add 75 grams of the reserved tap water and 75 grams of the flour mixture, whip, and leave at room temperature, covered as before, for another 24 hours, again whisking occasionally. You should see bubbles starting to form and the mixture increasing in bulk.

DAY 3

7. Transfer the *levain* to a clean 2-quart container. Avoid transferring any of the dried bits from the sides of the old container.

8. Add 75 grams each of the reserved flour and tap water, whip, and cover as before.

9. If at any point in this process the *levain* starts to smell a bit funky, discard half, replace with equal parts (by weight) flour and water, and whip more frequently. If the *levain* seems limp (not rising and bubbling), increase the frequency of feedings.

DAY 4

10. Feed the *levian* once again with the remaining 100 grams of flour and 100 grams water and let it sit at room temperature for 2 to 3 hours, and your *levain* should be ready for use, although it will continue to develop flavor over the next few weeks. Follow the care and feeding directions below.

Care and feeding of your levain:

11. Store the *levain* in a covered container in the refrigerator.

12. For the first few weeks, feed twice a week as described in the next step; afterward a weekly feeding is sufficient.

13. To feed, stir thoroughly and discard about 250 grams of *levain*. Replace with 125 grams water (straight from the tap is fine if your water isn't too chlorinated) and 125 grams flour (either unbleached bread or all-purpose) and stir well. Leave the lid ajar (so gases can escape) at room temperature for 2 to 4 hours before tightly covering the *levain* and returning it to the refrigerator.

14. If you bake regularly, feeding is simply part of preparing the *levain* for the bread, and no other feeding is necessary. You should always feed the *levain* several hours or the night before making bread, so replenish with the amount of *levain* the recipe calls for and you will maintain a constant supply of fresh *levain* with no effort.

15. Occasionally clean out your container with hot water (never soap) to remove the crud that forms on the sides.
16. If you want a stronger *levain,* leave it out overnight once in a while and feed with smaller "meals."
17. You may see a puddle of liquid forming on top, a product of fermentation. It can simply be stirred back in, but when it accumulates too much, I like to pour it off. Weigh your *levain* beforehand and replace the discarded liquid with the same amount of water and flour (in a ratio of about 3 parts water to 1 part flour). Then feed as usual.

Peasant Bread
(*Pain de Campagne*)

For the *levain:*
130 grams all-purpose flour   130 grams water

For the dough:
260 grams *levain*   ⅛ teaspoon instant yeast (also
400 grams unbleached   called bread-machine, fast-acting,
   all-purpose or bread flour   or RapidRise yeast)
60 grams whole wheat flour   292 grams water (at room
30 grams whole rye flour   temperature)
13 grams salt

1. At least 2 hours before beginning (you can do this the night before), feed the *levain* as follows: Remove from the refrigerator and add equal parts flour and room-temperature water (I use about 130 grams each, which replenishes what I'll be using in the bread). Stir well, incorporating oxygen, and leave on the countertop with the cover slightly ajar. The starter should be bubbling and lively when you begin your bread.

2. Place a large mixing bowl on a kitchen scale and add each ingredient in turn, using the Tare button to zero out the scale between additions. Mix thoroughly with a wet hand until the dough is homogenous. Cover and leave the dough to *autolyse* for about 25 minutes.

3. Remove the dough to an unfloured countertop and knead by hand for 7 to 9 minutes (or if you insist, you can use a stand mixer with a dough hook for 2 to 3 minutes) until the dough is elastic and smooth. During the first minutes of kneading, a metal bench scraper is useful to scoop up the wet dough that clings to the countertop.

4. Clean out the bowl (no soap, please), mist with oil spray, and replace the dough, topping with a piece of oiled plastic wrap. Ferment at room temperature (68–72°F is ideal) for 4 to 5 hours.

5. Remove the dough, which should have risen by about half, to a lightly floured countertop and gently press into a disk about 1 inch high. Form a *boule* by gathering the sides into the center, creating surface tension, then place seam side up in a colander covered with a well-floured linen napkin. Return the plastic wrap atop the dough and set aside to proof. Meanwhile, place a pizza stone in the lower third of the oven and an old cast iron skillet or pan on the bottom shelf. Preheat the oven to at least 500°F.

6. After 1½ to 2 hours, carefully turn the loaf onto a baker's peel that has been liberally sprinkled with rice flour or cornmeal. Sprinkle the top of the loaf with rye or rice flour (not white flour, which turns brown) to get that country "dusted" look.

7. Make several symmetrical slashes (*grignes*) with your *lame* or a single-edged razor.

8. Immediately slide the loaf onto the stone and add 1 cup water to the skillet (wear an oven mitt), minimizing the time the oven door is open. Reduce oven temperature to 480°F.

9. After 20 to 25 minutes, or when the loaf has turned dark brown, reduce oven temperature to 425°F.

10. Continue baking until the loaf registers 210°F in the center (about 50 to 60 minutes total) with an instant-read thermometer, or until a rap on the bottom of the loaf produces a hollow, drumlike sound. Return the bread to the oven, with the oven off, for about 15 minutes. Allow the bread to cool on a rack at least 2 hours before serving.

Pain au Levain Miche

This is a large (about three-pound) *miche* leavened only with the wild yeast *levain* that makes for a nice, yeasty loaf with plenty of character and chew.

500 grams *levain*	25 grams rye flour
500 grams all-purpose flour	17 grams salt
75 grams whole wheat flour	345 grams water

Follow the recipe for Peasant Bread (pages 330–332) with the following differences:

1. Don't be alarmed when this wet (70% hydration) dough flattens out on the peel; that's the classic *miche* shape we want for this bread.

2. This is a very forgiving loaf. I usually use a 4-hour fermentation followed by a 2-hour proof, but when it fits my schedule better, a 2-hour fermentation followed by a 4-hour proof (or 3 and 3) seems to works equally well.

3. Follow steps 5–10 of the Peasant Bread instructions for baking, except extend the cooking time to 60 minutes or more, until the center of the loaf registers 210°F.

Baguette à l'Ancienne

In France, this bread would be known as a *baguette à l'ancienne,* a designation that refers loosely to an artisan baguette, often made with *levain* and/or a delayed fermentation, although less scrupulous bakers (yes, they are still around) have been known to dust a little flour on ordinary baguettes and pass them off as *à l'ancienne.* The recipe calls for fermenting the dough overnight in the refrigerator, but I've made these the same day using a four-hour refrigerated fermentation with little difference.

Makes 4 minibaguettes

250 grams *levain*	¼ teaspoon instant yeast
375 grams all-purpose flour	215 grams water
10 grams salt	

1. Feed the *levain* the night before or at least 2 hours ahead.
2. Set a large bowl on a kitchen scale and add each ingredient in turn, using the Tare button to zero out the scale between additions. Mix thoroughly, cover, and *autolyse* for about 25 minutes.
3. Remove the dough to an unfloured countertop and knead by hand for 7 to 9 minutes.
4. Clean out the bowl (no soap), mist with oil spray, replace the dough, and cover with oil-misted plastic wrap. If you are doing an overnight fermentation, place the dough immediately in the refrigerator. For same-day baking, ferment the dough at room temperature for 1 to 2 hours, then ferment it in the refrigerator for an additional 4 hours.

5. Remove the dough from the refrigerator and wait for the dough to reach room temperature, about 2 hours.

6. Place an old cast iron skillet on the bottom shelf of your oven and a pizza stone near the middle rack.

7. Preheat the oven to 500°F.

8. On a floured countertop, divide the dough into 4 equal parts of about 212 grams each (don't go crazy trying to make them all exactly the same), gently shape into balls, and allow to rest, covered, for 15 minutes. (I sometimes omit this step if I'm in a hurry, but it does help to relax the dough for the next step.)

9. Press each ball into an approximately 3×5-inch rectangle, with the short side facing you. Fold the top third of the dough down toward you, press the edge to seal, flip the dough around 180 degrees to reverse the top and bottom, and fold the new top third down toward you, again sealing tightly, not unlike folding a letter for an envelope.

10. Fold once more, this time in half, in the same direction as before, as follows: Starting at one end of the loaf, make a deep indentation in the center of the dough with the side of your hand, using a tomahawk motion, while pulling the two sides up to meet, pinching them together, creating some sur-face tension. Continue moving down the loaf in this same manner, folding it in half, forming a nice, straight seam run-ning the length of the dough. Pinch closed any gaps.

11. Now, starting with your hands together in the middle, start rolling the loaf back and forth, using a light touch, moving your hands outward as you roll. You should have nice little blisters or bubbles of gas in the dough — leave them!

12. Proof in a floured *couche* or between folds of parchment paper for 45 to 60 minutes.

13. With four baguettes to place into your oven, it's sometimes

easier to use a wide baking sheet rather than your peel. Sprinkle the sheet liberally with cornmeal or rice flour (or cover with parchment paper), transfer the baguettes to it (I use a narrow piece of ¼-inch plywood as a flipping board, but you can transfer them by hand as well), and make several overlapping diagonal slashes on each baguette with your *lame* or a single-edged razor.

14. Transfer the baguettes to the stone with a clean jerk back of the baking sheet. Quickly add 1 cup water to the skillet and reduce the oven temperature to 480°F.

15. Bake for 20 to 25 minutes, until the crust is a rich brown and the center registers 210°F.

16. Cool on a rack for at least 1 hour before serving.

Pain de l'Abbaye Saint-Wandrille

This is the recipe I improvised at the abbey to fit baking into the monks' day of prayer, contemplation, and study. As I write this, two years later, the abbey *fournil* continues to turn out *pain de l'abbaye* three times a week.

Makes 6 bâtards

3 kilograms type 65 (or all-purpose) flour	80 grams salt
500 grams whole wheat flour	70 grams cake yeast (or 23 grams instant yeast)
250 grams rye flour	2,330 grams water
500 grams *levain*	

The night before baking, prepare the *poolish:*

1. Mix all the flours well, then make a *poolish* using:

    1 kilogram of the flour mixture

    1,300 grams water

    30 grams of cake yeast (or 10 grams instant yeast)

2. Mix well and refrigerate, covered, overnight.

3. Feed the *levain* well, keeping in mind you will need half a kilo of it for the bread.

The next day, make the bread:

4. Remove the *poolish* and the *levain* from the refrigerator 2–3 hours before beginning.

5. Combine the rest of the flour mixture with the *poolish,* the *levain,* 1,030 grams water, 40 grams fresh yeast (or 13 grams instant yeast), and the salt.

6. After a 25-minute *autolyse,* knead until the dough is supple and elastic, then cover and ferment 2–3 hours.

7. Divide the dough into six approximately 1,100-gram portions and form *bâtards* using the method described for making *baguette à l'ancienne* (steps 8–11), but making them stubbier, about 12 inches long. Preheat the oven to 500°F.

8. Proof the loaves in a floured *couche* for 1–2 hours and follow the instructions for baguettes (steps 13–16), baking at 480°F for about 35 minutes, until the loaves are a deep golden brown and 210°F at the center.

~ A Baker's Bookshelf ~

Beard, James. *Beard on Bread.* New York: Knopf, 1973.
———. *Delights and Prejudices.* New York: Smithmark, 1964.
Bertinet, Richard. *Crust: Bread to Get Your Teeth Into.* London: Kyle Books, 2007.
Calvel, Raymond. *The Taste of Bread.* With James J. MacGuire. Translated by Ronald Wirtz. New York: Springer, 2001.
Child, Julia. *My Life in France.* With Alex Prud'homme. New York: Knopf, 2006.
Child, Julia, and Simone Beck. *Mastering the Art of French Cooking.* Vol. 2. New York: Knopf, 1970.
Curry, Brother Rick, SJ. *The Secrets of Jesuit Breadmaking.* New York: Harper-Collins, 1995.
David, Elizabeth. *English Bread and Yeast Cookery.* Newton, MA: Biscuit Books, 1977.
Denzer, Kiko. *Build Your Own Earth Oven,* 3rd ed. With Hannah Field.Blodgett, OR: Hand Print Press, 2007.
Duff, Gail. *A Loaf of Bread: Bread in History, in the Kitchen, and on the Table.* Edison, NJ: Chartwell Books, 1998.
Dupaigne, Bernard. *The History of Bread.* New York: Abrams, 1999.
Fermor, Patrick Leigh. *A Time to Keep Silence.* New York: New York Review Books, 2007.
Glezer, Maggie. *Artisan Baking.* New York: Artisan, 2000.
Hamelman, Jeffrey. *Bread: A Baker's Book of Techniques and Recipes.* Hoboken, NJ: Wiley, 2004.
Hertzberg, Jeff, and Zoë François. *Artisan Bread in Five Minutes a Day.* New York: St. Martin's, 2007.
Jacob, H. E. *Six Thousand Years of Bread: Its Holy and Unholy History.* Garden City, NY: Doubleday, Doran, 1944.
Kaplan, Steven Laurence. *Good Bread Is Back: A Contemporary History of French Bread, the Way It Is Made, and the People Who Make It.* Durham, NC: Duke University Press, 2006.

Leader, Daniel. *Local Breads: Sourdough and Whole-Grain Recipes from Europe's Best Artisan Bakers.* With Lauren Chattman. New York: Norton, 2007.

Leader, Daniel, and Judith Blahnik. *Bread Alone: Bold Fresh Loaves from Your Own Hands.* New York: William Morrow, 1993.

Mayle, Peter, and Gerard Auzet. *Confessions of a French Baker: Breadmaking Secrets, Tips, and Recipes.* New York: Knopf, 2005.

McGee, Harold. *On Food and Cooking: The Science and Lore of the Kitchen.* New York: Scribner, 1984.

Norris, Frank. *The Octopus: A Story of California.* Garden City, NY: Doubleday, Page, 1901.

Pyler, E. J. *Baking Science and Technology,* 3rd ed. Kansas City: Sosland, 1988.

Rapaille, Clotaire. *The Culture Code.* New York: Broadway Books, 2006.

Reinhart, Peter. *American Pie: My Search for the Perfect Pizza.* Berkeley: Ten Speed Press, 2003.

———. *The Bread Baker's Apprentice: Mastering the Art of Extraordinary Bread.* Berkeley: Ten Speed Press, 2001.

———. *Brother Juniper's Bread Book: Slow Rise as Method and Metaphor.* Reading, MA: Addison-Wesley, 1991.

Robertson, Laurel. *The Laurel's Kitchen Bread Book.* New York: Random House Trade Paperbacks, 2003.

Schnitzbauer, Boniface, and Francis Kline. *Baking with Brother Boniface.* Charleston, SC: Wyrick, 1997.

Van Over, Charles. *The Best Bread Ever.* New York: Broadway Books, 1997.

Wing, Daniel, and Alan Scott. *The Bread Builders: Hearth Loaves and Masonry Ovens.* White River Junction, VT: Chelsea Green, 1999.

Wright, Kevin J. *Europe's Monastery and Convent Guesthouses: A Pilgrim's Travel Guide.* Liguori, MS: Liguori, 2000.

Additional References

Bamforth, Charles W. *Food, Fermentation, and Micro-organisms.* Oxford: Blackwell, 2005.

Campbell, Judy, Mechtild Hauser, and Stuart Hill. "Nutritional Characteristics of Organic, Freshly Stone-Ground, Sourdough and Conventional Breads." *McGill University Ecological Agriculture Products Publication* 35 (1991).

Carpenter, Kenneth J. "Effects of Different Methods of Processing Maize on Its Pellagragenic Activity." *Federal Proceedings* 40, no. 5 (1981): 1531–35.

Chapman, A. "The Yeast Cell: What Did Leeuwenhoeck See?" *Journal of the Institute of Brewing* 37 (1931): 433–36.

Colwell, James. "From Stone to Steel: American Contributions to the Revolution in Flour Milling." *The Rocky Mountain Social Science Journal* 6, no. 2 (1969): 20–31.

Dobell, Clifford. *Antony van Leeuwenhoek and His "Little Animals."* London: Stapes Press, 1932.

Evans, Oliver. *The Young Mill-Wright and Miller's Guide.* Philadelphia: Blanchard and Lea, 1860.

Fenster, Julie M. *Mavericks, Miracles, and Medicine.* New York: Carrol and Graf, 2003.

Ford, Brian J. *Single Lens: The Story of the Microscope.* New York: Harper and Row, 1985.

Fred, Edwin Broun. "Antony van Leeuwenhoek on the Three-Hundredth Anniversary of His Birth." *Journal of Bacteriology* 25, no. 1 (1933): 1–18.

Gieson, Gerald. *The Private Science of Louis Pasteur.* Princeton: Princeton University Press, 1995.

Goldberger, Joseph. "Pellagra: Its Nature and Prevention." *Public Health Reports* 33, no. 14 (1918): 481–88.

———. "A Study of the Treatment and Prevention of Pellagra." *Public Health Reports* 39, no. 3 (1924): 87–107.

Goldberger, Joseph, G. A. Wheeler, and E. Sydenstricker. "A Study of the Diet of Non-Pellagrous and Pellagrous Households." *Journal of the American Medical Association* 71 (1918): 944–49.

———. "A Study of the Relation of Diet to Pellagra Incidence in Seven Textile-Mill Communities of South Carolina in 1916." *Public Health Reports* 35, no. 12 (1920): 648–713.

Graham, Sylvester. *A Treatise on Bread and Bread Making.* Boston: Light and Stearns, 1837.

Hall, Ross Hume. *Food for Naught: The Decline in Nutrition.* New York: Harper and Row, 1974.

Kraut, Alan M. *Goldberger's War: The Life and Work of a Public Health Crusader.* New York: Hill and Wang, 2003.

Kruif, Paul de. *Microbe Hunters.* 1926. Reprint, New York: Harcourt Brace, 1996.

McGrain, John W. "Good Bye Old Burr: The Roller Mill Revolution in Maryland, 1882." *Maryland Historical Magazine* 77 (1982): 154–71.

Park, Y. K., C. T. Sempos, C. N. Barton, J. E. Vanderveen, and E. A. Yetley. "Effectiveness of Food Fortification in the United States: The Case of Pellagra." *American Journal of Public Health* 90, no. 5 (2000): 727–38.

Parsons, Robert A. *Trail to Light: A Biography of Joseph Goldberger.* Cornwall, NY: Cornwall Press, 1943.

Pedersen, Birthe, and Bjørn Eggum. "The Influence of Milling on the Nutritive Value of Flour from Cereal Grains." *Plant Foods for Human Nutrition* 33 (1983): 51–61.

Reustow, Edward. *The Microscope in the Dutch Republic: The Shaping of Discovery.* Cambridge: Cambridge University Press, 1996.

Roe, Daphne A. *A Plague of Corn: The Social History of Pellagra.* Ithaca: Cornell University Press, 1973.

Schierbeek, Abraham. *Measuring the Invisible World: The Life and Works of Antoni van Leeuwenhoek.* London: Abelard-Schuman, 1959.

Stiebeling, H. K., and M. E. Munsell. "Food Supply and Pellegra Incidence in 73 South Carolina Farm Families." *U.S. Dept of Agriculture Technical Bulletin* 333 (1932).

Swazey, Judith P., and Karen Reeds. "Today's Medicine, Tomorrow's Science: Essays on Paths of Discovery in the Biomedical Sciences." U.S. Department of Health, Education, and Welfare Publication No. (NIH) 78-244 (1978).

Terris, Milton, ed. *Goldberger on Pellagra.* Baton Rouge: Louisiana State University Press, 1964.

Watts, Alison. "The Technology That Launched a City: Scientific and Technological Innovations in Flour Milling during the 1870s in Minneapolis." *Minnesota History* 57, no. 2 (2000): 87–97.

Wilder, Russell M., and Robert R. Williams. *Enrichment of Flour and Bread: A History of the Movement.* Washington, DC: National Research Council (1944).

Further Information Online

For additional recipes, techniques, sources for materials and ingredients, photographs and videos of my year of bread making, a photographic tour of l'Abbaye Saint-Wandrille, and more, visit my Web site, williamalexander.com.

≈ **Acknowledgments** ≈

If one does not live by bread alone, one also does not make bread alone. I often needed help during my year of bread making, and I was astounded and gratified at how the mere mention of the word "bread" in any language opened doors and hearts. My deepest thanks to the following individuals for their invaluable assistance, advice, and support.

Laurie Abkemeier, "Petit" Ali Adimou, Rob Alexander, *frère* Michael Bozell, Mike Dooley and Bay State Milling, Jessica Dugan, Gary Edwards and Lallemand, Inc., Jack Fuchs, Brother Dominic Garramone, Steve Kaplan, Alan Kraut, Don Lewis, Stuart Moss, John Pelella, Clotaire Rapaille, Peter Reinhart, Chuck and Karen Rogalski, Ed Sears, Charlie van Over and Priscilla Martel, Nina White of Bobolink Dairy, Kevin Wright, and the late Erle Zuill of Jones Farm. I wish I knew his name, but thanks to the TSA official who allowed my *levain* onto the plane to Paris (he didn't have to do that). Of course, this project wouldn't have been possible without the unwavering support of my family, Anne, Katie, and Zach, who ate the bread and (more difficult) endured the baker, week after week, without complaining about either.

A special thanks to my editor, the immensely talented Amy Gash, whose skilled hands were indispensible to the final shaping of these fifty-two loaves, the entire Algonquin creative, production, and publicity teams, and my literary agent, Liz Darhansoff.

Finally, an extra special thanks to *frères* Bruno Lutz, Pierre Chopin, and Jean-Charles Nault and to the entire community of l'Abbaye Saint-Wandrille. May God bless them.

KATHERINE ALEXANDER

WILLIAM ALEXANDER lives and bakes in New York's Hudson Valley. He is the author of *The $64 Tomato: How One Man Nearly Lost His Sanity, Spent a Fortune, and Endured an Existential Crisis in the Quest for the Perfect Garden.* His website is www.williamalexander.com.